Legal and Paralegal Services on Your Home-Based PC

Other books in the Entrepreneurial PC Series

The Entrepreneurial PC Series brings the hottest new work-at-home options and essential information and advice to the new breed of PC-based home business owners—information they can use.

Health Service Businesses on Your Home-Based PC by *Rick Benzel*

Computer Consulting on Your Home-Based PC by *Herman Holtz*

Start Your Own Computer Repair Business by *Linda Rohrbough* and *Michael F. Hordeski*

The Entepreneurial PC: The Complete Guide to Starting a PC-Based Business—2nd Edition by *Bernard J. David*

The Information Broker's Handbook—2nd Edition by *Sue Rugge* and *Alfred Glossbrenner*

Information for Sale—2nd Edition by *John H. Everett* and *Elizabeth P. Crowe*

Bookkeeping on Your Home-Based PC by *Linda Stern*

Operating a Desktop Video Service on Your Home-Based PC by *Harvey Summers*

Mailing List Services on Your Home-Based PC by *Linda Rohrbough*

Legal and Paralegal Services on Your Home-Based PC

Katherine Sheehy Hussey
Rick Benzel

Windcrest®/ McGraw-Hill

New York   San Francisco   Washington, D.C.   Auckland   Bogotá   Caracas
Lisbon   London   Madrid   Mexico City   Milan   Montreal   New Delhi
San Juan   Singapore   Sidney   Tokyo   Toronto

1 2 3 4 5 6 7 8 9 0   FGR/FGR   9 9 8 7 6 5 4

Library of Congress Cataloging-in-Publication Data
Benzel, Rick.
    Legal and paralegal services on your home-based PC / by Rick Benzel, Katherine
Sheehy Hussey.
        p.   cm.
    Includes index.
    ISBN 0-07-005109-7 (paper)
    1. Legal assistants—United States.   2. Home-based businesses-
-United States. 3. Law offices—United States—Automation.
I. Sheehy Hussey, Katherine.
KF'320.L4B46 1994
340'.068—dc20   93-48742
                                                                    CIP

Acquisitions editor: Brad Schepp
Editorial team: Lori Flaherty, Supervising Editor
                Susan Bonthron, Book Editor
Production team: Katherine G. Brown, Director
                Rhonda E. Baker, Coding
                Tina M. Sourbier, Coding
                Rose McFarland, Desktop Operator
                Cindi Bell, Proofreading
                Joanne Woy, Indexer
Design team: Jaclyn J. Boone, Designer
                Brian Allison, Associate Designer
Cover design: by Lori E. Schlosser. Marble paper border
    by Douglas M. Parks, Blue Ridge Summit, Pa.   0051097
Cover copy writer: Michael Crowner   EPC1

Contents

Appendices

Illustrations

Acknowledgments

Many, many wonderful people contributed to this book. Most of all, I thank my loving, supportive husband, Bob, for his patience, good humor and his great cooking, which kept me going through the interviews and writing. Thanks to my son, Jim Sheehy, and stepdaughters, Diana Garrett and Alicia, and Sheila Hussey for their enthusiasm and encouragement. I am grateful to Stephanie Allen for getting Rick and me together on this effort and for her knack for finding new ways to use talents, experience, and aptitudes. I thank my wonderful friends for their suggestions and their patience during the book's gestation.

Katherine

The legal community is a web of interconnecting networks, and the paralegal network found me innumerable interview subjects. However, we could not have gathered all this information without the wonderful cooperation of all my NFPA contacts and the other legal professionals who generously shared their knowledge, experience, and Rolodexes with us.

In particular, I'd like to thank those people who shared their personal experiences so openly: Mary Susan Bach, Jane Bourgoin, Eileen Brown, Elizabeth Burda, Jan Burnham, Terrie Burton, Evelyn Cable, Phyllis Cardoza, Fran Chernowsky, Doris Childs, Brenda Conner, Judith Current, Laurel Davies, Doriana Fontanel, Mary Griffith, Debbie Hartzer, Patricia Hicks, Marti Holmes, Joanna Hughbanks, Jodie Hughes, Eileen Hyatt, Louise James, Jean King, Susan Kligerman, Lindi Massey, Carolyn McKown, Pam Miller, Diane Minter, Mary Mitchell, Sam Moretz, Nick Norman, Claire Palmer, Deborah Pietrzyk, Mary Ellen Robertson, Debra Schiff, Cathy Schultheis, Janet Shadeix, Cheryl Templeton, Shirl Thompson, John Trott, Fran Turner, Bonnie Twigg, Jamie Vance, Linda Will, and Sandy Williams. Thanks to Sue Colson and Virginia Dahlberg, who reviewed the sections on litigation and probate practice areas and provided thoughtful comments and to Linda Katz, J.T. Roy, Denise Templeton, Frances Whiteside, and Shelley Widoff, who referred me to so many wonderful interview subjects. Special thanks to the members of Rocky Mountain Legal Assistants Association's Experienced Paralegal Network.

The professional associations who serve as resources for these legal professionals were very helpful to us, particularly Lu Hangley and Jolene Miller of NFPA; the staff at NALA; Marshall Jorpeland of NCRA; Peter Beck of AALL; and Betsy Covington and Sandra Sabanske of AAfPE.

Thanks to my wife and two daughters for their support and encouragement throughout the past year as I worked on this project and others. Without their patience and love, I would not have been able to put my all into making this project a success. Thanks to my good friends and colleagues, Paul and Sarah

Rick

Edwards, whose work in this field is an inspiration to all. I also thank my parents for their support and help.

I also want to thank the many people who graciously assisted me by providing their time for interviews, which make this book real and personal: Rick Kraemer, Debra Bozanic Schechter, Laura Woodrow and Margaret Dalton, Richard Meyers, Cory Levenberg, Shelley English, Lu Hangley and Joleen Miller of NFPA, Eleanor Schub, Shirley Jantz, Stephanie Kelso of Z-Axis Corporation, Dan Laird, Susan Scott, Natalie Roberts, and Robert Reisch.

Finally, I want to thank Katherine for working with me on this book. Her knowledge and diligence are greatly appreciated.

Introduction

A succession of exciting stories and colorful characters involved in the legal profession are paraded in front of us almost daily, from Perry Mason to L.A. Law, *Twelve Angry Men*, *Presumed Innocent*, and other novels, television shows, and movies. Although our familiarity with the legal system is often skewed by Hollywood imaginations, it is difficult indeed not to have some knowledge of the interactions of judges, lawyers, and the American legal system.

Our society is founded upon a complex system of laws. As a democracy, our country depends upon thousands of codes and laws to keep the peace and ensure harmony. As a sophisticated industrialized nation, our economy depends on a plethora of business and tax laws to provide safety and fairness to consumers, ethical business behavior, and income to the treasury.

As a society of recordkeepers, we also maintain vast codes of laws that regulate many aspects of our lives, from birth to marriage to death. Some believe we are in a state of overregulation, overlegislation, and overkill—too many lawyers and others involved in the legal system. However, the rapidly growing legal nature of our society means a profoundly interesting career and a steady income for millions of others.

Today, more than 800,000 lawyers practice in the United States, of which 113,500 practice in California alone. Many lawyers work in one of the more than 60,000 law firms scattered across the country. And not to be forgotten are the many attorneys working for corporations, small businesses, and federal and state governments, as well as the growing number of independent practitioners.

Law is big business. In the past decade, more people are using legal services than at any other time. Large law firms bill between $50 to $100 million per year. In all, law firms grossed more than $100 billion in 1990 according to the Department of Commerce, as fees for legal services jumped into the hundreds of dollars per hour for most lawyers.

Not surprisingly, there are hundreds of thousands of support personnel, from paralegals to deposition digesters, court reporters, transcriptionists, courtroom graphics designers, legal consultants, even psychologists to study jury behavior and decision making. Computers have consistently become more important in the legal industry as well, creating jobs in software and hardware industries. Videographers have also tapped into the legal profession, videotaping depositions, hearings, and accident scenes for use in the courtroom.

The paralegal profession has mushroomed in part to help reduce fees for clients, but also to assist with a burgeoning legal business. Through the end of the 1980s and up to the early 1990s, the entire legal field was growing so rapidly that in 1987 the U.S. Bureau of Labor Statistics projected that the paralegal profession itself would be the fastest growing occupation between 1988 and 2000 with the addition of more than 60,000 paralegal jobs! While this figure was not quite as high as the expected growth in raw numbers in some other fields, such as medicine and computers, the projection suggested that change was in the wind and was worth paying attention to in the coming decades.

The growth of small & home-based businesses

In the meantime, another change was also taking place in the American workplace: the consistent growth of small and home-based businesses. In fact, hardly a day goes by in which a politician or business leader doesn't acknowledge that small businesses are the primary supplier of new jobs in the country.

There are many reasons for the rise of small businesses. In many parts of the country, a sluggish economy and a recessionary climate has forced some companies to downsize. Other companies have been able to fend off the recession only by paring their workforce. Others are simply operating leaner and not hiring as quickly as they once did in the 1980s. Consequently, many people have resorted to creating their own businesses or working for smaller companies for less pay but with more stability.

Another reason given for the popularity of small companies and home-based businesses is the maturing of the baby boom generation, many of whom are tired of corporate politics and the fast track. They want to be out on their own, running their own shop, creating their own future. They want to be able to have families, spend time with their children, and have a more balanced life. As a result, more people are starting their own business and succeeding, and many begin by working at home to reduce expenses and overhead. Although the vast majority of lawyers, paralegals, and other support staff still work in law offices, more attorneys are opening up their own practices, and more paralegals and other legal-related businesses are setting themselves up as a home-based or small business.

Depending on the type of business, some entrepreneurs are able to actually use their home as an office, while others work from home in the sense that their base of operations is their home, but they must physically go into a company or corporation several days a week to do most of the work. They might then take some of the work home to work on during the rest of the week or at night.

One large impediment to a home-based legal business is that most lawyer's work must be conducted in strict confidentiality or secrecy. Documents and conferences must be highly protected, and many law firms are reluctant to use home-based businesses. As technology moves forward, however, this barrier too will crumble, although the ethic of confidentiality will not change, and the sheer demand for people to be able to work from home will force some amount of flexibility on this issue.

This book aims to help those of you who want to learn more about the opportunities for home-based legal careers.

Why this book?

- Students who are thinking of a career in the legal profession.
- People considering a career transition into the legal profession.
- People reentering the job market.
- People interested in computers and jobs that involve computers and the legal profession.
- People who are currently involved in a legal career and want to move into another line of work.
- Experienced legal professionals who want to freelance or work from home.

Legal and Paralegal Services on Your Home-Based PC is a useful and comprehensive resource for anyone who wants to become a paralegal or one of the other affiliated legal professions covered, even if you are not seeking to be a home-based business.

Legal career paths are presented and disseminated, including a complete overview of the profession along with tips and advice on the educational background, skills, and personality traits you need to enter that career, regardless of whether it is located in a law firm, a corporate legal department, an agency employing paralegals or court reporters, a small business, or a home-based operation.

Because most legal jobs are still in law offices and corporations, particularly for paralegals, many of you will be obligated to work for a firm. If you are a paralegal student or new to the profession, you'll need to work for a few years at a law firm or for a company before trying it on your own. In fact, in-house experience is practically a requirement for an inexperienced paralegal. Few attorneys will hire a home-based paralegal who has not had two or more years of solid work experience within a law firm.

Even if you expect to be working in-house for a firm or need to gain in-house experience, this book can help you plan your career and prepare you for starting your own home-based business. We have consciously provided accurate, up-to-date, and realistic information about how to gain experience in a field, how to move from an in-house position to become an independent practitioner, and how to market yourself once you become independent. We have also provided profiles of successful entrepreneurs who have made the move to prove it!

Nearly two dozen paralegal and legal-related careers are covered, with chapters organized according to type of career. The first three chapters break down and profile the many types of paralegal specializations. The following

How this book is organized

three chapters describe other legal-related careers. Finally, the last chapter discusses general issues to developing any business.

Chapter 1 introduces you to paralegal careers. Information on the type of training needed to become a paralegal, including specific educational programs, is covered as well as personality traits that help make an individual successful as a paralegal and a review of national salary ranges.

Litigation, which represents the largest area of employment for paralegals, is discussed in chapter 2. This high-growth area offers many opportunities for those of you who are interested in developing your paralegal skills and computer expertise. The future of paralegal work in litigation is high technology—legal database research, computerized litigation support, and general office administration computer skills.

We also look at the skills and training needed by litigation paralegals, as well as the employment opportunities for both in-house and freelance paralegals, of which there are growing numbers. We discuss getting a first job as well as three ways to work from home using your present job as a paralegal as a stepping stone.

Chapter 3 reviews a dozen specializations for paralegals, focusing on those areas that are particularly suitable to freelance work. The chapter includes personal injury, family law litigation, estate planning, estate administration, corporate and securities practice, bankruptcy, real estate and oil and gas law, environmental law, water law, trademark and intellectual property, and criminal law.

In many legal cases, attorneys must interview dozens (if not hundreds) of clients and witnesses to obtain background testimony and figure out what happened. This is done in *depositions*, special legal proceedings in which attorneys are able to ask questions and explore evidence while witnesses tell their story and rebut accusations. All of this is covered in chapter 4, as well as the fast-growing fields of court reporter scopist.

One specialization of the legal field is the career of deposition summarizer, also called *deposition digester*, which is covered in chapter 5. The deposition summarizer takes the transcripts produced by court reporters, often amounting to thousands of pages and condenses them for attorneys. The deposition digester is frequently trained as a paralegal and is an important part of the legal team.

Chapter 6 covers specialized legal businesses, or niche markets, many of which can be started from a paralegal background but often include people from other backgrounds: computers, graphics, video, engineering, nursing, and even literature. Dozens of business ideas are presented: asbestos abatement consulting, computer consultant, consultant to start-up law firms, corporate service company, demonstrative evidence specialist, independent professional law librarian, mediation service, multimedia/video specialist, nurse/paralegal consultant, proofreader, Social Security claimant representative, and transcriptionist.

Chapter 7 presents ideas and tips on choosing your career and going into business for yourself and shows you how to determine whether or not self-employment is for you. A seven-step program for examining your goals and establishing your business is included to help you.

Finally, we have included a list of some major associations and organizations relevant to the legal field, information about the ethical considerations critical to the legal field, and a list of court reporter schools and information on how to locate a paralegal school in your community.

It is important to mention that this book largely addresses the various legal assistant/paralegal careers and other legal-related jobs that provide service directly to lawyers. It does not cover work by what has come to be called an *independent paralegal*, that is, someone who works directly with the general public. Although many states are now evaluating the relaxation of laws that prevent nonattorneys such as paralegals from preparing simple documents and assisting consumers with routine forms, our focus does not include information on this type of work except for a few situations where it is already legally sanctioned, such as paralegals working directly with consumers on social security disability claims.

1 Introduction to paralegal careers

This chapter provides an overview of the role of paralegals in the legal process, how the profession developed, and the various tasks paralegals perform. We also discuss the different job opportunities for paralegals, ranging from law firms and corporations to the growing body of freelance, contract, and home-based paralegal workers. We'll cover recent salary trends and earnings potential of the profession and define the background education, training, knowledge, and personality qualities you must have in order to be a success.

What a paralegal is

The role of paralegals, or legal assistants, in legal services developed largely because paralegals offered a significant cost savings to clients. Anyone who has had to hire legal counsel knows firsthand the shock of receiving a legal bill from a lawyer. Since most attorneys charge by the hour—at rates that vary by area of practice, expertise, level of risk, and even geographic area—the cost of legal services is sizeable. Enter the paralegal, who can be billed out at a lesser rate while providing a high level of skills and mastery. Whenever an attorney delegates work to a paralegal, the client saves money—as much as 50 to 75 percent of the attorney's fees. In the long run, however, the attorney actually benefits, because he or she can serve the client more economically.

In today's recessionary climate, companies need to economize anywhere they can. Many require their law firms to use paralegals in place of attorneys for routine support and research, where in the past a junior attorney might have been used. As a result, paralegals have become an integral part of legal services and a stunning variety of work opportunities are open to good, experienced legal assistants.

Years ago, some of the work now done by paralegals was done by good legal secretaries. The profession can be traced to the late 1960s and early 1970s when public legal service agencies began training legal assistants to help attorneys provide economical services for the poor. In time, specific academic programs for paralegals were developed throughout the United States. In the intervening decades, the profession has grown to tens of thousands of paralegal workers, and judging by statistics put out by the U.S. Department of Labor, the profession is still growing and shows continuing promise for years to come.

Paralegals work in law firms, in legal departments of corporations, in banks, insurance agencies, accounting and engineering firms, title companies, construction companies, and in government agencies at every level, from city attorney offices to a myriad of federal agencies. In all of these situations, paralegals can perform work that would otherwise be done by an attorney. In fact, the National Federation of Paralegal Associations (NFPA) defines a paralegal as:

A person qualified through education, training, or work experience to perform substantive work that requires knowledge of legal concepts and is customarily, but not exclusively, performed by a lawyer. This person might be retained or employed by a lawyer, law office, governmental agency, or other entity or might be authorized by administrative, statutory or court authority to perform this work.

Legal secretary, paralegal, legal assistant, or lawyer

The term *legal secretary* represents a job category that is very different from a paralegal or legal assistant. The duties of legal secretaries generally include such tasks as typing or word processing, filing, answering phones, and scheduling appointments and meetings.

The terms *paralegal* and *legal assistant* are completely interchangeable and represent a substantially different type of work from that of a legal secretary. Although many paralegals began as legal secretaries, especially those who started their careers in the 1960s and the 1970s when there were few legal assistants, a paralegal today performs a broad range of duties that requires specific legal education, knowledge, and experience. While some people make a distinction between paralegal and legal assistant, most often today, paralegals in the profession and lawyers recognize both terms to connote the same job duties. Note that most academic training programs use the term "paralegal studies."

The last distinction, paralegal/legal assistant vs. lawyer, is actually quite straightforward, though you need to know what is and is not the "practice of law." The simplest way to express it is that only a lawyer can "practice" law, and a paralegal cannot. This means that paralegals are not allowed to provide legal advice to clients, establish legal fees, or represent clients in court in any state. Paralegals must generally work under the supervision of an attorney who obtains the clients, provides the actual legal advice or strategy behind a case, and pleads in court when necessary.

Today, however, paralegals often work hand in hand with lawyers to interview a client, to research the background of a case, to develop ideas and strategies, to prepare documents for filing, and to perform a myriad of other tasks that attorneys often do. The line between paralegal and lawyer has been blurring, but it is nevertheless still there. The paralegal profession has been evolving over the past few decades, as paralegals have taken on more responsibilities and shown lawyers that they can handle more legal tasks. Nevertheless, a paralegal must never forget that lawyers are the ones with deeper and more specific legal education. They have spent long, difficult years, enormous mental effort, and a lot of money to earn a law degree, pass a bar exam, and obtain a license to practice law, and understandably might not be comfortable delegating to nonlawyers most of what they were trained to do.

On the other hand, most lawyers find that much of their work involves things nonlawyer legal assistants can be taught to do at considerable cost savings to the client—provided that the person has the training, knowledge, skill, and intelligence to do the task well. This is particularly true for legal work with much routine or boilerplate language. This work requires intelligence, training, and awareness, but not always a lawyer to do it.

To demonstrate how much the profession of paralegal has evolved and gained respectability, in 1968 the American Bar Association established a committee to study how lawyers could make use of legal assistants in some areas of the practice of law. The committee, now called the *Standing Committee on Legal Assistants*, also developed educational requirements for paralegal training programs and grants institutions their stamp of approval as an ABA-approved paralegal school. While there are more than 600 programs in the country, only about 150 of them have received ABA approval.

The American Bar Association also has its own specific definition of paralegal that aims to clarify and make official the distinction between lawyer and paralegal:

[Paralegals are] persons who, although not members of the legal profession, are qualified through education, training or work experience, are employed or retained by a lawyer, law office, governmental agency, or other entity in a capacity or function that involves the performance, under the direction and supervision of an attorney, of specifically delegated substantive legal work, which work, for the most part, requires a sufficient knowledge of legal

concepts, such that absent the legal assistant, the attorney would perform the task.

As this statement obviously shows, the ABA is firmly protecting the sanctity of the lawyer's privilege to practice law, but is also recognizing the substantive nature of the paralegals work as opposed to a legal secretary.

Paralegal tasks The nature of a paralegal's work varies a great deal according to the area of law in which he or she works. There are many fields to work in, including:

- Litigation—cases in which one party sues another, (e.g., personal injury accidents, malpractice suits, breach of contract suits, and so on)
- Corporate—incorporations, partnerships, securities filings, and so on
- Family—divorce, custody, adoption
- Estate planning—wills and trusts
- Probate—estate administration (following the death of a person)
- Real estate—Contracts, construction, mortgages, banking, foreclosures, title work
- Government—legislation, hearings, regulations
- Employment—employee policies and manuals, discrimination, labor campaigns, sexual harassment, and so on.

In general, all paralegals, regardless of specialty, perform similar duties that include the following types of tasks:

- Organize, review, analyze, and summarize existing documents in preparation for a trial or to understand the background to a case.
- Draft or create new documents.
- Research facts and information in a law or a public library, on computer databases, or through interviews and phone calls to individuals, businesses, or governmental agencies.
- Perform legal research. (However, many paralegals do little of this.)
- Coordinate between clients, attorneys, witnesses, courts, and agencies to make the day run smoothly.
- Interview clients, witnesses, and experts on the subject of the case.
- Prepare tax returns or determine the value of an estate or a person.
- Fill out government agency paperwork.
- Prepare business paperwork for events such as trade name notices that are filed with the county clerk and recorder, or federal securities registration statements that are filed with the Securities and Exchange Commission.

Whatever the task, the work done by a paralegal represents considerable cost savings to the client when it is work a lawyer would otherwise have to do. Chapters 2 and 3 detail much more extensively the specific tasks of paralegals in each major specialization field.

Without a doubt, the majority of paralegal jobs are inside law firms. According to a 1991 survey conducted by the National Federation of Paralegal Associations (NFPA), more than 75 percent of the responding paralegals worked for a law firm while roughly 15 percent worked for corporations. The remaining 10 percent worked for various levels of federal or state government or were freelance paralegals. While most of our focus is presenting information on self-employment and working from home, following is a discussion of all work opportunities for paralegals:

Full-time work at law firms is the route most paralegals take. Law firms offer many advantages, particularly for new paralegals. First, you are in daily contact with lawyers who need assistance on a regular basis and are usually able to keep a paralegal staff busy. Particularly at large law firms (more than 100 lawyers), paralegals have many opportunities to obtain solid work experience and a breadth of contacts.

Large law firms have a variety of support systems that make the paralegal's job easier and more enjoyable, including word processing (days and evenings), errand runners, librarians, computer departments, copy departments, and possibly case clerks or document clerks to take over the more routine document handling tasks like Bates stamping. They might also have better programs for training and performance reviews, regular paralegal meetings, and are likely to pay for professional association memberships. Large law firms offer wonderful training; they are excellent places to learn the best practice habits. Small law firms are also good learning environments; a paralegal in a seven-attorney firm might not learn how to give Cadillac-quality service, but he or she will learn a broader variety of skills.

There are also disadvantages to working within a law firm. First, the environment at law firms is often extremely stressful. New paralegals are hit with high expectations of productivity from the lawyers, who often give them little direction and are commonly known as poor people managers. The more experienced paralegal might be channeled into becoming highly specialized, taking on the same types of assignments time after time in order to become more efficient. One becomes, in effect, pigeon-holed. This is less common in smaller firms where paralegals can find themselves doing everything from making copies to conducting research and drafting briefs.

Like attorneys, paralegals in law firms must also keep track of every tenth of an hour of time (six minute increments) so that the time can be billed to each client as appropriate. In addition, overtime work is frequently required, especially when a trial approaches and the pace steps up as attorneys prepare for court.

The burnout rate is high for litigation paralegals, particularly for those in large law firms. After several years, many of them tire of endless document review

Where paralegals work

Law firms

and summarizing and from the critical deadlines and barked-out orders of frazzled attorneys about to go to trial.

Corporations

Paralegal positions are increasingly available in corporations as well as law firms, and there are many advantages to working in-house. The hours in most corporate positions are more consistently 9:00 to 5:00, or 8:30 to 5:30, while in law firms, the hours frequently extend into evenings and weekends, especially in litigation work. Corporate legal departments, having only one basic "client" (the company itself), are generally low-stress environments compared to law firms of any size, although this is changing as the character of in-house legal departments change. Most work follows some sort of schedule, and planning ahead seems to be a more routine practice than in a law firm. Fringe benefits are typically much better in a corporate setting than they are in law firms—better insurance, stock option plans, and more holidays and vacation days.

The disadvantages of in-house corporate work include the relative rarity of opportunities. Vacancies aren't as common, and sometimes are filled from within the corporation rather than the general paralegal community. When not filled in-house, the positions are often awarded to very experienced people, and many in-house positions require experience in the corporate and securities areas. Finally, for someone who enjoys the excitement of trial work, an in-house position might not have enough of a "charge," because the work does not provide as much variety or stress as in a law firm.

Self-employed & freelance paralegal work

Despite that the majority of paralegal work is done as an employee of a law firm or company, opportunities to work as a self-employed or freelance paralegal are increasing. Just as in other segments of the business world in the 1990s, law firms and corporations find that freelance, contract-basis paralegals provide a way to hire skilled people only when the need justifies it, without incurring the risks and costs of adding full-time staff.

At the same time, paralegals who want more flexibility and variety in their schedules than a full-time job permits, find that starting their own business and taking work on a freelance basis provides them with more control over their lives and work schedules. Jolene Miller, Co-Chair of the Education Task Force for the National Federation of Paralegal Associations says, "I think there are a lot of opportunities for self-employed paralegals, especially given the cost of doing business in large cities such as in New York. With a modem you can have any paralegal working out of their home, and the law firms benefit."

In this book, we use the terms *self-employed*, *freelance*, and *contract* to mean roughly the same thing: a person who is running his or her own business and is not in the consistent employment of a company or law firm beyond the scope of a specific project. Note that we also include people who work through a temporary agency and accept different projects for different law firms. Although this type of person becomes an employee of the temporary agency for a period of time, we included this because, like the self-employed freelance individual, the temporary employee has the ability to accept or reject the project or job, and when the job is over, the person must go out and find another project to work on, with or without the temporary agency.

Many types of paralegal work are particularly suitable for self-employed, freelance, and home-based work. We discuss each of these practice areas in more detail in the following chapters, and include here a brief overview to illustrate the number of paralegal areas in which you can work as a freelancer and/or home-based entrepreneur.

Litigation   While most litigation work is done inside law firms, there are freelance paralegals who specialize in litigation support. The paralegal in this field works with complicated and document-heavy lawsuits that might involve hundreds to thousands of documents produced by the various parties. Each document must be reviewed by a thoughtful person who understands the case and is aware of the parties and the issues in the law suit, and can therefore determine what the document is and how it fits into the attorney's strategy. Paralegals also participate in drafting responses to interrogatories.

Family law   In the family law area, a home-based freelance legal assistant can draft initial petitions for separation, prepare drafts of affidavits and separation agreements, and calculate financial affidavits and child support worksheets using a home-based computer and special software. Freelance family law paralegals consult with attorneys and can provide them with prepared documents by modem, on diskette, or in hard copy. The freelancer might also review and analyze documents, inventory a party's assets, and order appraisals of someone's property in order to calculate a divorce settlement. They may also help the attorney prepare for trial as in any other litigation (e.g., prepare interrogatories and responses to interrogatories).

Bankruptcy   In the bankruptcy area, a freelance legal assistant can take the clients' financial records to a home office where all initial documents, bankruptcy petition, and accompanying schedules can be prepared on special software created for personal computers. The prepared documents can then be returned to the attorney by modem, disk, or hard copy.

Natural resources/mining/oil and gas   In natural resources law, a freelance legal assistant can prepare a "chain of title" for a property, which shows the history of ownership. The person can also prepare an initial draft of the attorney's title opinion based on the results of the chain of title, using a home computer and even delivering it by modem, on disk, or as hard copy.

Real estate   In the real estate area, leases or loan documents can be transmitted by facsimile or picked up by the legal assistant to be reviewed at home. The freelancer can analyze the terms, and transmit the analysis to a lawyer by telephone, fax, or modem. A home-based real estate paralegal can also arrange for documents to be prepared for a real estate closing using the home telephone to contact title companies, realtors, mortgage lenders, etc., and can prepare settlement sheets and other documents from home.

Securities In securities law work, state securities laws, regulations, etc., can be researched from a home-office provided that the basic materials are available either on computerized database or in loose-leaf volumes. The person can also prepare filings on a personal computer, since the forms for securities work are now available in reasonably priced software packages.

Obstacles to working from home

There are a few obstacles that prevent more paralegals from working from home, although more and more of them are disappearing with the use of computers and modems. The primary obstacle is true of many professions: clients (the attorneys) expect to have paralegals on-site to meet urgent client demands. It might not seem practical or feasible to them to have to call someone located elsewhere to arrange for a client's work to be done. It is also easier to discuss what needs to be done in person, and it seems that most resources required for legal work are present in the law firm, and not available at home.

In addition, some paralegal tasks are not suitable to working from home, and many firms are not able to accommodate this sort of arrangement in certain typical paralegal practice areas. If the work includes a lot of involvement in attorney-client meetings, or assisting at the closing of financial transactions, for example, you need to be where the meetings or closings are taking place. If the work requires numerous legal forms, or use of a legal library for research, you might need to be located close at hand to the resources. In corporate law, for example, most tasks are not easily transferred to home-based work, since the work typically involves using many government forms and resources generally available only at a law firm. In order to work in this area outside the law office, a corporate paralegal would need an expensive and extensive supply of corporate forms, loose-leaf services, and legal publications, most of which need constant updating.

Another obstacle is attorney reluctance to allow clients' files and paperwork to leave the safety and confidentiality of the law firm. The practice of law is steeped in trust and attorney/client secrecy in every aspect and at every level. Not only is the information between the attorney and legal assistant as they work on a case confidential—even the fact that a particular client is represented by a particular firm or attorney is considered to be a confidential matter. In this light, attorneys are understandably reluctant to allow clients' files and private papers to leave the office for a destination where unauthorized eyes might be able to view them. Again, a very trusted legal assistant might be permitted to do this in certain situations, but it is not a common practice.

Finally, a home-based paralegal might need to hire a secretary or to work without secretarial support. Part of what makes paralegal work so economical in a law firm setting (especially larger law firms) is that considerable support is available to perform typing, copying, errand-running, etc., all of which frees the paralegal to perform more thought-demanding work, and billing time to clients at the firm's hefty hourly rate. A home-based paralegal working without secretarial support might be somewhat less efficient, and might therefore not be able to earn as high an hourly rate as a paralegal with support.

However, these obstacles are being slowly confronted by the realities of economics, and by good legal assistants who want flexibility in their schedules. Despite the obstacles, opportunities for home-based paralegal work continue to open up. Many such paralegals are based at home, but accept assignments that take them into the attorney's office for periods of time, where files are kept secure, extensive libraries are available, and secretarial support is provided. Furthermore, paralegals who are well-known and trusted by the attorney are able to work on some client work in their own homes, or able to work on computerized databases on portable hard disk or accessible by modem. While some paralegal tasks will continue to be limited to in-house performance, there is still a variety of work available to home-based legal assistants.

In the next two chapters, which cover paralegal employment, we will explain in more detail how to develop your career by working for a law firm or corporation, as well as how to take steps to become a freelance, contract, or home-based paralegal.

Becoming a paralegal (wherever the work occurs) is not a quick and easy process. In fact, it takes several years from the idea to the reality, since paralegal preparation involves education, specific paralegal training, and experience.

First, since the paralegal career began as such in the early 1970s, more and more paralegals currently have a four-year college degree. While many college courses have an application to the work done by paralegals, a number of skills contribute toward success as a paralegal, all of which are enhanced by a college education:

- Logic—a strong ability to organize, and to create order from chaos.
- Strong English language skills, including both writing and speaking abilities, but particularly the ability to write.
- Research skills—the ability to use a library and to use creative approaches to finding information.
- Analytical skills—the ability to analyze detail while keeping the "big picture" in mind.
- Problem-solving skills—the ability to tackle and solve problems.
- Computer skills, including familiarity with personal computers and information resources on databases accessible by computer.

Training, knowledge, & aptitudes required
General educational requirements

If you are still in college, English or library science are excellent majors, but almost any liberal arts background could apply.

Paralegal training

Specific paralegal training is almost mandatory for anyone entering a paralegal career, since legal knowledge, including an awareness of legal procedures and terminology, are critical. Most people today enter the paralegal profession with a certificate in paralegal studies. Twenty years ago, when the field was new and little training was available, nearly anyone could become a paralegal, but now paralegal training is practically required of new paralegal employees.

In fact, training for paralegals has become big business in the last few years; more than 600 programs exist across the country. There are correspondence schools, business colleges, community colleges, and even four-year institutions and post-baccalaureate training programs all offering training to become a paralegal. Many of these are creditable institutions doing an excellent job of training, but some are fly-by-night schools and programs that simply do not do a thorough job of training prospective legal assistants. Attorneys in law firms, corporate legal departments, and government agencies are all very cautious about who does their paralegal work, and typically review resumes carefully to evaluate the applicant's training. You do not want to invest time and money in a program that will not train you to be a good paralegal, or will not be an asset to you in your job search.

So, how do you make sure the school you want to attend is a competent and reputable institution? First, be aware of the fact that there is not a standard training program across the board at these schools, although several paralegal groups are currently trying to devise a uniform curriculum that schools would have to follow to become "accredited." Therefore, the first thing you should do is check the courses offered by the schools you are considering. At the very minimum, look for a program that combines legal theory with practical, hands-on experience: a curriculum that includes civil procedure and litigation, legal research and writing, legal ethics, a paralegal introduction course, and several specialized courses in specific areas of law all taught by teachers who are practicing attorneys and/or experienced paralegals. The program should also include an internship and the school should have a legal library available for students' use.

It is our recommendation that you not enroll in a correspondence school for paralegal training if you will be relying on your credentials to help you obtain your first paralegal job. Although many correspondence courses are available for home training, and some might do an excellent job within the necessary limitations of correspondence study, we do not recommend this route for training. The skills and experience needed in order to perform well as a paralegal are best learned in a classroom situation, including regular daily interaction with practicing attorneys and paralegals, and homework assignments that utilize good legal libraries and interaction with governmental agencies. In addition, good training programs include an internship period served in an office, working under the supervision of attorneys. Those elements are rarely available through correspondence training. Most good paralegal training programs fall into the following categories:

- Two-year associate degree programs, typically a community college.
- Four-year baccalaureate programs with a major in paralegal studies.
- Several-month, post-baccalaureate programs, frequently offered as continuing education through a college or university, with college credit and granting a certificate.
- Programs offered by private or proprietary institutions, such as business schools, usually several months long, that grant a certificate on completion. Some of these programs require a bachelors degree or passing a test before a student may enroll.

Contact one of the paralegal associations in your area or local community colleges for information on the programs offered in your area. A pamphlet entitled "How to Choose a Paralegal Education Program" is available from the ABA Standing Committee on Legal Assistants or the American Association for Paralegal Education (AAfPE) and other organizations (a list of associations and their addresses and phone numbers is provided in appendix A). The pamphlet outlines typical curricula and explains the approval process conducted by the ABA. It also sets out criteria you can use to evaluate programs in your area. Although the programs that meet the ABA's approval standards can be relied upon as thorough and creditable training programs, several other programs are good although they might not have completed the lengthy ABA approval process. The pamphlet can help you evaluate whether a program you are considering will suit your needs.

Good training is critical in order to compete as an applicant for paralegal positions of any sort. In many urban areas it is typical for employers to require, or at least prefer, someone with a four-year degree in addition to paralegal training. In smaller communities more variety in training background might be acceptable.

Join a paralegal association

While we are on the subject of training, it is worth a moment to discuss joining a paralegal association. In the early years of the development of the paralegal career, several professional associations were formed to respond to the issues arising for paralegals, and these associations have grown along with the profession. Today, membership in a professional association is critical to a paralegal working in any type of situation; it can contribute greatly to job satisfaction and success. The national associations keep their members informed on issues that have an impact on their careers, such as efforts to regulate paralegals through licensing or registration; court decisions on whether or not paralegal fees can be awarded in lawsuits, like attorney fees are; or developments in training and seminar opportunities.

The two major organizations are the National Association of Legal Assistants (NALA) and the National Federation of Paralegal Associations (NFPA). They each have national annual meetings, and periodic regional meetings where paralegals can meet compatriots from other areas, and share working issues and concerns. In addition, there are many state and local associations in major cities.

The most important advantage of joining an association is the networking opportunity—learn about job possibilities, pick up scuttlebutt on working conditions and salary levels, and support each other. This only happens through paralegal contacts, and association activities are the best places to find those contacts. Indeed, many of the issues raised in this chapter can be explored in detail through contacts and membership in a local, regional, or national legal assistant/paralegal association. Most associations prepare salary and job surveys for their geographic areas; these will be much more accurate than the general information we can provide here. Frequently a student membership or an associate membership in a paralegal association is available to persons not working as paralegals, and many associations also offer job bank services to their members. Appendix A provides a list of the major paralegal associations with addresses and phone numbers.

Personality characteristics for paralegals

For more than 70 years, the Johnson-O'Connor Research Foundation has inventoried aptitudes for a number of careers, recently including that of a paralegal. According to Steve Allen of Johnson-O'Connor's Denver office, aptitudes are characteristics that are inborn, as opposed to learned; they represent inherent qualities in people. Steve says people who do well and enjoy the career of a paralegal are those who:

- do not demonstrate a strong ego, but can adapt to and follow directions, can adapt to a group viewpoint, and can function harmoniously on a team;
- can organize concepts, arrange ideas in logical sequence;
- can reason inductively; that is, reason from the particular to the general, from evidence to a conclusion, and can draw a conclusion after learning a particular set of facts; and
- can handle paperwork and clerical tasks well, such as recognizing patterns of numbers, and balancing checkbooks.

More informally, the freelance paralegals we interviewed agreed that the following personality characteristics are very important:

- Self-motivated—A freelance paralegal must be able to take the initiative; you can't be passive or wait for work to be given to you.
- Assertive—You have to be assertive or even aggressive; you have to have confidence in yourself and be able to work with attorneys without feeling unintimidated, but still respect their authority and expertise. You must be assertive enough to demand certain working conditions and payment arrangements. While paralegals on a typical in-house job might or might

not receive close supervision and direction, freelance paralegals typically receive minimal direction. They must be able to seek out answers when needed, and to work without supervision most of the time.

- Detail oriented—You must be meticulous about your work. Any job, no matter how small, creates a client relationship. You need to do the best possible job, and every project should get the same amount of attention.
- Organized—You must be organized (mentally, at least), and be able to juggle conflicting priorities.
- Resilient and resourceful—Can you deal with ambiguity? You must be able to work with inadequate information and unclear instructions. What if your attorney goes on a business trip and expects the product done tomorrow? You need to be able to get the big picture somehow, from him, the secretary, or the file.
- Flexible—You must be able to change direction on short notice, and to take it in stride when the case settles and no one looks at the work you spent hours or weeks producing, without becoming disabled by a sense of time wasted. Often the issues in a case change, and the direction of work changes, and you need to be able to go with the flow. You must also be able to jump in for a heavy push when it's needed, including all-nighters.
- Dedicated—You must be able to set your priorities (and put your personal life on hold without resentment) even more so with freelance litigation work, because you don't get ongoing regular scheduled work. They don't call you in until there is a crisis, the day before something is due.
- Cool—You must be unflappable, calm in a crisis.
- People skilled—You will attract more business if you can get along with attorneys no one else can get along with. Learn to express a lot of tolerance, and avoid taking things personally. Sometimes it gets lonely working contract; you go in to work on one project for a large firm, and you are treated like an outsider; understand the situation and make your own little spot. You need to be even-tempered, pleasant, and tolerant of a variety of personalities. Attorneys exhibit the same range of personalities found anywhere, but seem to have an abundance of aggressiveness; most have strong egos and many lack good people-management skills.
- Emotionally mature—You must be comfortable getting your "strokes" from inside yourself, or finding friends and coworkers to support you. You cannot count on a lot of appreciation from attorneys. Fortunately, there are many exceptions to this, but don't count on finding them in most jobs! Actually, attorneys are one of the great advantages of this career, since so many of them are charming, interesting, exceedingly bright, clever, and funny. They make the work interesting, but they can also make it an emotional challenge.
- Able to laugh—A sense of humor is always indispensable in a difficult job.
- Honest—A high sense of personal integrity and character is most important. Attorneys are so cautious, and so aware of the risks in their profession, they are very reluctant to trust nonlawyers with substantive work. In addition, legal work is steeped in confidential matters.

Additional requirements for freelancers

Above all, it appears that substantial work experience is the most critical attribute for anyone hoping to become a freelance paralegal. The nature of law practice is that it involves work that must be done correctly and always on time. The consequences of errors are cost to the client, as well as legal liability and potential malpractice suits against attorneys. Thus attorneys are very careful about delegating work to nonlawyers, and select only well-trained, trustworthy, and experienced legal assistants for most assignments. You will have a hard time making a paralegal practice work if you cannot convince attorneys that your background and character merit their trust.

From experience you learn thousands of skills, specific facts and subtle aspects of law that make you an invaluable member of a legal services team. The following list provides some examples of what experience can teach you that training programs generally don't:

- Where each local courthouse is, when it closes, and whether or not there is a way to file a document after closing hours;
- How to get information for a courthouse in another city;
- How long it takes to get a document from a government office, who in that office can expedite it for you, or which document retrieval agency can get it for you the fastest at the most reasonable price;
- Which client questions you can answer as a nonlawyer, and which ones would involve the practice of law and must be handled by the attorney;
- How to work effectively with a difficult judge's clerk;
- How to find the answer to a difficult question when people you call keep telling you the answer cannot be found;
- How to handle a crisis in an attorney's absence;
- Which expert witness is reliable, prompt, and accurate;
- How to set up a trial office in a hotel in another city, what you will need in it, and how to move your materials there;
- The best system for analyzing 20,000 documents in six weeks' time;
- How to arrange a deposition and get a court reporter in another city;
- The best way to keep clients informed of what is being done on their behalf;
- When to edit an attorney's work and when not to—i.e., which are "magic words" and which can stand some improvement without changing the document's meaning;
- Which government offices really can do something in a day when they say they can't, and which can't do it no matter how you ask.

Given the range of inside knowledge required, it is understandable why, the contract and freelance paralegals we spoke with all stressed that a paralegal must have good, solid, varied experience—most recommended at least 5 years—before going freelance.

Income & earning potential

The salaries obtained by paralegals at law firms and in corporate legal departments can be quite good relative to other paraprofessional careers.

While the salaries for paralegals in regular, full-time jobs vary by region and by size of law firm, they usually range from approximately $20,000 for entry level paralegals to near or even exceeding $60,000 for experienced paralegals in technical practice areas working in medium or large firms or for corporations. Additionally, the employed paralegal usually receives benefits and sometimes a yearly bonus.

Tables 1-1 and 1-2 show the results of several recent salary surveys as compiled by the magazine *Legal Assistant Today*. In addition, Table 1-3 shows a comparison of the 1988 and 1992 salary surveys conducted by the Los Angeles Paralegal Association, exemplifying the increase in salaries that paralegals obtained in the course of four years.

Table 1-1
Paralegal salaries

City	1992 average salaries by city Average gross annual salary
Atlanta, GA	$33,986
Austin, TX	30,828
Boston, MA	33,597
Chicago, IL	32,232
Cleveland, OH	28,900
Columbus, OH	27,469
Dallas, TX	31,820
Denver, CO	28,157
Detroit, MI	29,942
Grand Rapids, MI	27,393
Greenville, SC	21,453
Hartford, CT	34,056
Houston, TX	32,579
Kansas City, MO	28,508
Los Angeles, CA	36,990
Memphis, TN	33,625
Miami, FL	32,598
Minneapolis, MN	35,788
New Orleans, LA	30,098
New York City, NY	41,488
Philadelphia, PA	31,908
Phoenix, AZ	39,583
Portland, OR	30,611
Sacramento, CA	28,233
San Francisco, CA	$36,468
Seattle, WA	30,931
Washington, DC	29,020
Wichita, KS	30,689

Table 1-2
Salary breakdown

	Average salary	Maximum salary
By years of experience		
0–2	$23,182	$39,270
3–5	26,079	45,000
6–10	31,058	67,475
11–15	33,939	65,000
More than 15	36,264	72,600
By practice specialization		
Workers' Compensation	24,713	36,000
Family law	24,753	39,270
Personal injury	26,295	55,000
Environmental	27,184	36,000
Litigation-plaintiff	28,408	65,000
Estate & probate	28,689	43,750
Bankruptcy	28,721	53,000
Litigation-defense	30,039	52,000
Real estate	30,156	58,000
Employment/labor	32,009	45,000
Corporate law	33,799	72,600
National		
Rural	24,803	42,000
Urban	28,059	62,000
Metro	31,043	72,600
By region		
Region 1		
Rural	24,791	31,270
Urban	28,770	48,750
Metro	33,280	67,475
Region 2		
Metro	28,833	45,000
Urban	$23,934	$42,000
Rural	21,700	27,300
Region 3		
Metro	30,776	65,000
Urban	26,344	52,000
Rural	19,500	20,800
Region 4		
Rural	20,832	30,160
Urban	29,000	34,500
Metro	31,124	55,000

	Average salary	Maximum salary
Region 5		
Urban	25,871	62,000
Rural	27,322	34,980
Metro	28,703	72,600
Region 6		
Rural	21,000	21,000
Urban	24,513	37,500
Metro	30,943	50,000
Region 7		
Rural	24,100	28,200
Urban	26,213	41,888
Metro	29,570	49,000
Region 8		
Rural	26,388	29,950
Urban	30,234	49,200
Metro	31,620	43,800
Region 9		
Urban	33,961	55,776
Rural	35,600	42,000
Metro	35,372	57,500

Key:

Region 1   Connecticut, Delaware, Maine, Massachusetts, New Hampshire, New Jersey, New York, Pennsylvania, Rhode Island, Vermont

Region 2   Maryland, North Carolina, Ohio, South Carolina, Virginia, Washington DC, West Virginia

Region 3   Alabama, Florida, Georgia, Mississippi, Tennessee

Region 4   Arkansas, Louisiana, Oklahoma, Texas

Region 5   Illinois, Indiana, Kentucky, Michigan, Missouri, Wisconsin

Region 6   Iowa, Kansas, Minnesota, Nebraska, North Dakota, South Dakota

Key:

Region 7   Arizona, Colorado, New Mexico, Utah, Wyoming

Region 8   Alaska, Idaho, Montana, Oregon, Washington

Region 9   California, Hawaii, Nevada

Table 1-3
Los Angeles Paralegal Association salary survey
comparison of 1988 & 1993 average salaries

Years of experience	Average salary 1988	Average salary 1993
0–1	$24,016	$30,136
1–2	26,318	30,614
2–3	26,865	29,441
3–4	28,779	34,682
4–5	31,106	37,883
5–6	31,857	41,002
6–7	35,977	39,670
7–8	33,915	39,422
8–9	38,176	42,425
9–10	35,647	46,014

Reprinted with permission, Copyright 1993 the Los Angeles Paralegal Association.

As for freelance paralegals, we discovered that many freelancers are making a good living, as good as those employed in law firms and corporations. However, no one indicated that income was their prime motive for going solo. Many paralegals changed to being home-based to get more freedom in their schedules, and variety in the work. In fact, several were hoping to work only part-time. Nevertheless, freelance paralegals say they typically earn incomes similar to employed paralegals, and many are making a good full-time living working this way.

Nationally, the figures for earnings of freelance paralegals are harder to come by and not easily verified. Many paralegal associations conduct salary surveys periodically in their community, whether it is local, statewide, or national. However, these surveys cover income from regular jobs and do not cover freelance paralegals. Experienced freelance paralegals in urban areas often bring in as much as $35,000 in a year, and many earn more.

But freelance paralegals rarely take home more than their salaried counterparts. Freelancers typically are paid hourly, and usually command from $25 to $40 per hour from the attorneys who hire them, but they must cover all their own employment taxes and benefits, including health insurance, from that amount. They find that in some weeks no work comes in, while in others they work evenings and weekends to get it all done in 50 or 60 hours. Of course, the more expertise a person has, and the higher the demand for his or her specialization, the more can be demanded as an hourly rate. At least one person we interviewed charges $75 an hour, and she had more work than she could do herself. However, she is highly computerized and extremely efficient in her practice.

Most of the paralegals we interviewed were highly experienced and had a consistent supply of work to keep them busy. They experienced slow periods, and extremely busy periods, but were able to earn a satisfying living overall. However, they all stressed the point that, at the beginning, work came in very slowly, and regular income did not become the pattern until at least six months after starting their freelance businesses.

Deciding about your paralegal career

Questions for students and new paralegals

If you are just starting to think about a paralegal career, or you are currently in a program training for paralegal work, the following checklist can help with your decision, or prompt you to think about considerations unique to your situation. Take a moment now to go through this list and check out your feelings before reading the next few chapters.

- Does being a paralegal appeal to me?
- Am I willing to work very hard and do very detailed work?
- Can I work with highly ambitious, motivated people such as lawyers?
- Can I work cheerfully with stormy personalities?
- Do I enjoy large quantities of paperwork?
- Am I unflappable under pressure?
- Can I handle ambiguity? Solve problems on my own?
- Do I enjoy examining the facets of an issue?

Questions for experienced paralegals

If you have already spent some time as a paralegal and would like to decide whether or not you should go freelance, consider the following questions:

- Do I want to have my own business?
- Do I have paralegal training and/or several years of paralegal experience in the practice area, or am I willing to invest to that degree as a foundation for this career?
- Am I a self-starter? Can I be assertive?
- Do I have the confidence in my skills and experience to complete assignments with little supervision and to question inappropriate assignments?
- Can I negotiate a sufficient billing rate for myself?
- Can I deal with delinquent accounts receivables?
- Do I have a year to get the business started?
- Can I work in a solitary situation, keep to a tight schedule, and be productive?

If you have answered yes to most of these questions, you might be a candidate to have your own business. Please read on in the next two chapters about the specifics of various paralegal work, as well as chapter 7 about establishing your own business.

2 Litigation paralegals

Everyone knows what a trial looks like—television and movies, with the help of the likes of Perry Mason, have seen to that. However, on television and in the movies the cases providing the most entertainment are criminal trials, usually intriguing murders. In the paralegal world, on the other hand, the type of litigation where most paralegals work is civil litigation. While there are paralegals working in the criminal area, the numbers are far smaller. Overall, it is estimated that more than half of all paralegals work in the litigation area, and in the case of freelance paralegals, the percentage is probably much higher because so many tasks in the litigation process are appropriate for freelance work.

What is litigation?

Litigation starts when two or more parties have a dispute causing them damage, loss, or injury that one party claims to be due to the other party's wrongful acts or failure to abide by promises made in an agreement. The complaining person (called the plaintiff) decides to have the problem resolved in a court of law and begins the litigation process by filing a complaint against the other party (who then becomes the defendant). The defendant is served with the complaint, then answers it, and the lawsuit process has begun. The plaintiff and defendant can be one or more persons, businesses, governmental agencies, or other entity, or a combination of them, so the suit can be one person suing another person, or numerous parties suing numerous other parties.

Once the defendants have been served, the suit proceeds to investigation through each side providing information to the other side (called "discovery"), then to preparation for trial and/or negotiation for a settlement (the "pretrial" stage). If the suit does not settle, the case goes to trial. After trial, there might also be appeals to higher courts. In brief, the stages of litigation are:

- Preliminary investigation and research
- Initiation of a lawsuit
- Investigation, fact-gathering, and discovery
- Pretrial
- Trial
- Post-trial motions and appeals

Let's review these stages specifically in regard to what the paralegal does in each step of the process. For simplification, we've assigned these tasks to specific stages in the litigation process. In real life, however, many tasks recur at several points in the process. Real life is never as neat as an outline!

Initiation

At the beginning of a litigation, the paralegal might investigate and verify facts, such as locating the defendants and verifying their names and where they can be served with the complaint. If the attorney represents the plaintiff, the paralegal might be asked to investigate the facts of the case to help in the determination of whether or not a case actually exists. They also might research the assets of potential defendants to determine whether it is worthwhile to pursue the action, or hire an outside firm specializing in asset location to arrange for such searches. Depending on the complexity of the issues involved, paralegals might help draft the complaint, especially paralegals who are experienced in certain areas and learn to handle routine complaints, or those that can be patterned closely on another similar complaint, such as the collection of an unpaid promissory note.

Paralegals might be asked to review the clients' documents and analyze them with respect to the lawsuit's issues, or to prepare a chronology of events as revealed by the documents.

From the beginning of the lawsuit on, there are myriad deadlines to be met and time frames to be observed, so paralegals are frequently the people charged with the responsibility of keeping calendars, tickler (reminder) systems, or docket control programs (a docket is a court calendar) to see that no critical dates are missed. The complaint, summons, and answer are just three of the many court-filed documents created during the course of the lawsuit. Paralegals are usually responsible for maintaining a current, accurate record of all filed court documents showing which party initiated the document and when it was filed in the court. They also typically set up all the files to be used in trial preparation.

Once the complaint has been prepared and signed by the attorney (paralegals do not sign court documents), the paralegal usually prepares the summons, arranges for a process server to serve the complaint and summons, and then has the documents filed with the appropriate court.

If the attorney is representing a defendant in a complaint, paralegals help research the facts and obtain information from the client to respond to the complaint from the defendant's point of view.

During the fact-gathering and discovery phase, there are innumerable opportunities for paralegals to be involved. The allegations made by both parties in their complaint and answer must be studied and verified. Evidence must be gathered and analyzed. For many litigation paralegals, in fact, nearly all of their work occurs during this time.

Fact-gathering & discovery

During the process called discovery, each side is required to provide information requested by the other. There are four ways this can happen.

Interrogatories   Interrogatories are written questions one side asks of the other. They are typically numerous and lengthy, and court rules provide for a certain time period within which they must be answered in writing. Paralegals often assist in drafting the interrogatories, and in reviewing the answers to them as they are received. Just a few years ago the answers were often supplied by number, without the questions being repeated. Coordinating the answers with the questions that had been asked was a time-consuming, cumbersome effort, often literally involving cut-and-paste jobs. Today, some court rules require the questions to be repeated along with the answers when they are provided; and now word processing and other special software is used to link up the questions with the answers. Paralegals are often responsible for working with clients to draft answers or objections to interrogatories asked by the other side.

Requests for production of documents & things   The name of this procedure is exactly what it says: the two sides are entitled to ask each other for documents and things. Each party typically sends the other an exhaustive list of the documents and things they want to see or review, and court rules specify a certain time period within which they must be provided. Sometimes the documents are provided for review in a conference room, and the attorney can review them and request copies of the ones he feels would be pertinent. At other times, copies are made of all the documents, and the copies shipped to the opposing side. The things requested can be any items of physical evidence; for example, X-rays, an automobile, a pair of skis, photographs—anything!

Paralegals help draft the requests for production. Then, once the document copies arrive, paralegals see that a "Bates" stamp number is applied to every document produced. (The Bates stamping is named for the type of stamp used.) The paralegal is usually assigned to index the documents by reading them and identifying key terms. As you might expect, this process has recently been enhanced by using special legal database software that allows the user to code the key words for each document. The database software then allows the paralegal or attorney to sort, search, and review documents quickly. This entire process has come to be known as *automated litigation support system (ALSS)*, and is discussed further in the section on computers in litigation.

When the paralegal's own client has been asked to produce documents and things, the paralegal and attorney must obtain all the appropriate documents and review them before producing them to the other side to be certain nothing is produced that might be privileged or protected information. The paralegal then assembles the documents and sees that they are provided to the opposing side in an order corresponding to the written request. An accurate record must be kept of all documents requested, received, and sent out in response to requests—more paralegal work!

In complex litigation, in particular, discovery becomes a monumental task as thousands of documents are commonly produced by either side that fill boxes and even roomfuls of file cabinets. This phase of the litigation might go on for years.

Depositions   Depositions are an opportunity for attorneys on one side of the case to ask questions of the sworn witnesses, persons who might testify on behalf of the other side. The testimony is recorded by a court reporter and a verbatim transcript is made. Paralegals typically

- Arrange the depositions (times, locations, and court reporters).
- Prepare and serve the subpoenas and notices of deposition.
- Help draft a list of questions to be asked of each witness.

Once deposition is scheduled, the paralegal prepares a file for the attorney who is conducting the deposition, containing all documents having any relationship to the witness being interviewed. Sometimes the paralegal also attends the deposition with the attorney, taking notes and maintaining the documents that are referred to during the questioning. A court reporter then produces a transcript of the deposition, which the paralegal might summarize or index. Many freelance paralegals do this step exclusively; see chapter 5, "Deposition summarizers."

Requests for admission   These requests mean essentially "Please say you agree with us that such-and-such is true." This helps the attorneys verify certain facts, and narrow the facts and issues that need to be argued at trial. Paralegals help draft these requests, by reviewing the documents and becoming familiar with the case. They also help attorneys coordinate responses to requests from the opposing side.

In any of the four types of discovery, if the opposing party fails to respond or responds incompletely within the required time period (or does not respond to reminders or correspondence also drafted by the paralegal), the attorney can draft or have the paralegal draft a motion to compel compliance.

Another important task the paralegal might fulfill during discovery is to prepare a chronology of events in the case taken from the documents produced by all the parties, deposition testimony, and any evidence obtained.

Throughout the discovery process, the paralegal might also act as another mind on the case, providing valuable assistance in spotting connections or inconsistencies among documents, deposition testimony, or evidence being gathered.

As trial approaches, the attorney is required to prepare documents for the court setting out the issues, the facts, the law, and the witnesses and exhibits to be used at trial. This process varies according to the rules of each particular court; it might be called a trial data certificate, a pretrial order, a disclosure certificate, or something similar. In complex litigation, the process might even occupy more than one attorney with paralegals. In small cases, paralegals frequently prepare the first draft of this document, since they have been so closely involved with all the elements of the case.

Pretrial

The court might require scheduling of pretrial conferences where the parties outline the issues to be resolved at trial, or settlement conferences where the parties attempt to negotiate a settlement. Paralegals might arrange for and sometimes attend these conferences, and can help draft a proposed settlement agreement. Should settlement turn out to be impractical, the parties continue to trial, and everyone working on the case becomes immersed in the trial preparation process that requires several steps:

Legal research and writing briefs   Paralegals, even litigation paralegals, usually do not do much true legal research since this is typically assigned to junior attorneys. However, there are exceptions, mostly among those paralegals who work on smaller cases or for small- or medium-sized firms if they have many years of experience. Legal research involves finding cases that support the arguments in the brief—or do not support them, which is just as important to know. A thorough knowledge of legal research resources is required, as well as a creative approach, to find all possible relevant cases. Today, computerized legal research plays an important role in certain steps of legal research (see the section on computers in litigation). However, most research is still done manually, especially reading past cases because online computerized research is usually expensive.

Fran Turner in Novato, California is an example of a freelance paralegal who does a lot of legal research. Usually an attorney asks her to learn what the client's liability is in a specific situation, or what the law is on a certain subject. Fran uses local law libraries to conduct research and writes the attorney a memo outlining what she has found.

Paralegal Bonnie Twigg does research for her attorney clients in the Santa Rosa, California area. She handles discovery, drafting, and answering interrogatories and requests, and she does a lot of the investigation, meeting with people, gathering documents, performing research, sometimes going to medical libraries in addition to her legal research.

Cite-checking and Shepardizing   At several points during the trial preparation stage (and in post-trial appeals) attorneys and some paralegals research various legal issues involved in the case and draft memos (briefs) to support motions they are submitting to the court on a particular issue. Whether or not the paralegals are involved in the actual legal research, they will probably be asked to "Shepardize" and cite-check the brief before it is signed and filed with the court. Shepardizing is the process of double-checking all citations used in the brief referring to precedent-setting cases that other courts have ruled upon, and with which the attorney hopes to bolster his case. It is critical that the cases being cited are properly named and have the proper cite number, and that they are still good law, meaning that they have not been superseded or overruled by subsequent rulings. Paralegals confirm this by checking the volumes of *Shepard's Citations* (a listing of all published cases by cite numbers and notes of any mentions of cases in any subsequent cases). Symbols are used to indicate, among other things, whether that particular case has been affirmed, superseded, questioned, or overruled. Litigation paralegals have developed efficient systems for the cite-checking and Shepardizing processes, and there are a number of computerized systems that help the paralegal to do it very quickly. In fact, *Shepard's* is now available on CD-ROM for extra speed and convenience.

Trial preparation

As trial approaches, work intensifies. Everyone on the case works long, hard hours and the stress level can increase dramatically. Exhibits must be organized, demonstrative evidence prepared, witnesses lined up, evidence organized. Paralegals might prepare visual aids for trial such as charts, diagrams, graphs, posters, photographs, and videos (commonly known as demonstrative evidence) or they might arrange for them to be professionally prepared by an outside service (see chapter 6 for a description and profiles of this business). Paralegals might also help expert witnesses prepare materials they need for their testimony, and they prepare trial notebooks made up of divided sections including research results on each issue, information on each witness, and copies of important documents to be referenced during the trial. They organize copies of any documents that might be submitted as exhibits according to local court rules (in notebook form or in files, as two examples). If needed, they also prepare subpoenas, and arrange to have them served or sent to witnesses.

With the growing focus on courtroom psychology, many attorneys in litigation might also involve the paralegal in getting the list of prospective jurors from the court shortly before trial begins, and researching any available information on them to help with jury selection.

Once trial begins, paralegals sometimes accompany the attorney to trial, or they provide support from the office. If they are at the trial, they assist by observing and taking notes, maintaining the documents that the attorney might need during trial, and keeping track of which exhibits have been admitted into evidence. They also keep track of witnesses, scheduling them appropriately and making sure they are available when needed.

Trial

Fran Turner, a freelance paralegal in Novato, California, often accompanies attorneys to trial. She organizes the files and gets documents together. Fran sometimes participates in conferences with the judge, works on jury selection, takes notes during trial to use in preparing for final argument or post-trial brief; she keeps track of exhibits; she passes notes to attorneys with a suggested question, and gives input on legal issues. She coordinates witnesses, sometimes leaving the courtroom to call for a witness to be available. Fran serves as go-between with clients, helping them understand what is going on and explaining the mechanics of the trial.

Fran cautions that, although paralegals would like to accompany the attorney to trial, it usually takes many years of experience before you get to do this. Large law firms usually have associates go to trial, so she's been lucky to have attorneys who use her this way.

After trial, the attorney might file motions or briefs for an appeal. Again, the processes of research, writing, cite-checking, and Shepardizing are performed by attorneys and paralegals. In addition, paralegals might need to arrange for preparation of the trial transcript, for the court files to be transferred from the trial court to the appeals court, and for the proper pleadings to be filed in the appropriate courts.

Appeals

Although it is true that most freelance litigation paralegals work heavily in the discovery stages, judging by the people we interviewed, freelance litigation paralegals do virtually *all the things listed in this section*, to varying degrees and levels of sophistication. How much they do depends both on what they are capable of doing, and what they can convince the attorneys to let them to do. A summary of what they might do in each stage of litigation follows:

Summary of litigation paralegal tasks

Initiation of a lawsuit

- Research facts and potential defendants, or obtain information to respond to the complaint.
- Draft pleadings and court documents.

- Arrange for service of process and court filings.
- Review and analyze documents.
- Keep calendars.
- Set up and maintain court document files and other case files.
- Research, investigate, and analyze facts.
- Track down evidence by searching public records, obtaining medical records or other documents, or assembling physical evidence.
- Locate and interview potential witnesses and in some cases arrange for an outside investigator.
- Locate and arrange for the services of expert witnesses.

Discovery

- Draft interrogatories, responses to interrogatories, requests for production, deposition questions, or requests for admissions.
- Analyze the other party's responses to interrogatories, production requests or requests for admissions, and coordinate them with the questions or requests.
- Schedule and assist at document productions and depositions.
- Obtain documents from the client, and review, inventory, and assemble documents to be produced.
- Number, review, analyze, index, organize, and maintain files of documents received from other parties.
- Review, summarize, organize, and maintain deposition transcripts and exhibits.
- Draft correspondence and motions related to discovery.
- Keep the issues in mind and help the attorneys to coordinate the discovered facts, documents, and information with the issues.

Pretrial

- Help prepare the pretrial certificate.
- Schedule and attend pretrial or settlement conferences.
- Perform legal research and draft briefs and motions.
- Cite-check and Shepardize briefs.
- Prepare trial notebooks and exhibit notebooks.
- Obtain a jury list and develop background information.
- Prepare and serve subpoenas for witnesses.
- Arrange for and support expert witnesses.
- Coordinate witness scheduling, preparation, and appearances.
- Arrange for preparation of demonstrative evidence.

Trial

- Attend trial, observe, and take notes.
- Maintain communications with witnesses.
- Keep track of documents, exhibits, and demonstrative evidence.
- Confer with attorneys regarding testimony and trial strategy.
- Act as liaison with the client.

As you can see, the variety of tasks is extensive and complex. Most paralegals who work in the litigation area indicate that the work is fascinating and they enjoy their jobs. Many say that they enjoy the adrenaline-surge that accompanies preparing for and participating in a trial, or the satisfaction of seeing a suit settle prior to trial actually taking place.

Computers & litigation

As you can see, litigation is an information-intense business, with documents, exhibits, transcripts of depositions, and many bits and pieces of information floating around. As a result, this is one area in which paralegals and lawyers are recognizing the advantages of using computers to increase their efficiency and productivity. Instead of paralegals or attorneys physically searching through 5,000 or 50,000 documents to find what someone said about a person or how many memos were written about a certain event, or whatever piece of information the attorney is looking for, computers can automate such searches by allowing documents to be indexed, coded, abstracted, and even fully transferred as a text file to the computer.

The computerization of litigation has been growing so rapidly that there is now a clear paralegal specialization in litigation support. To put it succinctly, the more you know about using computers and litigation support software, the more valuable you will be and therefore the more opportunity for jobs you will have. This means that it is worth knowing about the many types of hardware and software systems that have been created especially for the legal field. Without a doubt, the litigation support area is becoming the domain of paralegals who learn to use the systems. Paralegals are the ones put in charge of managing the entire operation of litigation support, and so you might as well become the computer expert.

Although some litigation support systems are very complex and cost from tens of thousands of dollars to millions of dollars, most are priced so that even a home-based paralegal can afford to own them. Here is an overview of the major categories of software programs that a paralegal needs to know about:

Full-text management software

This category of software allows the transcripts delivered by court reporters after a deposition to be searched, summarized/annotated, and indexed rapidly. These are all critical features that attorneys need when faced with dozens of depositions that must be understood and correlated.

Full-text management software is more powerful than a simple word processor. For example, most software packages such as CAT-Links, Summation, and Discovery ZX allow the user to either have two windows on the screen, or to call up a small electronic memo box so that as one reads through the transcript, you can either write a summary of the material or add a comment about the material on screen. Paralegals and attorneys use such comments as reminders of questions they want to ask other deponents, or to flag issues that become important as they read the deposition.

The additional power of full-text management software programs is that they contain powerful search engines that allow the user to search one or many deposition transcripts using key words to find every page where something particular was said. For example, the attorney might want to find every transcript that contains a name, a date, or a specific word. Some programs can produce a complete word list of every word used in transcripts as a way to review the testimony and see what words pop out that might be more important than were previously thought. Sophisticated features of many full-text management packages also allow Boolean searches (find x and y but not z), and proximity searches (find every instance of x within ten words of y). The newest software has many other bells and whistles to facilitate working with lengthy deposition transcripts, such as the ability to organize a deposition transcript according to dates (since the original testimony might have been discussed in a haphazard time frame). Other software allows the attorney or paralegal to search an entire transcript by topic, or to review the transcript and make notes on any page as tickler reminders of questions to ask the witness. Such software exists for both PCs and Macintosh computers.

Three example screens from CAT-Links in Fig. 2-1 demonstrate the power of a full-text management program. Figure 2-1A illustrates how the user can browse through a transcript or use any of the commands at the bottom of the screen, such as Search. Figure 2-1B shows how the software allows the user to review a transcript in split screen mode, using the lower portion to create a digest while scrolling through the actual deposition in the top portion of screen. Figure 2-1C illustrates how CAT-Links can produce a word list of every word in a transcript with the number of occurrences.

2-1A
(A–C) Example of full-text management software: CAT-Links. Copyright 1993 by CAT-Links, Inc.

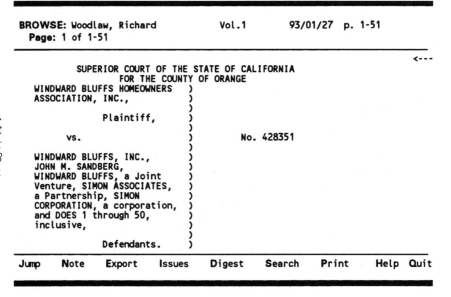

```
BROWSE: Woodlaw, Richard          Vol.1        93/01/27  p.1-51
    Page: 1 of 1-51


            SUPERIOR COURT OF THE STATE OF CALIFORNIA         <---
                  FOR THE COUNTY OF ORANGE
WINDWARD BLUFFS HOMEOWNERS    )
ASSOCIATION, INC.,            )
                             )
            Plaintiff,        )
                             )
        vs.                   )        No. 428351
                             )
─────────────────────────────────────────────────────────────────
DIGEST Edit                            Ln:   1 Cl:  1   Insert     2-1B
LP......R LE.........................................R  L..........R

16:15     Woodlaw prepared all of the specifications on     STANDARD
          the Windward Bluffs project.  Did not use         SPECS
          standard instructions or specifications;
          followed specification masters on file in the
          office but modified them to adapt to specific
          job.


 Use Alt:  Edit  Block  Go to  Print  Search  Transcript  Other   Help Quit
```

```
WORDLIST    Pattern:  A*              1040 total occurrences of 83 words
Transcript: Woodlaw, Richard    Vol.1       93/01/27  p.1-51
─────────────────────────────────────────────────────────────────
    Word                            Occurrence(s)

    A                                    438
    able                                   1
    About                                 19
    Academy                                1
    accepted                               1
    acquaint                               1
    acted                                  1
    actually                               1          2-1C
    adapt                                  1
    admired                                1
    adopted                                2
    Adrienne                               1
    advice                                 1
    after                                  7
    Again                                  3
    ago                                    1
    agree                                  1
─────────────────────────────────────────────────────────────────
 Press Enter to add to Search List.
 Use ↑, ↓, PgUp, PgDn, Home, or End to move.        F9 Help  Esc Quit
```

Document-management software is different from full-text management software in that it relies on a database. However, several software packages are now integrated, and include both functions.

Document-management software allows the legal team to store abstracts of documents (or sometimes the full text of a document) along with several pieces of commonly coded important information in database fields, such as

Document-management software

Document Type, Author, Recipient, Address, Date, Issues/Topic, and so on. The value of this is that rather than needing to physically review thousands of documents looking for a word or name, once the abstract or text is typed into the computer, the user can search the file and locate which documents to review immediately. With programs that integrate both full text and a document-management database, this means that if you were looking for every instance the word fire, for example, you could generate a complete report of all documents that contain that word, as well as see the actual transcripts where the word was used.

With document-management software, there is a lot of initial work typing in abstracts of documents and coding in key words indicating important items that might need to be searched, but such up-front work saves endless hours of time when the attorney needs to find something. Instead of reviewing boxes of paper, the paralegal can simply sit at the computer and type in a search word, and voila, the software lists every document that fits the bill. (Of course, you might need to go find a box to get the original hard copy document if the full text has not been keyboarded into the computer, but the software usually includes a place where you can type in the document's location according to a box, file, or Bates number.)

Document-management software has proven to be a godsend for attorneys, and represents the increasing sophistication of specialized software. Many programs are now being designed by people in the field. For example, CASE-Links (CAT-Links, Inc.) was designed by and for paralegals, according to Margaret Dalton, General Manager of the company, and Summation Blaze was designed by a team of litigation lawyers. As a result, the search algorithms reflect the types of searches (e.g., Boolean and proximity searches) that lawyers commonly perform (see Fig. 2-2).

SUMMATION's Main Menu

2-2A
(A–C) Summation Blaze is an integrated program that allows for both full-text retrieval and document management. Copyright 1993 by Summation Legal Technologies, Inc.

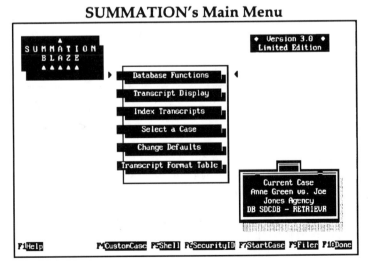

Annotating Transcripts

2-2 B

Searching All Case Data at Once

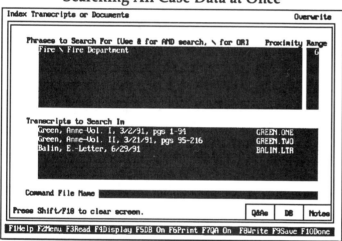

2-2 C

Summation Blaze is an integrated program that allows for both full-text retrieval and document management. Figure 2-2A (Main Menu) shows several different functions provided by the software. Figure 2-2B (Annotating Transcripts) shows how an electronic comment can be created to accompany any portion of transcript as a reminder to the attorney of the testimony's relevance. Figure 2-2C (Searching All Case Data at Once) shows how the user can key in a term and indicate which documents to search. The software then searches all selected transcripts to locate every mention of the term. If desired, Summation Blaze can also print out a report in chronological order showing the summary of each document, thus helping the attorney to understand the events and build a case for the client. (Fig. 2-2D)

SEARCH PHRASE: ANYTEXT CONTAINS "Fire Department" or ANYTEXT CONTAINS Fire

#RE	DOCDATE	DOCTYPE	ISSUES	SUMMARY
1	July 2nd 0000	BLUEPRINTS	Blueprints Fire Safety Water Flow	Blueprints for building. All fire safety mechanism were intact and up to specification.
2	July 20th 1980	AGREEMENTS	Policies Background Check	Shows that it was Anne's responsibility to respond to emergencies, such as the fire, and call and direct the needed emergency services.
3	April 30th 1991	SCHEDULES	Background Check Fire Safety	Shows that Mr. Bill Presley was scheduled to work on 4/4/90, the day of the fire.
4	June 2nd 1991	LETTER	General Damages Policies Fire Safety	Sprinklers had been tampered with so the fire would easily spread.
5	June 10th 1991	LETTER	Rebuttal Testimony	Mary saw Bill Presley at the scene of the fire.
6	June 24th 1991	LETTER	Mental Health Medical Record OSHA	Ann Green was seeing a therapist prior to the fire.
7	June 29th 1991	LETTER	Rebuttal Testimony	Mr. Presley was seen outside Boboli's Donuts after the fire.
8	August 1st 1991	LETTER	General Damages Policies Timing	Termination letter citing the inadequate response of Anne to the fire as their reasoning.

Recent document-management software has even gone further, taking advantage of optical character recognition (OCR) so that original documents can be scanned into the database and converted to text (scanning treats a document as a graphic image, so the computer cannot actually read it until OCR software converts the image to ASCII text). This allows many more documents to become searchable.

In addition, the newest imaging software uses higher level imaging technology and CD-ROM laser disks that hold huge amounts of data (between 15,000 and 20,000 pages) to store actual graphical images of documents, including those with handwriting and signatures that cannot be converted to text. Such systems can be taken into the courtroom where the attorney can immediately look up a document rather than lugging around boxes and boxes of paper. This means that lawyers need not fumble through boxes of documents or exhibits in the middle of a trial or deposition, but rather can easily locate what they want within seconds.

For example, two products from a company called inVzn® help attorneys maintain control over runaway documents. Exhibit-Link® and Trial-Link® both take documents that have been scanned onto CD-ROM disks and allow them to be retrieved instantly. The attorney can call up any document with a bar code wand waved over a sheet of paper containing all the bar codes identified by exhibit. The document then appears on the computer screen or monitor for jury and judge to see. Trial-Link® is even fancier; it is interactive, allowing the lawyer to circle words or highlight passages on his computer screen; the jury sees the same highlighting on their television screen.

Although much of this technology is still developing, it is clear that the legal profession is changing rapidly toward what is already being called *the paperless trial*. In fact, as we write, the current litigation between women with breast implants and the manufacturers is being done using CD-ROM disks to save on the huge costs of copying millions of documents that over 800 attorneys representing plaintiffs want to see. Instead, the documents will be stored on CD-ROM disks that attorneys can order for $25 each (although they must have a CD-ROM player for their computer, costing from $300 to $500).

For most cases, document-management software is sufficient, since you can store an abstract of all documents and select only key documents to store full-text (when you need to read exactly what the document said). For most people, scanning and imaging thousands of documents is not necessary, but the technology is improving so quickly that in the near future, it is likely that a combination of all three systems will become inexpensive and in common use everywhere. Together, a combination delivers what is often called the three-pronged approach to litigation support: full text (the complete text of any document); images (allowing the attorney to be able to see the actual original document); and hierarchical database ability (allowing searches of any type so that the attorney can quickly retrieve any document or section of a document based on his or her search criteria).

The following is a list of several of the most popular litigation support packages.

CAT-Links (full text)
CASE-Links (document management)
CAT-Links, Inc.
2100 N. Broadway, Suite 320
Santa Ana, CA 92706
(800) 825-4657

For the PC

Discovery ZX (full text)
Discovery Base (document management)
Discovery Video (document management including video)
Stenograph Legal Services, Inc.
3000 Executive Parkway, Suite 530
San Ramon, CA 94583
(800) 527-8366

Folio Views (document management)
Folio Corp.
2155 N. Freedom Blvd., Suite 150
Provo, UT 84604
(801) 375-3700

INMAGIC (document management)
INMAGIC Plus (document management including imaging)
Inmagic Inc.
2067 Massachusetts Ave.
Cambridge, MA 02140
(617) 661-8124

Exhibit-Link (document management)
Trial-Link (multimedia trial presentation system)
inVzn Development Corp.
1478 North Tech Blvd.
Gilbert, AZ 85234
(800) 828-8884

Summation II (integrated full-text and document management)
Summation Blaze (integrated full-text and document management)
Summation Legal Technologies
595 Market St., Suite 2050
San Francisco, CA 94105
(800) 735-7866

For the Macintosh   Ready for Trial!
Robins Analytics, Inc.
245 E. 6th St., Suite 821
St. Paul, MN 55101
(800) 767-3239

Sonar Professional
Virginia Systems
5509 W. Bay Ct.
Midlothian, VA 23112
(804) 739-3200

For more information, *Legal Assistant Today* magazine has had many articles on the use of computers in litigation support. Contact them at (714) 755-5450 for back issues. Also read *The Lawyer's PC*, a newsletter available from Shepard's/McGraw Hill (call them at (719) 488-3000). This newsletter is an excellent resource for learning about the computer needs of small law offices, including hardware and software reviews. There are many additional legal newsletters such as ComputerCOUNSEL, a national monthly newsletter devoted to computing in the legal profession by Richard L. Robbins, and *Leader's Legal Tech Newsletter*, edited by the Law Firms Group of Ernst & Young.

Although paralegals are not always involved in doing legal research, they need to be familiar with the online databases that are commonly used for legal research: LEXIS and WESTLAW. Both are available as online services (meaning that you must dial into them with a modem), for which you pay a subscription fee plus online time charges.

Online database research software

LEXIS was introduced by the Ohio State Bar in 1967, and has been subsequently marketed by Mead Data Central. LEXIS is a full-text retrieval system that searches the full text of federal and state databases of cases, court decisions, digests, and statutes. In litigation, which is heavily dependent on precedent-setting cases, the paralegal and/or lawyer must frequently research previous cases that are similar to the case at hand, in order to learn how the courts held in those cases. A computerized search of these databases therefore provides an efficient and up-to-date method of finding the information rather than going to a law library and looking up the cases in books. (Books also take months to typeset and print, whereas electronic databases are quickly updated with new information.) The researcher keys in Boolean or proximity searches, and as with all online databases, the key to a successful search is to use the right combination of key words so that the computer can find only those cases that most closely apply. Whereas one combination of key words might find 50 cases, a different combination of key words might bring you closer to your target, finding only five cases that should be researched.

LEXIS also allows the paralegal to access other services such as Shepard's Citation Service to Shepardize a brief, among others.

WESTLAW is similar to LEXIS but differs in the numbers of cases it carries and the dates to which it goes back. It is developed and marketed by West Publishing Company and requires the payment of a subscription fee and online connect-time charges per hour.

In addition to legal research, the paralegal is often responsible for factual research as well. Just as with LEXIS and WESTLAW, there are dozens of online services such as NEXIS, DIALOG, CompuServe, GEnie, Dow Jones News/Retrieval Service, BRS Information Technologies, and dozens of others through which specific databases can be accessed to find information ranging from general news articles to highly technical information in any field. Some of these databases are full-text, while others carry only abstracts of the original articles. The paralegal can use general online databases to find out facts and information on literally any topic. He or she might need to research the history of a business, the patent behind an invention, the viability of a new product, the origins and use of a chemical—just about any topic. There is a wealth of information available at one's fingertips through online services.

The key to using an online service is knowing how to log onto the service (since each vendor has its own log-on procedures) and how to formulate the request using the right key words. In this regard, the paralegal might do some of the same things that an "information broker" does, and as a result, in some cases it might be cheaper to call a professional researcher than to spend time and money doing the research.

Other software used by paralegals

In addition to the preceding software, several other types of software are commonly used by all paralegals.

Word-processing software   This is obviously the most commonly used software and is now a fairly standard expectation for a paralegal. The word processor of choice in the legal profession is WordPerfect, which by all accounts is used in nearly every law office in the country. According to Ken Merritt, public relations specialist at WordPerfect, some of the reasons for this dominance in the legal market is that the software has hooks into other important software used by law firms: JurisSoft, LEXIS, NEXIS, and WESTLAW. Knowing how to use a word processor is critical in the paralegal profession today, as it offers greater productivity and efficiency than using a secretary in many cases.

Calendaring & docket control software   This type of software automates the tracking of important dates that must be maintained for cases: pleadings, motions, court hearings, and even client meetings. If a lawyer has dozens of cases, as most do, using paper calendars to keep track of all deadlines is very cumbersome and often leads to mistakes. Calendar software simplifies the entire problem. Once dates are input into the program, the software acts as a tickler system that automatically reminds the paralegal what is due when each day.

Time-keeping and billing software   This type of software, of which TimeSlips is the most commonly used, lets you track exactly how much time is spent on each project, by whom, and on which task. In essence, the software can work in either of two ways. It can reside in the background of a computer, silently keeping track of how much time you spend word-processing a document, reading a memo, or talking on the phone (you need to push a button to tell the software when to start and stop counting), and then tally for you the time for each activity or project. Alternatively, you simply use the program at the end of each day to record your time on all your projects, and it tallies the total times on a daily, weekly, or monthly basis. Time-keeping software has become very important to the more business-oriented law firms of today. The software is used to calculate attorney and paralegal hours, to prepare billing statements, to record income, and to monitor overdue accounts.

Graphics software The major use of graphics software in the legal field is to prepare presentations and courtroom graphics of evidence. Because this field is becoming more specialized, we present more detailed information on this field in chapter 6, in which we profile several people and companies that produce "demonstrative evidence."

For an excellent in-depth explanation of the growing use of computers in the legal profession, read *Computers and the Law* by Peggy N. Kerley, published by the National Federation of Paralegal Associations, Inc. You can buy a copy of the book directly from NFPA for $30.

Fran Chernowsky
Litigation Resources & Consulting

Business profile

Fran Chernowsky is an example of a paralegal who has used her knowledge of computers to expand what was a home-based paralegal business into Litigation Resources & Consulting, a litigation support business in Van Nuys, California with several employees. She also provides a temporary support personnel service.

Fran uses computers a lot in her work. She travels with a laptop to depositions or to court where she takes notes, and she makes presentations of how to use computers to her attorney clients. She relies heavily on modems and has one in all her computers so she can log onto CompuServe and other online databases for research on professional articles, general news articles, and technical journal articles. She uses CompuServe bulletin board networks to exchange information with others. When Fran is on the road she can upload and send something to herself on CompuServe, and download it when she returns to the office. She sends work such as memos and letters to clients via CompuServe. She also has accounts in GEnie (GE information services), and Delphi (Internet, which has access into universities and government installations). The three services she uses all have research capabilities, and specialized services for searching public records and government materials. Fran even travels with surge protectors, digital converters, and modem cords so that she can always be ready to dial up.

In addition to her paralegal work, and in conjunction with the computerized litigation support she provides, Fran does computer consulting to lawyers. She has helped attorneys set up computerized procedures to make their offices run more efficiently. For example, she helped one attorney set up a calendar system that helped his office run more smoothly. In another law firm, Fran trained the in-house paralegal on computer software; her input benefited the paralegal, and the firm is giving Fran business.

Fran began her freelance service from her home for the first two years, but has since moved to an office. However, Fran is now considering moving her business back home to take advantage of all the benefits of working from home. She particularly enjoyed being able to take an occasional break, since she works such long hours. She also liked being more informal; "You can work in pjs" as she says, and "work any hour of the day or night." However, Fran's business has now grown to the point that she keeps several additional employees busy.

Fran is a 19-year veteran of paralegal work. She has always been active in paralegal associations and is currently President of the California Association of Freelance Paralegals (CAFP). Between her paralegal business and her activities with the California Association of Freelance Paralegals, Fran seems to have endless energy and is an example of how successful a creative, active, and resourceful entrepreneurial paralegal can be.

Skills & aptitudes of litigation paralegals

It is clear from the variety, complexity and quantity of tasks listed for litigation paralegals that a variety of skills are required for this career, including:

- Communications skills
- Excellent listening skills, including the ability to get all the information you need from a conversation, whether with an attorney or an information source.
- Analytical ability, to be able to review a series of documents and spot patterns or significance among them.
- Research skills, to know where to go for both legal and factual information.
- Organizational skills, to be able to set up a system that makes sense to others.
- Ability to juggle myriad details without letting any drop through the cracks, and still keep the big picture in mind.
- A broad knowledge about the litigation process and the variety of contributions paralegals can make to the process, (often you can or must create the job description for an assignment).
- Ability to work with poise under stress and pressure.
- Attention to detail, e.g., with cite checking.

In addition, in order to perform as a freelance litigation paralegal, a person must have considerable in-house litigation experience. As Susan Kligerman, a freelance paralegal in Mt. Laurel, New Jersey says, "No attorney is comfortable with the types of questions a new person would have to ask. You need several years working under supervision;" Susan recommends 5 years as did most of the people we interviewed. This enables you to get a thorough knowledge of the resources available in litigation, and how to get everything you need without bugging the law firm for backup to help you. An attorney once told Susan, "Never tell me it can't be done; find the answer." You need the ability to find everything, even if it is not the answer the attorney wants.

Marti Holmes, a freelance paralegal in Denver, found that contract paralegals are given more responsibility as case managers than in-house paralegals are. Attorneys who are paying you to manage the case will listen to your ideas on how to organize it, and have more respect for you. It's vital that a contract paralegal undertaking case management have sufficient background to meet that expectation. Marti suggests litigation paralegals look for attorneys whose qualities their own traits complement. In those situations, experienced paralegals provide a needed perspective. Background and experience build a foundation of maturity that freelance paralegals need, in order to attract business and to perform as well as they will be expected to.

The litigation paralegals we interviewed, even paralegals who began this career before such formal training was universally available, feel paralegal training is critical for this career. One person recalled an experience when she worked against a paralegal for opposing counsel. The paralegal was a very bright person with both a B.A. and M.A. but she did not have a paralegal background. That lack showed because she did not know discovery rules and laws. The aptitudes and traits freelance litigation paralegals must demonstrate include:

- Independence—ability to set the necessary agenda and follow it.
- Ability to meet strict deadlines.
- Ability to work long, solitary hours on a project—If you are a very social person and need to work around people, this is not the job for you, unless you accept strictly in-house assignments.
- Team-player—You must be comfortable supporting a team effort and willing to do what it takes, for as long as it takes, to get the job done without whining!
- Assertiveness—Many steps along the way will seem formidable, information will be unavailable, or the result you want impossible. You must be able to insist and persist, without alienating the people whose help you need (a court clerk, a hesitant witness, your own support staff or an outside service company), until a way is found.
- Creativity—You can come up with unusual routes to the result, when the usual route doesn't work.

- Sense of humor—Everyone we interviewed mentioned this so it must be pretty critical!
- Business "smarts"—This is running a business, not just paralegal work.

Marti Holmes believes empathy is another important quality for legal assistants in litigation. Paralegals need to be able to hold clients' hands, and attorneys don't as a rule do that well. Furthermore, attorneys are very expensive by the hour.

Advantages & disadvantages of working in litigation

One very practical reason to go into litigation is because that is where most of the jobs are. However, it is also where most of the paralegals are working, so there is some corresponding competition for the jobs. Other advantages are more personal. According to many, the variety of subject matter is very attractive—there is always something new to learn. Every lawsuit you work on introduces you to a new field of knowledge—perhaps the mechanics of a ski lift, what it is that accountants do, what affects the viscosity of wheelchair cushions, or what causes home foundations to fluctuate, to give a few examples. By the time you have worked with the documents in the case, interviewed witnesses, read the interrogatories and the answers to them, designed or even created trial exhibits, and helped as the attorney sets out the trial strategy, you have become an expert in the area.

Other advantages of litigation work include the fast pace of work, especially as trial approaches. The level of excitement and tension builds and you become more and more invested in the outcome of the case.

There are disadvantages to the field of litigation. Just as you get "invested" in a case so that it begins to take over your thoughts and your night dreams, it might settle and suddenly you have nothing more to do on it but organize the files and send them off for storage. The settlement is probably an enormous relief, and of course a cost savings, for the client and the opposing party, but for you it is anticlimactic. The sudden drop-off is even more dramatic if you are working freelance, because not only are you suddenly bereft of what has been the focus of your days for weeks or perhaps months, you are also out of work.

If the case does not settle, as it approaches trial you might experience another disadvantage: long hours. Litigation paralegals, more than any other field of practice, have periods where the hours they put into trial preparation become very, very heavy. This is unavoidable, but it is not constant. It builds prior to actual trial. In some areas, there is a high percentage of settlement prior to trial, so the hours might not be as intensive. But as a rule, litigation work is trial preparation work, and long hours will be a factor.

Another disadvantage is that because litigation is the practice area utilizing the largest number of paralegals, litigation paralegals are more interchangeable than paralegals with narrower specialties. While experienced people have an easier time getting jobs than less experienced or inexperienced people, there is more competition for litigation jobs for people with just a couple of years of experience, because there are many such litigation paralegals in most legal communities.

Some paralegals find that the adversarial process is a "downer"—litigation inevitably means dispute and conflict, and the hardball tactics used by some attorneys can be offensive. This element of the practice contributes to paralegal burnout.

Finally, many litigation attorneys have very strong egos—(think about how much acting goes on at trial). Many are part performer, part charmer, part genius, and very much in charge of everything going on around them. They can have a very dramatic temperament, and be very demanding. Of course, they can also be extremely bright and fascinating personalities. Some litigation paralegals tire of working with such strong personalities and find them a drawback to this area of law.

Now that you have an idea of the nature of litigation paralegal, answer the following questions to see if you might want to go on.

- Are you a self-starter?
- Do you thrive on excitement in your work?
- Do you work well under pressure?
- Can you handle long, heavy hours from time to time?
- Can you work in solitude?
- Do you enjoy working on computers?
- Can you organize things well?
- Do you enjoy learning a lot about a variety of things?
- Can you work comfortably with strong personalities?
- Do you take creative approaches to solving problems?
- Do you have, or are you willing to get, a few years of experience in the litigation area?

Deciding if this business is for you

The usual route to paralegal litigation work is to spend a few years at a law firm or corporation to obtain the necessary experience before going solo as a freelancer. For this reason we discuss the steps both to getting a job and building a freelance business.

Getting started

Litigation is the largest specialty of paralegal employment within law firms. As we pointed out earlier in the chapter, nearly one-half of all paralegals employed in firms work in the area of litigation, and employment trends in litigation have been quite steady.

Working for a law firm or corporation

To get a first job as a litigation paralegal in a law firm, you will be most successful if you have graduated from an ABA-approved school with a paralegal certificate, excellent research and writing skills, good organizational ability, and a strong interest in litigation. Furthermore, it is obvious that today, the more you know about computers, the more likely your chances will be to land a law firm job, because more and more hardware and software is being developed for the litigation area, given its dependence on keeping track of documents and gathering information.

Finding a position as a paralegal in a law firm or corporation requires following many of the usual steps that most people utilize to locate a job: resumes, networking, cold calling, answering ads, contacting job placement agencies, and so on. Most paralegal schools and training programs not only have placement services but also do an excellent job of teaching students how to prepare resumes and conduct themselves at interviews, so we do not cover these areas comprehensively. However, we have a few suggestions based on the experiences of paralegals and paralegal coordinators who hire them:

Resumes, your cover letter, and writing samples you provide are your work samples   Be absolutely certain there are no spelling, punctuation or grammatical errors. That should be obvious, but people who hire paralegals say "You'd be surprised!" Furthermore, your writing style, for example in a cover letter, should reflect energy and enthusiasm, and show that you know something about the firm or company and are eager to work there. Everyone says they want a "challenging" position—make yourself stand out by saying something true but more distinctive.

The first thing about interviews is to get into one   Do not hesitate to contact everyone you know who might be able to introduce you to a hiring person, whether it is someone in human resources, a paralegal coordinator, or an attorney. See if they will meet with you just to talk about what you want to do, give you some information about the local legal community, or what paralegals do in their firm, or just their advice. Most people like to talk about what they do, so offer to take them to lunch so you can pick their brain. Be pleasant and brief if they are not interested, and try someone else. Not only will you learn what they have to offer, you can let them meet you and get to know you, and there can be a ripple effect from that.

Be prepared when an actual job interview comes along   Read all the reminders you can about interviews, get lots of sleep, look your best and be bright, enthusiastic, professional, and friendly. Be prepared to talk about what you have done before that shows how promising you are.

Don't be discouraged   The first job is not easy to get these days—it's probably not you, times are hard in many legal communities. Be persistent. The most important factor in getting that first job is timing—it's getting your resume or placing a telephone call just when an opening happens. A lot of that is luck, a lot of it is staying in touch with what's going on in local law firms and corporations. You can learn what's going on through your paralegal association contacts, through reading local bar journals and business papers, and classified ads, and through constantly talking to everyone—at church, at the store, at PTA, at parties—about what you are looking for.

Call the temporary paralegal agencies   Some place permanent positions, but if necessary, consider taking temporary work to get the experience everyone wants you to have. Consider accepting a combination paralegal/secretary position if there seems to be promise of real paralegal work.

Be client-oriented   In all your interactions with potential employers, remember that the law firm or attorney is your potential client and concentrate on their interests rather than your aspirations and intentions. Be thinking of what you can do to help them out, particularly to make their practice more profitable, efficient, and client-oriented. Find out what they need and what is involved in their practice, and then be the solution to their problems. For example, if they have too much work and are disorganized, you can do some of the tasks the attorneys might be doing now, and suggest how you would organize a typical case for trial. If the attorney has not used a paralegal before, stress how you can be billed out at a rate more than sufficient to cover your salary and benefits. For attorneys who have used paralegals, stress the tasks that you can do that they might not have thought of as paralegal work.

You can find further advice available on paralegal job hunting through the "Career Advice" column in *Legal Assistant Today*, written by C. B. Estrin; and two recent books:

Paralegal: An Insider's Guide to the Fastest Growing Occupations of the 1990s, by Barbara Bernardo, (Peterson's Guides, 1993)

How to Land Your First Paralegal Job: An Insider's Guide to the Fastest-Growing Profession of the Nineties by Andrea Wagner (Estrin Publishing, 1992)

There are three options you can pursue if you are establishing or seeking to establish your own freelance paralegal business. Following these are a brief review of each.

The self-employment route

1. Turn your regular job into a home-based job via telecommuting or working some of the time at home.
2. Work through a temporary agency to get freelance work at law firms, corporations, or government agencies; contract on a project-by-project basis.
3. Set up your own business and seek your own clients. The same employers of full-time employed legal assistants are all potential clients: private law firms, corporations, and government agencies.

Convert your in-house job to a home-based job

In a few situations, paralegals employed in permanent positions have been able to become home-based paralegals without leaving their regular positions, by convincing their employers to let them perform their jobs from home. Attorneys are notoriously slow to adapt to changes in work style, however, so very few law firms have established procedures for paralegals to take work home regularly or telecommute to their jobs. The individuals who have managed this working arrangement are paralegals whose work can be performed off site. They are often highly experienced and valued employees whose attorney-employers have absolute confidence in their paralegal's integrity, motivation, and productivity. These people are usually mature as well, and assertive enough to demonstrate that they have what they need to get the job done well.

One obstacle to working from home is that attorneys frequently do not believe it is possible to work off site, when in fact the task is quite manageable. For example, documents in a complex litigation case can be coded and indexed from a home office, and the database updated and manipulated on a personal computer. Reports can be printed and faxed or sent by modem to the office. Discovery documents can be reviewed and analyzed, pleadings and correspondence drafted, depositions summarized, etc.

Before approaching an employer with a request to become home-based, take the following steps.

1. Ask yourself, "Do my attorneys respect my professionalism, trust and value me as an employee?"
2. Review your work carefully and plan how you would do it from home.
3. Review the obstacles discussed in the previous section and prepare a response addressing each one.
4. Be sure you have the assertiveness, maturity, and communication skills to be able to get what you need from the office and to work productively at home.
5. Discuss your proposal informally with the senior partner you work with, or another attorney who might be supportive, and get their suggestions for how to proceed.
6. Prepare a written proposal setting out briefly how the arrangement would work, how your compensation might be adjusted, how the proposal would affect your billed hours numbers, and your willingness to be flexible, to be at the office when necessary for meetings or other obligations.
7. Agree to meet periodically while the arrangement is in process, to evaluate the success of the program.

It is important to bear in mind the concerns and needs of the attorneys with whom you work about the security of the files, the need for prompt response to clients, your productivity, accessibility, and responsiveness. But studies show that, preconceptions aside, telecommuting employees are highly productive compared to employees working on-site in the office. As indicated in an article entitled "Wired for Business" in the April 1993 issue of LAMA Manager (a publication of the Legal Assistant Management Association), participants in an IBM program called "Flexiplace" cited productivity gains of up to 50 percent, resulting from uninterrupted work time, reduction in the number of meetings, longer work hours because of lack of commuting time, and the ability to work in the evening if desired. In addition, some clients' needs can more easily be met outside the 9:00 to 5:00 work day. This can be useful in today's global economy, in which the ability to respond to requests from different time zones is becoming mandatory.

Employers who value your work and can see the feasibility of your working from home might far prefer to adapt to that arrangement for you, rather than lose you as an employee to one of the following arrangements for home-based paralegal work.

Evelyn Cable
Dallas, Texas

Evelyn Cable was able to move her corporate paralegal job home when she had a baby in May of 1993. She had been working for a corporation's general counsel as in-house corporate paralegal, but when she had her baby, she and her boss together worked out an arrangement that allowed her to resume her work from home. Evelyn continued the arrangement for five months without any difficulty (although she later decided to devote herself to child raising for a while). But Evelyn's boss was enthusiastic about the arrangement and encouraged her to continue it because he valued her work and hoped to keep her in her job.

From home, Evelyn did a variety of tasks formerly done in the office, such as minutes for board meetings, working on departmental budgets, telephoning people at the company in her department and in others to stay abreast of news. She supervised in-house work at the office via phone, relying on her efficient secretary. The latter reviewed each day's mail with her by phone, letting Evelyn tell her how to handle each item. Not surprisingly, adjustments had to be made in the work. For example, Evelyn found that the company used outside service companies more than when she was at the office.

Evelyn believes a working paralegal in a similar situation can convince an employer to start a similar arrangement. "You need to have enough experience to be able to answer questions for yourself, not relying on someone at the office to watch or direct every project closely. You also need the self-discipline to get up and do the work, and not procrastinate."

There is also a financial commitment involved in equipping your home office with equipment compatible to your employer's; for example, a computer, word-processing software, and a modem. In Evelyn's case she also had the same spreadsheet software, so she could do calculations, budget projections, and work on the company's stock appreciation rights plan, using the spreadsheet to track the amounts that had been issued.

There were some disadvantages to the arrangement: There is still a lot of work that must be done at the office; some things you can't do at home. For example, the company minute books are kept in the office, and there were occasional meetings to attend, so she wasn't totally free from some commuting. Also, she did feel some isolation being removed from the day-to-day things at the office and the camaraderie of her colleagues.

Evelyn says the special people skills paralegals develop in working with attorneys are the same ones that made this working-at-home arrangement successful. That is, the paralegal has to have earned the attorneys' respect, for her and what she could do. "Show them your ability to work independently all along, then they are willing to give you that opportunity. They need to be comfortable that when they give you something to do you will get it done, and they are not afraid to have you out of their sight."

Employment from a paralegal service agency

Temporary services are also a major source of jobs, since they get most of their calls from firms that have a sudden need for litigation paralegals. Agencies are often called for a number of paralegals to staff a document production, to summarize depositions, or code (index) documents. They also have assignments requiring case managers, to supervise legal assistants on preparation for a trial.

Many freelance legal assistants working from home receive their assignments through a paralegal service or temporary agency. The person signs on with a service, and the service maintains a list of available paralegals. When an assignment comes in from a law firm, corporation, or government agency, the service will match the job requirements with individuals on their list of available paralegals, taking into consideration the specific experience needed, the area of practice, the degree of management skill required, and even personality characteristics.

One advantage of working through a service is accessibility to more jobs—the service does the work of finding the jobs and negotiating with the employer for a good rate of pay. Temporary work might, therefore, provide more experience than if you had a permanent job. In addition, doing temporary work clearly gives you more independence, as you can accept or turn down jobs at your preference. You might also be able to get workers' compensation insurance from the agency, and because the agency is your employer, they will usually deduct taxes and FICA from your check so you do not have to deal with calculating and paying estimated taxes. Last, the service might also have equipment available for your use (computers, dictating machines, copiers, etc.) and even provide free training on computers and software to improve your skills.

A disadvantage of working through a service is reduced income. A service usually will keep a portion of your pay to cover their overhead and profit. In addition, you have less control over your schedule and where you are sent to work. The job might be a poor match of personalities. Good services attempt to match people, but they work under a limitation, since it is very difficult for the service to have met each specific attorney with whom the contract employees will be working. A lot of the placement is trial and error. Another disadvantage is that the job might terminate abruptly if a lawsuit settles unexpectedly. In such cases, there is rarely any termination bonus—you are just suddenly out of work and needing another assignment. Whether or not you are eligible for unemployment compensation depends on local laws and regulations.

Finally, you are often not free to accept a permanent position with the employer where the service has sent you, should you and the employer wish that to happen. The employer might be able to "buy you out" of your contract with the service—it depends on the terms of the contract you have signed with the service. Some paralegals do well accepting work from employers with whom they have individual relationships (not established through the service) and accepting other assignments through a service when time permits, or when the assignment is appealing. This combination might work for you.

While most temporary services prefer to utilize experienced paralegals, and most jobs require paralegal experience, there are increasing opportunities for paralegals with training but without experience especially for jobs involving Bates stamping and document indexing. Many services give a test to new contract paralegals before sending them on jobs in order to verify skills and aptitudes for certain types of work. The majority of jobs available through services are in the litigation field because this is where attorneys often face sudden crunch periods with "real" deadlines, according to Susan Scott, founder of Paralegals Plus, Inc. in Dallas, Texas. (But there are also placements available in the areas of real estate, corporate, domestic law, personal injury litigation, and workers compensation litigation.) Most positions available through services are performed on-site at the law firm or corporation, although there are a few jobs that can be performed from a home office. Deposition summarizing, for example, is frequently done at home.

In many urban areas where such services exist, competition is fierce, both among the services and among available contract legal assistants. But two owners of temporary service agencies, Joanna Hughbanks, owner of Paralegal Associates of Denver, and the aforementioned Susan Scott of Paralegals Plus, Inc. in Dallas, Texas both believe that the need for temporary legal assistant services continues to grow, and that working through a service is a good alternative for many paralegals. Like many such services, neither owner needs to advertise for paralegals to fill her needs.

Business profile

Jane Bourgoin
Denver, Colorado

Jane is an example of a long-term litigation paralegal who gets assignments from a service agency to manage litigation or to oversee a number of paralegals working in the discovery phase of a law suit. Jane signed up with a service as soon as she left her corporate position, took one week of "R-&-R," and had only one week of quiet before the service had work for her. When we spoke with her, several months later, she had not had any time without work. How did she stay so busy? Jane has an excellent track record as a case manager and good experience is a plus in getting good work from services, as it is getting work directly from firms. In particular, services look for people they know will make them look good on the job, people with maturity, judgment, excellent skills, and congenial personalities. If you can offer those benefits to a service, you will stay on the top of their list for good assignments.

Jane started out in legal aid in Maine, where she learned to be a paralegal. Because Maine lets paralegals practice in administrative forums, she could represent clients in nonadversarial proceedings, like social security hearings, and unemployment compensation. She learned to know first hand what an attorney needs to have at trial. Jane has had a few years of corporate experience, four of which were in a corporate legal department. Inside the corporation Jane coordinated litigation and outside counsel, and saw cases from the client's perspective.

Tips for getting temporary employment

Joanna Hughbanks, owner of Paralegal Associates of Denver, has several suggestions for contract paralegals who wish to stand out, and receive regular, good assignments:

- Demonstrate integrity in every assignment, and in your dealings with the service as well as with the employers where you are sent to work.
- Approach every job with diligence and perform with excellence. A paralegal whose work reflects well on the service will always be on the top of the list for the best placements.
- Be resilient, able to work with a positive attitude in a variety of situations and with a variety of personalities.
- Develop an attitude of loyalty toward the service. In other words, although you might wish or even need to sign on with more than one agency, never renege on an assignment with one agency to take a better assignment with another. When a plum assignment comes along, you can be sure a paralegal who has reneged on a prior assignment will not be on the top of the list of those to be called.
- Be honest about how your job went. Good services monitor the quality level of the work their contract employees perform. Joanna sends a quality assurance letter to the client after the assignment, to get feedback. In addition, she keeps in touch with the supervisor of the employee (ideally that is another employee from the same service, acting in a supervisor role). The service also makes follow-up phone calls during the project.

In exchange, it means a lot to the service operators, like Joanna, that they keep the best paralegals on their list. Joanna tries to do this by understanding their preferences and their personalities, and knowing the sort of work they do best, so she can send them on jobs with a high expectation of success.

Susan Scott
Paralegals Plus, Inc.

Susan Scott, founder and owner of Paralegals Plus, Inc. in Dallas, Texas, recognized the need for a temporary agency specializing in paralegals nearly a dozen years ago when she herself was a longterm paralegal working for a large law firm. At that time, she would often find that there was simply too much work for her to handle alone, and other paralegals in the firm did not have the same specialization as Susan to help out. So when a friend opened up a temporary agency for paralegals, Susan joined right in, knowing first hand how valuable such a service would become. A few years ago, Susan then moved on to found her agency, and in just a short time, it has grown to include offices in both Dallas and Ft. Worth.

Today, Paralegals Plus furnishes temporary paralegal services to lawyers in corporate, real estate, litigation, and estate planning. The agency particularly supplies paralegals to work in litigation because this field often demands freelance services due to the extensive amount of work under tight deadlines. Paralegals Plus employs a variety of people, most of whom work on-site at a law firm, although they also hire deposition summarizers who work at home or at Susan's place of business. Susan says that her agency distinguishes between two levels of paralegals: those who are essentially straight out of college with a paralegal program behind them, and those with more than 2 years of work experience in a law firm. It is, of course, much easier to place someone with experience, but Susan says she does not turn away high quality new talent.

Paralegals Plus is a good example of the employment opportunities one can find by working through a temporary agency. Many of the paralegals Susan places end up working at a firm for several months, and some have even stayed at the same job for as much as two years. Although this does not seem efficient, Susan says that some firms prefer to work on this temporary basis since they save on paying benefits. Of course, this means that the temporary paralegal must be prepared to pay his or her own health insurance, taxes, and social security.

If you want to work through a temporary agency, Susan offers the following advice to make a good impression when you apply at an agency:

- Call the agency and ask for an interview or send your resume first; but do not wait passively for the agency to call you back. Susan suggests that you be aggressive and show the agency that you are a go-getter by following up with a call.

- Be sure your resume and cover letter contain no errors of any kind. Nothing is less impressive than a paralegal who makes spelling mistakes or writes poorly.
- When you go for an interview, look appropriately professional. Susan indicates that in her experience, appearance says a lot about the care a person takes on the job, and is an indicator of whether or not they are punctual and how they handle themselves in general.
- Although Susan doesn't require that you have gone to an ABA approved paralegal school, she does look for an undergraduate degree and a paralegal certificate.
- Once you get a job through an agency, Susan reminds you to be flexible and have a can do attitude; lawyers don't like squaring off with a temporary worker who doesn't want to work. Susan adds that in her experience, law firms treat temps very well, although they seldom get the level of responsibility that an in-house paralegal does.

Susan's best advice is, in her own words, "Remember that not all paralegals see themselves as professionals and some are on their way elsewhere; these are transitory paralegals. You need to view your attorney as a client rather than as a boss; clients purchase professional services, bosses direct activities of employees. The best paid and most valuable paralegals are those who embrace new technology and take chances, not the paralegals who merely wait for directions."

Self-employment for freelance paralegals

Many home-based legal assistants today are simply setting themselves up in business on their own. They work directly for law firms or corporate legal departments on a case-by-case basis, particularly with attorneys who knew them before and were familiar with their work capabilities. Self-employment is especially ideal for people who want a great deal of control over their work schedules, and who have garnered enough experience and respect in the local legal community that they can attract sufficient work entirely on their own reputation. Many legal assistants support themselves entirely through their own entrepreneurial activity. Of the dozens we interviewed for this book, nearly all were very happy with their newfound freedom.

Most home-based paralegals get their work from networking with attorneys or paralegals in law offices. They might get work from a sudden, critical need for help on a specific job, or they might have regular assignments that they do consistently for a firm. Many freelancers also say that advertising in legal directories or legal newspapers can help because it enhances your name recognition. Advertising helps you look serious and professional. It also helps to show that you are an independent freelancer, so your clients are not at risk that you might be declared an employee for tax purposes—a risk they want to avoid if they have hired a freelancer.

Paralegal Susan Kligerman recommends that you ensure your advertising is professional-oriented with a professional appearance, in an appropriate legal publication if you can afford it. She says, "The Yellow Pages is not the right place for attorney clientele, and also, by avoiding Yellow Pages, you can get away with using your home phone number." Susan also mails brochures to firms with fewer than five attorneys, despite the fact that she does not get immediate results. "If they see ads in state and county bar publications, and also get a brochure with a letter, name recognition will be there. The multiple exposure provides that." She further recommends involvement in local bar associations and paralegal associations where you can get exposure to your follow professionals. Being well-known gets you referrals from persons whose opinions are respected. We provide more information on marketing a home-based business throughout the remaining chapters in this book.

The advantages of freelance self-employment, according to the paralegals we interviewed, include a higher rate of income than is available through a service, and more control over their personal work schedule. In addition, for some reason not easily explained, these legal assistants often enjoy more respect and independence from attorneys. However, only legal assistants who have considerable experience and who have earned a reputation in their area of practice have been able to garner enough work directly to make this situation work well.

Some paralegals, like Terrie Burton of Denver, are well enough known to attract regular work without any marketing effort at all. Terrie is even able to turn down assignments when she wants vacation or personal time; and she still earns a full-time living at a nice income from her contract work. Terrie has been a litigation paralegal in the Denver area for 16 years, including 12 as a contract legal assistant working on her own. Although Terrie is home-based in the sense that she does not have an office elsewhere, she has always performed the work she does at the premises of the attorneys for whom she works. Terrie manages and monitors sizeable litigation cases, and frequently has other, less-experienced legal assistants working under her supervision.

Some of the disadvantages of freelance work parallel those of working for a service. For example, the work might terminate before you expected, and you cannot count on an even supply of assignments. Many people become accustomed to the "feast or famine" aspect of legal work, and are able to stay busy during the "feast" times, while enjoying the famine time as almost a vacation. Another disadvantage common to contract paralegals working freelance (and working through a service) is the need to constantly adapt to a new working situation, especially since much work cannot be done in a home office, but must be done at the employers' offices. Unless you are able to garner sufficient work from known firms or employers, you will find yourself constantly living a "first day on the job," learning where the coffee machine and the restrooms are, facing unfamiliar people around each corner (who might be wondering who you are and why you are there), feeling like an "outsider" (if they have a party in the lunchroom, are you welcome?). A freelance paralegal must be able to thrive on a series of "new jobs," and not be intimidated by those aspects of contract assignments.

Another disadvantage is that if you find you need temporary help, agencies will not send people to your home to work. In litigation, lawyers typically call at the last minute with an outrageous quantity of work, and the paralegal needs to get others involved to meet the deadline. Space also becomes an issue if you have a large project—you need extra room and people, and you might have them working in your kitchen, the dining room, and the living room, in difficult crowded conditions. For many of these reasons, and because litigation is a labor-intensive, document-heavy practice, you might need to move into an office away from home.

Another downside of contract work is that you often find yourself walking into the middle of a case. While you bring in expertise, you weren't there to absorb the innuendoes of the case that became obvious as the case was developing; employers can't see why you aren't as effective as they might have expected. You need to try to absorb information quickly from the files and from questioning the attorney in an unstressed moment to get up to speed.

A freelancer who gets ill also has a big problem. There might be assignments due, but without the energy or health to perform them, they will either be done late, done poorly, or not done at all. You might lose the job or the client. One solution is to establish an informal arrangement with another freelance paralegal in your practice area, who might be able to pick up the threads and help finish the project. A side benefit to this sort of arrangement is that both of you have someone to help when workload is too heavy, or to be a potential source of overload work.

While a service agency pays less than direct freelance work, the agency takes the burden of fee negotiation off your hands. The freelancer must, herself, negotiate a fee arrangement before beginning the work. This probably need be done only once for each employer, when arrangements can be agreed to which will cover subsequent assignments as well. However, since the call to the paralegal is made at a time of critical need, the employer is likely to neglect this step unless the paralegal insists on it. With a new client, freelancer Terrie Burton will sometimes make an arrangement to work for less than her usual rate for the first 40 hours, until they get to know her, and then she raises to her normal fee from then on, if they are pleased enough to continue to use her. There is a certain amount of negotiating involved in this. She says she is not so good at it, but "you pick a day when you feel good" to take on the negotiating job.

Bonnie Twigg

Bonnie Twigg, a freelance paralegal in Santa Rosa, California, believes that there are many advantages to freelance work. She says that the freelance paralegal is more appreciated than an in-house paralegal on the same case. Once someone has become a regular in the office, "no matter how appreciated or loved they are, they become taken for granted. As trial approaches, there can be a lot of blame and finger pointing if things aren't going well, and the attorney egos come out at trial time." But Bonnie finds that if someone is upset at her, she does not hear about it. Of course, they might not hire her again, but she also doesn't need to work for them again if they treat her poorly.

The other benefit is that Bonnie finds she gets an immense amount of feedback on her projects, whereas the in-house paralegals usually do not. In fact, the complaints she hears from in-house paralegals are about getting yelled at and never getting feedback.

Finally, Bonnie feels she enjoys greater accessibility to the attorneys when she does not work in-house. As many working paralegals can attest, it is frequently hard to get time with the attorney, to get clarification on assignments or background on the case. But since she's not there all the time, Bonnie finds she can knock on their door and they won't get annoyed. If she tells an attorney she is too buried in work, they still call her back if they know her and have used her before.

Bonnie cites two disadvantages: You can get stuck doing a lot of running around, which seems to waste a lot of time. When they hit the panic point, and maybe partly because same attorneys have used her for a long time, they call and want something right away, and sometimes that means going to 4–5 offices in one day. The other problem is that the income is less regularly dependable—partly, she admits, because she has a problem with her own billing practices. It's hard to keep track of your time when you're on-the-go, so she probably loses some billable time.

The independent practice of paralegal work (working directly with consumers) and the status of paralegal regulation and licensing issues are all currently undergoing major review and scrutiny in nearly every state. In addition, you need to be aware of many ethical issues that are particularly sensitive for freelance paralegals. Please see appendix B on regulation and ethics for information on these topics.

Most of the paralegals we interviewed recommended joining and participating in a professional association to stay abreast of these issues. Through their representatives, conferences, and publications, associations keep you informed of legislation, rules, movements, and all new events in the profession that might affect freelance paralegals.

We also highly recommend that you maintain regular contact with other paralegals to develop a camaraderie and exchange information on employers (which are good to work for and which are "screamers") as well as tips on where you can get the fastest service on legal forms, which court reporters are the most accurate, news on the latest technology, and of course, where jobs might be.

In addition to the publications and papers put out by professional associations, we also recommend subscribing to *Legal Assistant Today* magazine, which comes out six times a year and provides a wealth of information on all aspects of paralegal practice. (Call (714) 755-5450 for subscription information.)

It's your choice

Despite the debate, most freelance paralegals would not return to a regular, secure in-house job. The independence they feel is too valuable. Cheryl Templeton, a probate and estate planning paralegal in Canoga Park, California, says the best thing about working at home is "I can work in my shorts!" She has a sign on her wall which reads: "An entrepreneur is someone who's willing to work sixteen hours a day seven days a week just to avoid having to work eight hours a day five days a week for somebody else."

Many people are afraid to try independent contracting paralegal work. Ask yourself, "What's the worst that can happen?" You might end up back in a salaried position, similar to where you were before you took the risk.

3 Other legal practice areas for paralegals

This chapter reviews nearly a dozen other practice areas that comprise the 50 percent of paralegal work other than litigation. Most of these fields are completely open to freelance paralegal work for people working from home. The areas include:

- Personal injury
- Family law litigation
- Estate planning
- Estate administration
- Corporate and securities practice
- Bankruptcy
- Real estate and oil and gas law
- Environmental law
- Water law
- Trademark and intellectual property
- Criminal law

In each area, we provide general information explaining how the law works and its application in that area, and we detail the tasks paralegals commonly perform. We also explain the specific skills, background, and preparation for working independently in the area, the personality traits that suit the practice area, and the advantages and disadvantages of this field. Throughout the chapter, we also profile many paralegals now working in these fields to show what some successful paralegals have done.

Personal injury litigation

Outside of family law, the area of law with which people are most likely to have contact in their lives is personal injury. This is largely due to automobile accidents, but also acts of negligence that lead to injury. Personal injury is a specialized practice area of litigation. About 25 percent of paralegals who are employed in law firms do some work in this area. It is also an important work area for freelance paralegals, some of whom have built successful small and home-based businesses around it.

In personal injury (as in workers' compensation, product liability, or medical malpractice), there are typically plaintiffs' attorney firms and defense attorney firms, but few firms take on both types of cases. Thus, as a personal injury paralegal in a law firm, you would be working primarily in one area or the other. There are distinct differences. Plaintiffs' attorneys represent the injured or ill individual. Their fees are usually paid on a contingency basis, that is a portion of the award or settlement amount. A freelance paralegal working for a plaintiffs' attorney should be sure to have an agreement to be paid regularly by the attorney—not wait until settlement, trial judgment, or, worst, collection before getting paid. Defense firms often work for insurance companies and are paid by the hour. As a freelance paralegal, you should be paid a typical hourly rate that the insurance company would probably cover (happily, no doubt, since your hourly rate is considerably less than that of an attorney who would have to do the work if you were not doing it).

What personal injury paralegals do

Personal injury cases follow the same litigation process as general litigation. However, most personal injury cases do settle, and the preparation for settlement constitutes a large part of the paralegal's work.

During the fact-gathering and discovery stage, in addition to the steps mentioned in the preceding litigation section (locating evidence and records, identifying witnesses, as well as all the steps of the discovery process) the paralegal carefully reviews the medical records of the injured person, from both before and after the accident (in case any of the injuries the victim is claiming occurred in the accident might be pre-existing conditions).

The paralegal puts together evidence documenting the extent of the injury and the extent to which the injury has affected the life of the injured person. Often, the paralegal assembles a settlement notebook with this information, including photographs as well as medical information. In other cases, the plaintiff's attorney or paralegal might have a video produced, commonly known as "a day in the life," which shows the injured person dealing with his injuries on a day-to-day basis. Video is particularly effective if the injured person is confined to a wheelchair or otherwise seriously impaired. Chapter 6 contains information on the videography businesses that make such videos.

Another document a paralegal might prepare is a medical chronology, a short synopsis of the medical treatment of an individual in time sequence order.

The chronology outlines only pertinent information, usually containing only what the records reflect without personal opinions or interpretations.

As a subset of personal injury, workers' compensation deals with injuries alleged to be related to a person's employment. This area of law is governed by specific statutes and regulations that differ considerably from state to state. The field is particularly suitable for paralegal work because it is highly systematized, i.e., one case proceeds very much like the last one. The plaintiff is usually represented by a personal injury attorney; the defendant is the employer, and has workers' compensation defense counsel, who might handle hundreds of these cases at once for a large employer. Clearly, this is a practice area that responds well to a system, making it a good area for paralegals. In some states, the paralegal can even represent the consumer before the Workers' Compensation Appeals Board, thereby creating an income area for the entrepreneurial paralegal.

Workers' compensation law

Whether the paralegal is working for an attorney or directly representing the client, it is likely that he or she will be in regular contact with the local workers' compensation authorities, verifying claim status and evaluating employer and insurance carrier status. Medical records must be obtained, and doctors' appointments made for the injured party. The paralegal contacts vocational rehabilitation counselors and claims adjusters, among other third parties, attends depositions, and summarizes transcripts. Hearings are held in administrative offices, not in court rooms, and the paralegal must be familiar with the process of requesting or arranging for these hearings, then attending the hearing with the attorney.

After the hearing, there might be appeal briefs to draft if the party disagrees with the proposed settlement. Throughout the process, the paralegal monitors changes in statutes, regulations, and case law in the area.

A few workers' compensation paralegals assist attorneys on a contract basis, but very few do their work in a home office, with the exception of people who regularly digest depositions in these types of cases. Marti Holmes, who has a contract paralegal business in Denver, handled a number of cases on a contract basis for FELA, the workers' compensation program for railroad employees, working in an office setting. FELA cases are also subject to systematizing, and are thus good paralegal work.

In addition to the standard skills and knowledge required for litigation work, a paralegal who wants to work in the personal injury area should have considerable experience in medical-related litigation and should be very familiar with medical records formats and medical terminology. In addition, experience should have taught the paralegal how medical records are used in preparing for settlement and in supporting the case of the plaintiff or defendant. Much more medical background is required, however, in order to take on consulting.

Skills & aptitudes for personal injury

As you might guess from the preceding description, many paralegals who have a nursing degree have made themselves invaluable to law firms working in this area. Some freelance nurse/paralegals have even built their businesses around summarizing depositions in medical-related cases together with reviewing medical records and interpreting them for law firms.

The American Association of Legal Nurse Consultants, a professional association for registered nurses working in the legal consulting field, is working to develop standards for their profession. (Their address and phone number is listed in appendix A.)

The job market for personal injury

As previously mentioned, about 25 percent of employed paralegals do some work in the personal injury area and in workers' compensation. However, although a large number of paralegal positions are in this field, there are not a lot of home-based or freelance personal injury paralegals. However, freelance paralegal work in medical law fields is an excellent career choice for people with both nursing and paralegal backgrounds, and can provide a great deal of independence and professional respect, especially when combined with medical records consulting. (See also chapter 6 for a profile of the special profession of Nurse/Legal Consultant.)

Business profile

Pamela Miller
Personal Injury Paralegal

Pamela Miller has a home-based business in Jacksonville, Texas, a small community outside Dallas. She calls herself a nurse/paralegal, and works as a personal injury paralegal and a medical records consultant. She has been home-based since January of 1992.

Pamela is a Licensed Vocational Nurse (the same thing as a licensed practical nurse (LPN)) as well as an experienced paralegal and a CLA (Certified Legal Assistant). After several years' experience as a medical/surgical nurse she got into the legal field because a friend had passed the state bar and needed someone to type for him. Since then, she has been doing legal work for over 15 years, some full-time for that attorney, and later in downtown Houston, where she started finding attorneys who wanted to use her medical knowledge and training, and worked on a lot of medical records.

The main part of Pamela's work is reviewing medical records for both insurance companies and attorneys. The vast majority of the medical records she reviews are from automobile accidents. For example, an insurance company, or an attorney, wants to know how badly the victim is hurt, or not hurt, as the case may be, so they hire her to review the records and interpret them, or advise them as to the extent of the injuries. Pamela works for both plaintiff and defense (of course, not on the same case), having some defense and plaintiff attorney clients and some insurance companies who will hire her prior to the onset of litigation. Insurance company adjusters feel the greatest benefit of her work is that it is a third party's objective evaluation. As a result, she probably prevents some litigation, a factor in her work that is very satisfying.

Pamela really enjoys her home-based business. Some days she works two hours, some days fourteen. She enjoys the flexibility, and the opportunity to home-school her 12-year-old son. She also enjoys being able to apply all her experience and knowledge to her work. She is always busy; in the last 18 months, she has had only two occasions when she could "breathe."

Pamela says her husband's marketing experience helped her get her business going. She gets most of her business by word of mouth, but initially she started going around to attorneys she knew and had worked for, and told them she was going into business for herself, and could provide an economical rate for reviewing medical records and preparing medical chronologies. She also contacted an adjuster she knew at an insurance company, her "the foot in the door" there. Those few clients got her started. She also started marketing, using a good introductory letter with samples of her work product, which she sent to area attorneys who were close enough that she knew she could provide good, prompt service; she followed up after sending out the letter, and obtained six to eight very good clients. She gets business from her paralegal association contacts, as well. Pamela still occasionally sends out a newsletter—a bulletin that gives an overall view of what she can do. She sends them to half a dozen attorneys at a time, and follows up with a personal visit to those nearby.

Pamela has clients in the towns in her area, and some in Dallas. She arranges for courier service, for prompt pickup of files and delivery of her work product, and feels her close personal service means a lot to her clients. Pamela feels she competes favorably with a corporate medical records reviewer, both in her reasonable rates and by giving personal attention to her clients, showing concern for their business and giving them what they need.

Pamela's equipment includes two computers, a fax machine, and medical resource books. Besides WordPerfect word processing she uses Medline, a medical research line through the National Library of Medicine, Bethesda, Maryland. She uses it for research on the latest in medical research information. She forwards Medline's per search charges on to the client. For database she uses Microsoft Works for Windows, and she has a large database of all doctors and attorneys in Texas. She also does her billing in Microsoft Works. Pamela enjoys the magazine *Home Office Computing*, where she finds a lot of good information, and believes, from what she reads there, that the business world is shifting more towards home-based businesses.

Pamela recommends that someone wanting to do personal injury work from home have some type of paralegal training, extensive experience, and a certificate or degree. A certain amount of marketing is necessary—you need to be able to get out there and obtain clients. Her medical training served her very well, but she concedes that many personal injury paralegals do not have that degree of medical training. Someone wanting to concentrate heavily in the medical area would need to know which resource books and medical books are available. And, Pamela stresses, you need good business sense, to be able to keep your business going.

Paralegals in family law

Many of us have had some contact with family law in our personal lives, either within our own families or among our friends and coworkers. The field concerns all issues related to divorce, alimony, child support, and child custody. Because this area of law has such an impact on peoples' private lives, many legal assistants are drawn to practice in the area where they feel they can have a positive impact on what is a difficult period in peoples' lives. According to the *Legal Assistant Today* 1993 Salary Survey, about five percent of the respondents work in the family law area, and the Los Angeles Paralegal Association 1992 Employment and Salary Survey showed roughly the same percentage.

Because it involves resolution of conflict, courtroom procedures, trials and hearings, family law is actually a subdivision of litigation. However, it has its own terminology and procedures, and in many places separate courts and separate rules of procedure dedicated to family law matters.

Family law is process- and forms-heavy, which make it an area particularly suitable for paralegals. A family law paralegal becomes a specialist in child support calculations, in listing and evaluating assets, and in accessing available related services such as therapists, mediators, custody evaluators, accountants, and appraisers. Another reason paralegals are critical to this practice area is that the clients are usually very distraught; they might have awful things happening in their lives that they do not understand, and they need a lot of hand-holding. The attorney's focus is on strategy and the necessary legal steps, and typically his or her time is too costly for hand-holding. The paralegal can do a lot of listening for a lot less cost, and can sift out the critical information the attorney needs to know.

Much family law work is done in small offices and by sole practitioners, attorneys who typically are reluctant to hire a full-time paralegal, lest there not be enough work to make it profitable. Freelance paralegals can fill a need in those cases, providing dependable assistance when needed with no financial burden when the work is not there. In other cases, when a firm finds itself working on high-asset divorces, or those with many issues to be litigated, freelance paralegals permit them to add to their existing paralegal staff on an as-needed basis.

One difference between family law and general litigation is important to bear in mind: family law clients are private citizens who are often not able to pay unlimited amounts for legal fees. Consequently, paralegals are an answer to providing good, economic legal service.

The family law case, whether it is divorce or custody, follows a format similar to general litigation, with a few differences. In family law, for example, instead of plaintiff and defendant, the parties are called petitioner and respondent. Divorce is usually termed "dissolution of marriage."

In family law, the action begins when one person files a petition, usually for dissolution of marriage, sometimes for legal separation, or sometimes a petition just for custody (if the parents are not married). There might be a need for a restraining order as soon as possible, such as the possibility of physical danger to the spouse or child. There is often a temporary orders hearing early on, to set up support and custody arrangements during the temporary period leading up to the permanent orders hearing or final judgment. The case then proceeds through the fact-gathering and discovery stage, through pretrial and trial, and sometimes through the appeals stage. The major stages of a family law case can be summarized as follows and are briefly detailed in the following sections. As with litigation, the "stages" and tasks are not really as discreet as described, but it will give you the general idea.

- Initiation of the action.
- Temporary restraining order (occasionally).
- Temporary orders.
- Fact-gathering and discovery.
- Pretrial.
- Trial (permanent orders).
- Post-trial and appeals.

Initiation

The action itself begins with the filing of the petition for dissolution of marriage or custody, but the paralegal's role begins before that stage. Often the attorney will include the paralegal in the initial client interview, when the client tells the story and the attorney informs the client of the steps that can be taken. The paralegal will be sure all necessary information is obtained, and that the client uses the paralegal as the main contact person throughout the process. Most offices have a form intake sheet that the paralegal will complete during this interview, or during a subsequent conversation with the client, including all information required to be submitted on the initial petition and affidavits.

In a "Family Law" column in the March/April 1992 issue of *Legal Assistant Today*, Lindi Massey explains her firm's practice regarding chronologies:

In our firm, upon being retained, we ask the client to prepare a chronology of events. If the matter is a divorce case, we generally like the client to begin with when they met their spouse. If it's a modification case changing custody, we ask the client to begin from the date of divorce.
The chronology helps you obtain valuable information concerning the background of the parties, leads for deposition questions, and an initial list of potential witnesses. In addition, it provides therapy for the client. Many times, while compiling the chronology, your client will remember pertinent information that has been buried or forgotten.[1]

Unlike general litigation, where complaints vary in complexity and are frequently drafted by attorneys, petitions for divorce, and the usual accompanying documents, are quite standard in most cases, and are prepared by the paralegal on type-in-the-blank forms, or increasingly by using computer software. Here is another area where computers are being more heavily used by paralegals, and we can expect more software to be developed to handle this paperwork in the future. (For more detail, see the discussion "Computers in family law" later in this chapter.)

Depending on the situation and the local court rules, there might also be affidavits with respect to the children of the marriage, or affidavits to support a restraining order if there has been domestic violence or if there is a need to freeze assets of the parties, for example. Often, these follow a standard format and the paralegal will gather the relevant facts and tailor the document to the situation.

If there is potential of physical danger to the client, the paralegal will prepare forms for a temporary restraining order, including an affidavit by the client setting out the facts that justify such a drastic step. In these cases arrangements must be made for a hearing as soon as possible.

The attorney will review and sign pleadings. If there are affidavits for the client to sign, the paralegal will arrange that and will see to servicing or processing the filings with the court. Just as with general litigation, the paralegal is responsible for docketing all court dates and deadlines, and for maintaining a calendar.

Temporary orders Typically the permanent orders hearing (trial), which settles all the disputed matters, will not happen for several months, or even years. Some matters must be settled so the parties can establish routines to abide by during the process of the divorce case, such as designating a residence for the children and a routine for paying the family's bills. The temporary orders hearing will result in orders that the parties are to live by between that date and a

• • • • • • • • •

[1]Copyright 1993 James Publishing, Inc. Reprinted with permission from *Legal Assistant Today.* For subscription information, call (714) 755-5450.

permanent orders hearing, regarding payment of support, custody and visitation, and the ability to draw on assets of the parties for living expenses, and forbidding the dissipation of assets. (Often, the attorneys negotiate temporary orders and do not go to a hearing.)

The paralegal usually prepares the motion for temporary orders and any necessary injunctions and affidavits; arranges to set the hearing dates and send appropriate notices to the other party; assists in settlement negotiations; and continues to be the client's main contact.

During this temporary period, the parties must prepare affidavits or sworn inventories to establish their financial status, income, expenses, debts, and all assets, separate and joint. The paralegal works with the client to obtain accurate information and exhibits, such as tax returns and pay stubs, and might also contact the client's accountant for information and records. She or he might even need to call appraisers to verify the value of the family's assets, before the affidavit can be finalized and signed by the client. Once the financial information has been obtained, the paralegal also calculates the child support payment amounts, depending on the local codes and regulations.

The temporary custody arrangement, whether sole custody with visitation or shared or joint custody, will be strongly considered at trial. This is, of course, because the children will be established in an arrangement that might be working well for them and the court might be reluctant to make changes. Consequently, much research regarding the issue of custody might take place before the temporary orders hearing. Although it is not common to have such extensive litigation of custody early on, the paralegal might interview witnesses and arrange for them to appear at the temporary orders hearing. If there is a possibility of mistreatment by one parent, the paralegal might arrange for supervised custody to be available, should the court wish to order that alternative.

In Colorado, as in many states, the statute sets out a specific formula for calculating child support payments, based on the income of the parties and various other factors. Today, software is frequently used to compute the payments.

Fact-gathering & discovery

This stage in family law litigation resembles the same stage as in litigation outlined in chapter 2, except that the information you are seeking concerns the issues of custody and financial settlement, who the primary parent should be, what the assets are, where they are, and what they're worth, and how they should be divided. When child support is at issue, the paralegal researches the occupations of both parties and their earning potential. Expert witnesses might be called in to testify on these questions. The paralegal arranges for child custody evaluations and summarizes the reports submitted by any experts. As with general litigation, there are many witnesses to be located and interviewed, and records to be reviewed, analyzed, and indexed.

The discovery process uses exactly the same four procedures as in litigation, i.e., interrogatories, requests for production, depositions, and requests for admission, depending on the factual information that needs to be verified. The paralegal drafts interrogatories asking about the identification, valuation, and location of assets, the facts to support the other side's requests regarding custody, support or financial settlement, and the witnesses and exhibits expected to be produced at final hearing.

Document productions occur in family law as well, although they are usually far smaller than in commercial litigation. In some cases, there might be heavy documentation to verify the value of a family business, or credit card statements, tax returns, and checkbook records to verify expenses and the disposition of assets. Often one or both parties to a divorce will be a participant in a pension or retirement benefit plan. Those records must be reviewed to determine, depending on the law of the specific state, whether any retirement benefits are marital property that can be divided as part of the divorce settlement.

Paralegals also schedule the depositions to obtain information from the parties, expert witnesses and other witnesses. For example, paralegal Brenda Conner worked in the family law area as a contract paralegal in Denver for two years. (She has since used her paralegal background to move on to become Assistant to the Executive Director of Opryland Music Group in Nashville!) Her description of what she did at this stage gives numerous good examples of the paralegal's role. She helped locate assets and review financial statements for the couple, made lists of their assets, and ordered appraisals when needed. On one sizeable case, for example, they had three different appraisals done on each property to get an average. Brenda called banks for copies of bank statements, and all bank account information, which she reviewed. She reviewed credit card statements and analyzed expenses. She accompanied the appraiser to the properties for inspection and inventory, and actually went into each of the houses and made lists of the furniture in each house. In the case mentioned, the parties had a lot of expensive artwork. Brenda made lists of it, because there was suspicion that one party was hiding some of the assets, and in fact some valuable ones surfaced in the attic the day before trial. Finally, she prepared questions for trial relating to each of the assets.

During discovery, Brenda also summarized depositions of doctors, psychiatrists, and in one case the bookkeeper for the opposing party to verify the stated income (that turned out to be higher than claimed). She subpoenaed records, and interviewed other people in the same profession regarding income potential. She interviewed family friends regarding treatment of the children and people suggested by the parties as character witnesses.

Pretrial preparations in family law are also patterned after those in general litigation, listing witnesses and interviewing them, getting exhibits, preparing trial notebooks to organize all documents for trial. The paralegal might also work with the attorney to plan the case presentation, and the paralegal might also attend trial, take notes, help with exhibits, and call witnesses when the attorney is ready for them.

Often, legal issues are disputed between the parties, and, just as in other civil litigation, legal research must be performed; memos, motions and briefs drafted; and cite-checking and Shepardizing done on the memos and briefs. Paralegals are more likely to research issues in the family law area than in civil litigation, partly because many family law attorneys are sole practitioners and usually do not have a junior attorney to whom they can assign the research. Another reason is that the issues in family law are frequently closely related to prior cases, so the paralegal can work more independently using established procedures. All the family law freelance paralegals we interviewed performed legal research as part of their work. In addition, some family law paralegals maintain files of research results on issues that commonly arise in family law.

The paralegal might also propose a separation and settlement agreement, which can be revised until the parties come to an agreement on all issues. Many cases settle at this stage, rather than arguing in court. (The only cases that often go to trial are ones with difficult custody disputes or sizeable assets.)

After trial there might be appeals that involve more legal research, motions, and briefs with which paralegals assist. Even if there are no appeals, however, steps remain to be taken. Typically, as in temporary orders, one of the attorneys will be asked to reduce the judge's findings and orders to written form for signature, and that is often the paralegal's assignment. In addition, any orders with respect to transfer of title of property must be implemented.

Initiation

- Participate in the initial client interview.
- Identify and verify information for initial filings.
- Prepare all initial pleadings and affidavits.
- Prepare documents for restraining order, if necessary, and arrange for hearing as soon as possible.
- Arrange for service of process and court filings.
- Act as liaison between client and attorney.
- Keep calendars.
- Set up and maintain court documents files and other case files.

Temporary orders

- Draft motions for temporary orders, injunctions, and affidavits.
- Set hearings and sends notices.
- Assist in settlement negotiations.
- Work with the client, the clients' records, and outside experts in preparing the financial affidavit.
- Calculate child support obligations.
- Interview witnesses regarding child custody issues.
- Arrange for supervised visitation when necessary.
- Continue as client's contact.
- Attend temporary orders hearing.
- Draft the order after the hearing.

Fact-gathering and discovery

- Help locate assets, list assets, and arrange for appraisals, sometimes accompanying the appraiser.
- Order copies of and review bank and financial records.
- Analyze expenses.
- Review pension and retirement records.
- Arrange for the services of accounting, property evaluation, or child custody experts.
- Prepare questions for discovery or for trial regarding the assets.
- Help assemble lists of witnesses, and interview witnesses, regarding family, business, and financial matters.
- Arrange for depositions and subpoena records.
- Summarize experts' reports and deposition transcripts.
- Draft motions.

Pretrial and trial

- Perform legal research and draft memos, motions, and briefs.
- Maintain files of briefs and memos on common family law issues.
- Contact and interview witnesses.
- Prepare witness lists and exhibit lists.
- Set the final hearing and send notices.
- Subpoena witnesses and records.
- Prepare trial notebooks.
- Assist attorney in planning trial agenda.
- Draft and revise settlement agreements.

After trial

- Draft the permanent orders.
- Perform research, and drafts appeals, motions, and briefs.
- Prepare documents to transfer title to assets.
- Arrange for filing and recording of transfer documents.

There are family law software programs available that do the types of financial calculations frequently needed in family law cases. The ones specified by the people we interviewed were all software developed by William Reddick and put out by his company, Custom Legal Software Corporation, (3867 Paseo Del Prado, Boulder, CO 80301, (303) 443-2634). There are three programs from Custom:

Legal Math Pac performs numerous financial calculations, such as determining arrearage to the party with accrued interest from date of each payment; preparing amortization schedules; figuring the present value of funds needed to send kids to college; calculating interest on irregular debt transactions; determining the present value of future payments, future lump sums, or future value of expected periodic investments. Each prints out in a matter of moments and is easy to use.

Colorado Child Support Guidelines calculates child support payments from basic information regarding income and expenses of the parties, and prints out the Worksheets required by Colorado statute.

Family Law Financial Affidavit prints out the standard forms required by law.

Similar programs are available in many other states, and there are also some nationally available programs:

Divorce, Alimony and Child Support Tax
(Shepard's McGraw-Hill)
P.O. Box 1235
Colorado Springs, CO 80901
(719) 577-7639

Divorce Settlement Assistant
(Lanier Business Systems)
2310 Parklake Dr.
Atlanta, GA 30345
(404) 270-2000

DissoMaster
(CFLR)
107 Caledonia St., Suite E
Sausalito, CA 94965
(415) 332-9000

SupporTax and Community Property Divider (Calif.)
(Norton Family Law Systems available from the Rutter Group)
15760 Ventura Blvd.
Encino, CA 91436-3022
(800) 747-3161, ext. 2 or
(818) 990-3260, ext. 2

Amortizer Plus
(Good Software Corp.)
13601 Preston Rd., #500 W., LB 226
Dallas, TX 75240
(214) 239-6085

In addition, many state bar associations or continuing education programs provide standard, approved forms for pleadings and court documents on word processing disks.

The family law paralegal job market

Family law is an area where much of the work is performed by small law firms and solo practitioners, and paralegals are commonly used because the issues are usually similar from one case to another. All the steps done by family law paralegals in law firms can be done by freelance paralegals as well. Judging by the experiences of the paralegals we interviewed, the area is open to many more freelance paralegals.

All the family law paralegals agree that networking is extremely important. In cities that have paralegal associations, there might be a family law section as part of the association. There are many family law sections of state bar associations, which might provide for paralegals to join as associate members, or welcome paralegals to meetings and seminars. Continuing education seminars, which you need to attend to stay current in the practice, are also a great place to introduce yourself to attorneys in the area who might be interested in using your services.

Business profile

Cathy Schultheis
Paralegal/Mediator, Longmont, Colorado

We chose Cathy for a business profile because her situation is unique. Cathy has had a home-based paralegal/mediation business since May 1989. She left a paralegal job in downtown Denver, Colorado to work from her home near Boulder to do more mediation, a form of alternative dispute resolution used in a broad variety of disputes. A mediator helps the parties come to a mutually satisfying solution to their dispute.

Cathy's work setting is truly pastoral. Her home/office is an old farmhouse set on a little more than an acre in a rural area near Boulder where she lives with her husband and children, ages 8 and 14. Instead of piped-in background music or the sounds of city traffic, her work is done to the sounds of crowing roosters or tree branches rustling in a breeze. She meets clients at her big wooden dining table, in a large lodgelike room with a wood-burning fireplace, shiny wooden floors, hanging plants, and children's art on the walls.

Cathy has observed that legal proceedings can be terrifying to a lay person, so her home is a comfortable place for initial interviews—she can get more pertinent information than she could in a downtown attorneys' office with a big conference room, cold white walls, and sparse furnishings. She is quite up-to-date, however, and has a fax machine, copier, computer, and laser jet printer. She uses WordPerfect for creating documents and a special family law program, Bill Reddick's financial affidavit MathPac. The latter is a software program that prepares financial affidavits, child support worksheets, and amortization schedules for payment of promissory notes. She also uses a database program for indexing documents, and Quicken for her business finances and other financial applications.

Cathy cites the many advantages to working at home; she can adapt her schedule to her children's needs, work and meet clients in a warm, nonthreatening atmosphere, and save commuting time. She tries to minimize interruptions by not answering the phone until a set period when she will gather the messages and return calls. She has found at least one disadvantage to using her home as an office where clients come—she must keep it clean most of the time.

Cathy's areas of expertise include family law and general litigation. She attracts paralegal work from a number of attorneys in Boulder who know her and trust her for both paralegal and mediation work. Cathy's work comes from word of mouth, repeat clients, and referrals. One attorney, for example, sends her work about every other day. He might call her to draft something like a motion; she calls him when it's done, and he comes by to review and sign it. She follows up, having the motion properly filed and delivered. Although most of her work is done in her home, Cathy does sometimes go to attorneys' offices to review documents for discovery.

Cathy uses a brochure and has also tried a promotion—offering a free hour of service to new clients. Cathy recalls "spending a bunch of money on brochures early on that were expensive, and I had to pay for postage—and I got nothing from it." However, she did say that some attorneys kept her brochure and now remember her name. She also puts an ad in the bar newsletter, which does not get new clients but helps her with name recognition when she meets attorneys at bar meetings.

Cathy advises people starting a family law paralegal practice in a small community like Boulder to attend bar association meetings when possible, join the chamber of commerce, attend breakfast meetings, and meet people and get acquainted. She adds, "The best marketing technique second to a personal referral from another lawyer to a new lawyer is taking the attorney you want to get to know out to lunch. You have 60 minutes of undivided attention and you're paying the bill; they'll listen to you. Find out first what type of work they do, so you know if they would have a need; find out the types of cases and sell yourself by telling them specifically how you could help. Attorneys are generally not good at delegating; they tend to keep it all, but then can't do it all. Tell them exactly and in great detail how you can save them time and money."

In Cathy's opinion, freelance paralegals need to be able to sell themselves, be detail-oriented, bright, enthusiastic, have a high energy level, know they can do it, maybe even be downright aggressive, and have a lot of ideas—running a freelance business is not easy. You have to want to do it very much. Some people Cathy knows have given up and gone back to a firm. She would not suggest freelancing for someone just getting out of school. In the early years of your career, you need someone supervising your work. It is helpful when you don't do something right to have some feedback and constructive criticism from professional supervision.

A note about pro bono work in family law

Family law is a good area for *pro bono* work opportunities. *Pro bono* is work done without compensation as a donation to people who need it. Many bar associations and paralegal associations have programs established where you can volunteer to help attorneys train individuals to do their own divorces or assist them in the divorce process. These programs are good places to keep family law skills sharp, and are also excellent opportunities to meet family law attorneys and paralegals.

Skills & aptitudes needed by family law paralegals

All the qualities, skills, and traits listed for litigation paralegals apply to freelance family law paralegals, with some slight differences. First, more financial work is involved. It is important for family law paralegals to be comfortable working with numbers, financial statements, and balance sheets, because they must calculate the equitable division of property and assets.

Much family law work also involves direct client contact, so the family law paralegal will enjoy more people contact than a paralegal in litigation. Family law paralegals, accordingly, must demonstrate empathy and active listening, as well as be able to respond affirmatively and positively to what the client is saying, which encourages more communication. They must be able to exude a sense of calm, because the divorce or custody dispute process is emotionally difficult for clients, who need to know you have matters well in hand.

Finally, while civil litigation frequently has winners and losers, family law seems to have only losers. No matter how a divorce or custody dispute comes out, few parties ever feel like winners. You need to be able to find your strokes and compliments elsewhere, or provide them for yourself, because clients are not always delighted with the outcome of the work.

Advantages & disadvantages of family law work

There are many advantages to this area for paralegals. First, it is an area that has a lot of work paralegals can do with minimum supervision once it is learned. A lot of fact-gathering and financial analysis is involved from the beginning, including refinement through the process, so someone who enjoys financial analysis will enjoy it. There is abundant opportunity for client contact. Because clients are often emotionally distraught, there is the opportunity to be supportive through good listening as well as legal help. There is also abundant opportunity for contact with opposing counsel, providing opportunities for more networking as you demonstrate your competence and professionalism in dealing with them.

As Terrie Burton puts it, "In freelancing in family law, you walk into a case load, and there are all these different nuances going on, and you have to shoot from the hip for a while while you figure it out. It's fun if you don't get bogged down in the emotions."

The main disadvantage is that you can find yourself working on a myriad of cases at once, with overlapping deadlines and numerous calendars to keep track of. Emergencies occur frequently, e.g., one party may try to hide or take assets from the other. There are many large divorce cases, where large assets are at risk, but there are many more typical cases that have only a few issues in each. The other obvious disadvantage of family law is the emotional component of working closely with people in turmoil. It can become depressing. When clients have very limited resources, it can be even more depressing. If you can keep it from getting to you, you might be able to enjoy this very human area of the law.

To help you stay current with changes in the family law practice, *Legal Assistant Today* inaugurated a regular "Family Law" column by Lindi Massey, a family law legal assistant at the firm of Burleson, Pate and Gibson in Dallas, Texas.

Estate planning & estate administration

Estate planning and estate administration are two practice areas so closely related that we cover them both in this section. It is not unusual for a paralegal to work in both areas.

Estate planning involves preparing the disposition of a person's assets after death, typically by will or trust (property held by one person for the benefit of another), or by joint title. Estate administration practice involves winding up affairs when someone dies. Probate involves the action by a court to validate and accept a will and see to the distribution of estate assets to the appropriate creditors, heirs, devisees, and beneficiaries. (People who inherit under a will are called *devisees*, and those who benefit from a trust or insurance policy, or are named such on investments, are called *beneficiaries*.) Most paralegals in these areas do just estate administration, but some have become trained in estate planning and do considerable drafting of wills and trusts.

What estate-planning legal assistants do

How often have you said "I (We) really must get a will!" Well, when you finally decide to do it, you will probably make at least one visit to an attorney to see what is involved. At that time, you might well meet an estate-planning legal assistant. Estate planning is an area where paralegal practice begins at the first client contact and continues through execution of all the necessary paperwork in order to put the client's estate plan into action.

Attorneys in estate planning typically ask their clients to fill out an extensive questionnaire listing all their assets and their locations, investments, insurance policies, family relationships, children and other potential heirs, and other similar information. Either before or after filling out that questionnaire, the attorney holds an initial interview with the client, possibly including the legal assistant. Shortly after, the legal assistant reviews the questionnaire with the attorney and begins to draft the appropriate will and/or trust documents for that client's situation.

As part of the estate-planning process, tax calculations must be performed to determine the most advantageous plan for the client's situation. The paralegal might perform the tax calculations and review the state statutes or the Internal Revenue Code and regulations to be sure the plan complies with the codes. Once a plan has been selected and the will or trust agreement drafted, the legal assistant might draft a summary of the terms for the client to read in "plain English." In addition, the legal assistant will probably review any insurance policies to find and analyze any provisions that need to be considered in the estate plan. During the process, the paralegal is frequently in contact with the client and the client's accountant or other financial advisors. The work is then reviewed by the attorney.

When a plan is ready and contains the terms the client desires, the client signs the documents with the legal assistant present to either act as witness or as notary. The papers might include the will and/or trust documents, and the necessary papers to change beneficiaries on insurance policies, investments, or retirement accounts, or to transfer title to assets that might be a part of the overall estate plan. The paralegal then takes the necessary steps to implement the plan, arranging for change of beneficiary on insurance policies or retirement or pension plans, recording documents necessary to effect transfer of title on any documents and taking steps to complete trust registration. The paralegal might also draft a letter informing the client of any requirements regarding the trust.

Estate-planning paralegals

- Participate in the client interview.
- Analyze and inventory the client's assets.
- Review current documents, insurance policies, and investment documents.
- Perform tax calculations.
- Review or research questions in state codes or Internal Revenue Code and regulations.
- Assist in drafting of wills and trust agreements, and summaries of provisions or procedures.
- Assist at signings and act as notary.

- Prepare and file change of beneficiary forms and transfer of title documents.
- Draft living wills and powers of attorney.
- Prepare gift tax returns.

What paralegals do in estate administration

When there has been a death, whether or not there is a will, the law suddenly becomes involved in the lives of the survivors and the disposition of the property of the person who died (the decedent). If there is a will, in some states the will must be probated, or proved, to make sure it's valid. In other states, the will only needs to be probated if there is real property solely in the name of the decedent, or if the property in the decedent's name exceeds a certain value; otherwise, the personal representative or executor can distribute everything according to the will without probate.

When probate is required, the court will want to be able to verify that the terms of the will have been properly carried out, and that the rights of creditors have been respected and bills paid. If there is no will, state law will determine what is to be done with the property and debts of the decedent.

Paralegal involvement starts from the first contact. When the decedent's family calls an attorney to assist in the probate process, there is an initial interview in which the attorney reviews the will and obtains from the client (usually a close survivor) the names and addresses of all of the known heirs, devisees, and beneficiaries. The legal assistant often attends the interview, taking notes. From here on, the administrative steps are largely in the hands of the legal assistant. The attorney continues to supervise the process, signs court pleadings, addresses any disputed matters concerning the estate, and intervenes when there are legal issues. However, in most routine estates, the legal assistant can follow through on all administrative work.

Because estate administration practice is filled with many forms and many steps, it is well suited to considerable paralegal involvement. In addition, it is an area that deals closely with normal people who are going through a difficult period in their lives. Paralegals have more time to listen and deal with the concerns of a bereaved spouse. The fact that a paralegal is accessible, helpful, and patient makes the probate process much more tolerable for the survivor.

The advantage of using paralegals in this practice area is clear. Because people often do not have a lot of money to spend on legal assistance, clients cannot afford the lawyer's fees, so the more a paralegal is involved in an estate administration matter, the less expense. In all cases, paralegal involvement is also important because it frees the attorney to perform higher income-producing work for other clients.

The steps in estate administration

The first steps in estate administration, after the initial interview, involve reviewing the will and determining whether the estate must be probated formally or not. If there is a will, you must go through it word for word because it governs the entire process—from who gets the money and the jewels to who pays the taxes. Based on the will, the size of the estate, and the situation (e.g., whether there are likely to be any disputes), the client, attorney, and paralegal determine whether to open formal probate or proceed informally (an option available in many states). In either case, the paralegal prepares the necessary paperwork.

In informal probate, the initial steps involve preparation of a series of forms for submission to the court for appointment of an executor or personal representative. Throughout the process of a formal probate, other submissions are made to the court to report accounting information and (in both formal and informal probate), to notify the court if additional heirs, devisees, or beneficiaries appear on the scene. The estate administration process then involves numerous steps, all of which might be done by the paralegal.

All these tasks involve plenty of detailed paperwork and specific steps in a specific sequential order. In some cases, such as change of beneficiary notices, the work must be done on separate forms provided by the insurance company or investment entity. In many cases, however, the forms are available on computer, tailored to the specific state and its statutory requirements.

Courts usually have detailed rules governing the probate process including specific deadlines that must be calendared. The Internal Revenue Code and regulations, and state codes and regulations, will also have absolute deadlines that must be adhered to. Part of the duty of the estate administration paralegal is to maintain detailed calendars and be constantly aware of approaching deadlines.

The paralegal serves as the client's primary contact person throughout the entire process, so the work also includes numerous telephone conversations and communications, not only between client and paralegal but between the paralegal and the insurance companies, banks, investment advisors, accountants, real estate brokers, appraisers and other specialists who might need to be consulted during the process.

Summary of estate administration paralegal tasks

- Make a thorough and detailed inventory of all the assets of the deceased.
- Calculate or obtain the exact value all assets, including bank accounts or investments as of the date of death, sometimes involving appraisals of personal property.
- Verify debts of the decedent.
- Notify creditors.
- Open an estate bank account and obtain a tax identification number for the estate.
- Review life insurance policies and arrange for payment to the beneficiaries.
- Arrange for the transfer of title on real property and distribute personal property.
- Distribute assets according to the will.
- Prepare gift tax, estate tax, fiduciary, and inheritance tax returns, as well as the decedent's final income tax return.
- Make a final accounting (filed with the court in formal probate) for all assets and debts.
- Close out the estate with the court.

Computers & estate administration

Computerized forms for the basic court filings in a probate matter are available in most states through bar associations or continuing education programs, and also through software publishers. For example, in California, official forms are available through the California Continuing Education of the Bar (CEB). Other software publishers have gotten into the market, but whatever forms are used in California must be basic ones approved by the California Judicial Council. Most states will have similar requirements. Again, the local bar association will be able to provide information.

In the case of federal tax forms, many paralegals use Shepard's McGraw-Hill programs for estate administration, specifically their Federal Estate Tax Returns: Calculation & Preparation; Federal Accounting for Trusts and Estates; Federal Gift Tax Return; and Fiduciary Tax Return (Shepard's McGraw-Hill, P.O. Box 1235, Colorado Springs, CO 80901, (800) 525-2472).

ProBATE Software also offers a package called 706 Plus, which performs complex calculations such as the interrelated computations required when state or federal death taxes are payable out of property used to fund marital or charitable deductions. The screens in the program resemble federal tax forms for ease of use. (Available from ProBATE Software, 3545 West 12th Street, Suite 102, Greeley, CO 80634.)

Business profile

Phyllis Cardoza

Phyllis Cardoza is a freelance probate paralegal who works out of her own office in Los Angeles, California, although she previously operated her business from her home for three years. Phyllis started as a legal secretary years ago, in a small office where she was encouraged to do a lot of drafting work. She worked in litigation, corporate law, and probate during those years. When she was expecting a baby, and still working part-time as a secretary, a former boss called and asked her to work on a probate matter at home. She soon had even more work, and he began telling other attorneys about her.

Phyllis has a well-equipped library in her office that represents a sizeable expense in periodicals, subscriptions, and memberships. She has probate practice books, a loose-leaf estate and gift tax reporter from Commerce Clearing House ($300–400 a year, used for doing federal estate tax returns); a book on trust administration in California, the California probate code, the California resident taxation code section regarding California estate tax; and West's California Code Forms Book on Probate. She also subscribes to two daily newspapers and professional association journals.

Phyllis uses a variety of computer software in her practice: official California estate forms from California Continuing Education of the Bar; Shepard's McGraw-Hill Federal Estate Tax program, which also has some state estate tax programs; In-house Accountant, a general ledger program for accounting to the court, (which Phyllis describes as an old program that was difficult to learn but turns out a beautiful product, courts love it). Her secretary uses Quicken for bookkeeping; Amortizer Plus if the estate owes money or is owed money, to help calculate the principal balance due; and Family Tree when family relationships are so complicated that the court wants to see a family tree to show who is related to whom; and Timeslips (Timeslips Corporation, 239 Western Ave., Essex, MA 01929, (800) 338-5314) for timekeeping and billing.

Although there weren't any paralegal training programs available at the time she began her paralegal work, Phyllis eventually took paralegal courses through several local colleges, and frequently attends continuing education courses for attorneys in the probate area. Phyllis has also been vigorously active in the probate sections of the Los Angeles Paralegal Association and the Beverly Hills Bar Association, and has worked on legislation changing the California statutes regarding probate as well as the recoverability of paralegal fees.

Phyllis strongly recommends that new freelance paralegals join a paralegal association and attend as many local bar functions as possible, especially probate section meetings where you can sit at tables with new people. Phyllis is active on committees and has addressed bar meetings, as well as paralegal associations, on topics ranging from committee announcements to legislation she has worked on. She says she was very uncomfortable speaking publicly at first, but has become more accustomed to it over the years. It has contributed to her professional image and she is now recognizable in the Los Angeles probate bar community. Phyllis has, of course, attracted a good deal of new business over the years through her activities, whose variety has provided her with name and face recognition.

Most of the skills listed previously for litigation paralegal apply to estates paralegals as well (communications, organizational ability, research skills, analytical ability). In addition, accounting training and skills are important, as well as strict promptness and attention to the calendar.

Skills & aptitudes needed by estate & probate paralegals

In order to work as a home-based freelance estates and probate paralegal, you should also have several years experience working in the area. This is particularly true of probate, because so much of the process is handled by paralegals without regular close contact with attorneys. You really need to have mastered the process, the regulations, and the deadlines.

Traits necessary to be a good freelance estate paralegal include:

- Strong independence—Ability to set an agenda and follow it strictly
- Responsibility and reliability—You'll have little direction from the attorney
- Empathy and responsiveness—Especially toward clients who are usually in a very difficult period

- Ability to work with clients directly
- Motivated self-starter

Jobs in estate planning & probate

According to the *Legal Assistant Today* 1993 Salary Survey, only a small percentage of the responding paralegals work in probate and estates. However, the area is a very popular one with freelance paralegals; the Los Angeles Paralegal Association 1992 Employment and Salary Survey shows that many of their freelance respondents work in the probate area.

Both the areas of estate planning and estate administration are promising fields for the future, for at least two reasons. First, the clients are likely to be senior citizens and the population in the United States is clearly an aging population; the "baby boomers" are just entering middle age, the estate-planning years, and will be approaching a time when more and more probate services will be needed. Second, estate planning is very closely married to tax laws and regulations, and tax laws change frequently. Such changes keep estate-planning lawyers and paralegals busy. No matter the size of the estate, tax laws affect what people do when they plan their estates.

Advantages & disadvantages of probate & estate-planning work

This is a wonderful area for people who want direct client contact as well as independence. Even in a law firm setting, probate paralegals work more independently than those in other areas, because so much of the process is systematized. It is not unusual to develop rewarding relationships with clients. One Denver paralegal received a five-pound box of chocolates from a client after an estate was closed. Most probate cases do not involve litigation, so there is less conflict involved in the process, although there are often very interesting and sometimes antagonistic relationships among the surviving family members. Moreover, the facts—as well as the individuals—in each case are very different. Phyllis Cardoza enjoys the opportunity to see a spectrum of financial situations. It allows her to be involved with corporations, litigation, and taxes, so it is never boring.

One of the great advantages of working in probate, of course, is that there will always be business. Due to our country's aging population, this can only increase. Phyllis says some estate administration attorneys in California are seeing some decrease in business because of the increased use of inter vivos trusts, which require little probate work. However, she has not experienced this; most middle class consumers do not need or use those devices, and the routine probate work that is much of what she does continues to be needed in the same numbers.

Finally, a great advantage to this area is income potential. A probate paralegal who has experience and knowledge in the area has a higher earning potential than freelance paralegals in other areas. According to the Los Angeles Paralegal Association 1992 Employment and Salary Survey, probate paralegals reported an average hourly rate of $57, as compared to $35 for litigation, $41 for corporate, and $39 for general practice paralegals.

Although salaries are admittedly higher in the Los Angeles area than in most areas of the country, the relative differences would still apply.

However, there are a couple of disadvantages to work in this area. First, it is apparently a little harder for some probate paralegals to collect their fees than for paralegals in other areas. This is particularly true where the attorney is paid by the estate after closing. The paralegal will need to collect fees more regularly than that, usually on a monthly basis. You need to be sure your understanding with the attorney is that you are paid directly by him, rather than by the estate following closing. Don't let the attorney tell you that you will be paid when he or she is paid.

The second significant drawback to this practice area is the cost of your continuing education and resource materials. You need form books, practice books, computer programs and tax reference books, many of which need constant updating. You will also need to read all tthe updates which might come weekly or bi-weekly, in order not to miss critical changes in laws or regulations. In addition, as part of keeping yourself current on changes in the practice area, you have added costs of continuing legal education, seminars, and bar section luncheon meetings. All practice areas require a certain amount of this, but in the probate area, which involves so much tax work, the investment is higher than other areas. The cost is not just in the fees for the training, but also in the lost work time.

For more information, read the excellent article in the May/June 1992 issue of *Legal Assistant Today*, "Federal Estate Tax Returns" by Diane St. John, which goes into great detail about the day-to-day work of estate administration paralegals.

Corporate & securities

The corporate and securities practice field is a major one in the paralegal world. According to the *Legal Assistant Today* 1993 Salary Survey, about 10 percent of the responding paralegals work in the corporate area. This is, however, a difficult area for home-based businesses, at least at present. In addition, over the past several years since the nation's economy has been in recession, there are fewer corporate paralegal positions now than in previous years, and the trend does not seem to be reversing yet. Highly experienced corporate paralegals seem to have little trouble staying busy, either in a law firm or working in-house at a corporation, but it is not the most promising field for new paralegals.

Much of corporate work involves working on transactions, mergers and acquisitions, public or private offerings of stock, and purchases and sales of business. Other corporate work involves setting up corporations and maintaining corporation's records and minute books, including calling their annual meetings, drafting proxy statements, and helping to prepare filings that must be regularly made with the Securities and Exchange Commission (SEC) by corporations whose stock is publicly held. And there is always a ton of document filing and retrieval in all areas of corporate and securities work.

All this work is most easily done by someone who has been present in the office enough to be familiar with the client's corporation and its records. Many of the documents to be drafted are patterned on the last such document prepared by the firm (which, admittedly would not be hard to work on from home). Furthermore, the corporation's minute books are likely to be housed at the attorney's office. Attorneys are understandably reluctant to have these critical original documents removed from their safe places at the law firm.

Two major coporate work areas: Federal securities & Blue Sky

Federal securities work   Paralegals frequently research questions in federal securities laws, regulations, rulings, etc,. that are available full text in CCH loose-leaf volumes of the *Federal Securities Law Reporter*. They prepare simple filings from single page fill-in-the-blank forms and complex multipage documents; and assist in drafting lengthy registration statements and prospectuses. This work is feasible by freelance paralegals who might be called on a project-by-project basis to work in the law firm; they are not very feasible for working from home, because frequent conferences are needed with the attorneys to discuss the specific language necessary for describing the corporation. There is such heavy liability attached to securities law practice that attorneys proceed with extreme caution, and understandably want the work done under very close supervision.

Blue Sky work   Some securities paralegals work with state securities laws (called "Blue Sky Laws") that regulate the advertising and sale of shares of stock in corporations, the registration of stock brokers and salesmen, and the regulation of stock advisors (to put it very generally). These laws, regulations, and policy statements are available in full text loose-leaf binders put out by Commerce Clearing House (CCH).

In a number of states Blue Sky work is appropriate paralegal work because it involves a lot of similar procedures: namely a lot of forms filings; and reading and interpreting laws, regulations, and policy statements that change regularly. But it is critical that the work be done absolutely correctly; there are significant consequences for both the client and the law firm if filings are made incorrectly or late.

When a client wishes to sell stock, for example, whether in a private offering or a public offering, paralegals do research and prepare (usually copious) filing documents in order for the securities to be either registered, or qualify for exemption from registration, in the states where they will be sold. This work is most feasible in the law office setting, but paralegals are often called in on a project-by-project basis to perform the work at the firm.

The full text of the CCH's loose leaf binders is also available on a computer program called Blue Sky Advantage, also put out by CCH Legal Information Services (49 Stevenson Street #900, San Francisco, CA 94105, (415) 227-0763). The program costs in 1992 were approximately $9,000 per year for a setup on one PC (updates are biweekly and are included in the annual fee). This program is full text, so research can be performed on it, searching for statute or rule numbers, by terms, and in a variety of ways. The program prepares summary reports on various types of state securities questions, and it also prepares and prints out all filing forms, including cover letters and in-house memos. While this is expensive for a home-based paralegal, a paralegal working for a firm that utilizes the software could conceivably arrange to use it from her home, accessed by modem.

Another software program is available to help Blue Sky practitioners—The Blue Sky Filer, (LegalDoc Software Corporation, 4725 Kynnelworth Drive, Suite 10, Bettendorf, IA 52722, (319) 332-5008) that reportedly prepares all the forms for Blue Sky filings in all states. This program was selling for $5,000 at the time of this writing, with an update cost of $2,000 per year (updates provided quarterly). It is encouraging that these programs are becoming available; little by little, they permit Blue Sky paralegals to do at least some of their work on a home-based PC.

Ultimately, because so many corporate and securities tasks must be done in the law firm, lawyers are reluctant to consider home-based paralegals as part of the team. Furthermore, because of the nature of the practice, attorneys are accustomed to having the paralegal handy to take care of this or that small detail, here and now, and the thought of a home-based person being helpful is a foreign concept. Still, there are a few signs that the field can adapt to freelance and home-based work in the future.

How do corporate freelance paralegals get work?

There have been a number of situations where paralegals working in an office have encouraged their firms to allow them to work from home, at least during a temporary period; for example, during or directly following maternity leave. Evelyn Cable, who was profiled in chapter 2, did this in the corporate paralegal practice area for her corporation employer for about five months, and it worked well. In most cases, corporate paralegals who have left full-time work are called back by previous employers on a project-by-project basis, to work in the firm setting. This is understandable; the paralegal is familiar with the clients, and the type of clients the firm handles; she knows the forms file and can quickly access what the attorney is looking for; and she probably knows how to use the corporate law library available there in the office.

Advantages & disadvantages of corporate paralegal work

The corporate and securities area is great for people who have an interest in the business world. You are actually part of companies starting and building their businesses. The work is intellectually very challenging—SEC regulations are almost as complex as IRS regulations to understand, and it is a great feeling to know you have mastered something other people have a hard time comprehending. As you gain experience, you learn to wend your way through various states' procedures and rules in the corporate and securities area, and earn the respect of clients and attorneys with whom you work. Furthermore, most transactional work involves parties who all want the deal to go—unlike litigation where there are apt to be winners and losers with a lot of antagonism. Most corporate and securities work is upbeat.

Another advantage to this field is that experience in these areas can lead to an in-house position in a corporation where hours and fringe benefits are usually better than in law firms. Of course, however, you might want to stay independent once you have experienced the pleasures of running your own business.

The main disadvantages cited by paralegals in these areas include less opportunity for direct client contact, and the piecemeal nature of many corporate assignments. For paralegals in this area, most of the contact is with attorneys, and the attorneys work with the clients. This is not exclusively true; in smaller law firms, for example, with smaller corporate clients, paralegals enjoy a lot of client contact. In large firms, however, attorney fees are very high, and sometimes corporation officers feel that they have earned access to the senior partner, and are not satisfied to have the paralegal be their prime contact. (Of course, this is not a disadvantage for a paralegal working in-house in a corporation.)

The other disadvantage is that much of the work comprises phone calls to this or that agency or service, requesting documents, figures or copies. A corporate paralegal can find herself mired in a variety of unrelated tasks, rather than focused on one client, case, or transaction. This can be less satisfying than other paralegal work.

Finally, some paralegals working in the Blue Sky area find that they have frequent telephone contact with clients as they obtain information needed for their filings, but they often have a hard time getting enough supervision from the attorneys in charge of the client's transaction. Attorneys view Blue Sky work as tedious and are so involved in the critical aspects of the transaction that it's hard to get their focused attention.

Business profile

Doris Childs

Doris Childs is a part-time freelance paralegal who works in the corporate practice area. She does not solicit new jobs or work full-time, but she works a couple of days a week, helping out a friend of hers who is a corporate paralegal at an entertainment law firm. Doris' friend does very sophisticated corporate work, and since the firm's client companies have a number of entities whose corporate records need regular attention, Doris provides those services, what the corporate law field calls *maintenance*. This work involves maintaining minute books, drafting minutes for routine corporate board and shareholder actions, and monitoring compliance with various routine state filing requirements. Occasionally new corporations need to be formed or obsolete ones dissolved, and through all three procedures corporate files need to be maintained. Doris manages this work in a couple of days a week. It is work that must be done in the law firm office since minute books are considered valuable originals and are generally kept under very secure conditions.

By only working a couple of days a week, Doris is freed up to do volunteer work, a situation she finds is ideal for someone who doesn't need full-time income.

The prime disadvantage Doris finds to working in the corporate area is that many corporate transactions are scheduled to wind up at end-of-year, and many corporations have a fiscal year that coincides with the calendar year, so much routine corporate work is clustered around certain times of the year; for example, proxy materials must all be prepared at the same time, or annual meetings are all scheduled closely together.

Doris finds some very interesting aspects to her work, especially since it is in entertainment law. She has also worked in a corporation as a corporate paralegal, which was interesting because Doris enjoyed working on securities offerings, drafting prospectuses, and having a variety of things to do.

Bankruptcy

As incongruous as it might seem, bankruptcy is an area similar to estate administration, because the steps are similar. In both situations there are estates involved: in estate administration, it is the estate of the decedent, and in bankruptcy, the estate of the bankrupt. Both cases require an inventory of assets and debts, petitioning to the court for disposition of the assets and debts, and a final closure of the matter. Furthermore, in both practice areas, paralegal involvement is very appropriate because of the abundance of paperwork.

The field of bankruptcy, like the estates field, continues to grow. Dun & Bradstreet reports that nearly 90,000 businesses failed in 1992, compared to 60,000 in 1991. Bankruptcy work is heavily detailed and time-consuming, so it is logical that attorneys would rather delegate it to a paralegal, and the ultimate cost to the client is far less than it would be if an attorney performed the work. From the standpoint of a home business, however, very few home-based paralegals are working in this field. Accordingly, we will not devote as much space to this specialty as we have to the previous specialty areas.

What a bankruptcy paralegal does

Much like probate, bankruptcy practice is forms-heavy, process-heavy, and the tasks are repetitious. The paralegal takes the case from initial interview through filing of initial forms and schedules in the bankruptcy court. Like probate, the practice involves the location, identification, and evaluation of assets and debts, which often involves sorting through the client's records and organizing them; listing the assets and debts; and verifying the true value of the assets and the actual amount of the debts.

Generally speaking, bankruptcy paralegals in large law firms have a much different job than those in small firms. Perhaps the real difference is between paralegals who work on large, commercial bankruptcies and those who work on individual and small business bankruptcies. In large cases, firms sometimes represent exclusively one side, either the debtor or creditors (those seeking the money the debtor owes them). The practice is very specialized, fast-paced, and document-heavy.

Freelance paralegals work in this area when they are hired on a contract basis, usually to work in the law firm, because of the fast pace of change in these bankruptcy cases. Bankruptcy is closely related to litigation, especially in the large cases. As creditors argue the issues of whether the debtor should be permitted to dispose of certain assets, and what their rights are, volumes and volumes of documents accumulate. A big difference, however, is that things proceed at a much faster pace in bankruptcy than in general litigation. Hearings are scheduled and held on short notice. Attorneys want even contract paralegals working on these cases to be at the office and accessible on a moment's notice.

In smaller firms, and/or on smaller bankruptcies, paralegals often work for debtors, reviewing their records and preparing and filing the petition and initial schedules (lists of assets, creditors, and debts). It is not unusual for this to begin with the individual debtor, or small business owner, bringing in a couple of corrugated boxes filled with loose papers—his records. Time to bring order out of chaos.

Paralegals might also work for the trustee, the person appointed by the bankruptcy court to gather all the debtor's assets and see that creditors are paid as much as possible from the bankrupt estate. The lawyer is in fact sometimes hired to act as counsel for the trustee—in fact, sometimes the attorney is appointed to serve as trustee.

The initial interview in bankruptcy is an opportunity, as in other areas, for the attorney to help the client determine the appropriate course of action. The next steps are very time-consuming—identifying all the creditors correctly, verifying the exact amount of each debt, and the value of each asset. Much detective work might have to be done to be sure the information the debtor has provided is complete, accurate, and up-to-date. All the transactions entered into by the debtor for several months before filing the bankruptcy must be scrutinized for appearance, or the reality, of fraudulent transfers. In bankruptcy the status of the debt must also be verified—whether it is secured or unsecured, and for secured debts, locating and verifying the status of the security (e.g., an automobile or equipment). The focus is on dealing with the debts so as to protect the debtor, while treating the creditors as fairly as possible under the circumstances.

There are always files to be set up and organized, and many notices to be sent—when nearly anything is filed in the bankruptcy court all creditors must receive a copy. And the paralegal is often the person, in a small office, to make visits to the bankruptcy court to read the court docket sheet (the court record of every step that takes place on that case) to see what is going on. When hearings, or the Section 341 Creditors' meeting (the first meeting to which all debtor's creditors are invited) need to be scheduled, that will also be the paralegal's job.

An experienced bankruptcy paralegal who wants to start a home-based business can specialize in the paperwork involved in Chapter 7 bankruptcies (liquidations, often filed by individuals and small business). Brenda Conner worked this way in her freelance business, charging on a per-case basis. Others charge a flat fee of $150–$200 to do a simple Chapter 7 filing. Some paralegals can also offer services as a bankruptcy typist to consumers who work on their own "self-help" bankruptcies. (However, be sure to read appendix B about the independent practice issues in this area.)

The basic library for a freelance bankruptcy paralegal includes, of course, the U. S. Bankruptcy Code and the Bankruptcy Rules, as well as a copy of the local rules for the local bankruptcy court. Also important are standard forms in printed form (Blumberg and Matthew Bender provide forms), or on disk as obtained from the attorney; they are also available on disk from Matthew Bender, which updates them periodically as changes occur in the Bankruptcy Code.

The bankruptcy paralegal job market

Most bankruptcy paralegals work in large or small law firms. We did not interview any freelance paralegals who specialize in bankruptcy, and due to the frequency with which court documents are filed and served, and the quickly changing status of the case, this type of practice is actually very difficult to work on from home. Freelance litigation paralegals are sometimes called on a case-by-case basis to work in a law firm on a large bankruptcy case, especially if they have some bankruptcy background. Most such paralegals are called by attorneys in the area whom they worked for in the past. If you have experience in the bankruptcy area and wish to attract more business, be sure to join the bankruptcy section of your local paralegal association, and attend meetings or join the bankruptcy section of the local bar association. Attend bankruptcy seminars and introduce yourself to attorneys who work in the area. Take any opportunities you can to demonstrate your expertise by appearing on panel discussions; for example, a program showing attorneys how to work with paralegals in the bankruptcy area—paralegal associations and bar association sections put on such seminars from time to time. If you are experienced, you might talk with a local paralegal training program about joining their faculty.

If you have a paralegal job where you currently work on small bankruptcies, try to talk your attorney into letting you do the work from home. The forms and process make this a very feasible option. You could pick up the client's records from the attorney, take them home where you prepare court documents and complete forms on your computer, and return the completed forms to the attorney. Once the client has reviewed and signed the petition and other documents, you can be the contact person with the bankruptcy court, filing the documents and monitoring the docket sheet. There is no reason this cannot work very efficiently.

Knowledge & skills needed by bankruptcy paralegals

All the skills and traits listed previously in the litigation section apply in the bankruptcy area. In addition, you must have facility working with numbers and an interest in financial matters, be detail-oriented, and have good investigative skills. Good people skills are also critical in dealing with this difficult issue. In a *Legal Assistant Today* article, Laurie Roselle suggests apprenticing yourself to a top-notch bankruptcy lawyer as a good way to learn the ropes. And of course, as with every practice area, paralegal training is strongly recommended.

Advantages of working in bankruptcy

According to the previously mentioned *Legal Assistant Today* article, job satisfaction is very high with bankruptcy paralegals. Brenda Conner enjoyed the field for the client contact and the reward of knowing you have helped someone work through a difficult period. It is a field with continuing opportunity and the pace is much faster than litigation, since bankruptcy cases rarely drag out for several years. Finally, it is a practice area where paralegals can exercise a lot of responsibility throughout the process.

Real estate & oil & gas law

The practice areas of real estate and oil and gas law have much in common; they both have to do with land—real property. When real property changes hands (especially commercial property), there are usually large loans that must be documented. The property must be perfectly described, and mineral interests accurately described and protected. As in most paralegal areas, paperwork abounds. In many states, particularly in the eastern U.S., paralegals can perform title searches in connection with purchases and sales of residential and commercial properties—work customarily done by title companies in the western states.

Although we did not interview any paralegals working in these areas in home-based businesses, we do know of situations where home-based businesses have worked in oil and gas law and real estate. There are two primary tasks for these areas that can be done from a home office: title opinions and foreclosures.

Title opinions   Every piece of property has a "title" that officially tells who owns it. When property changes hands, or someone wants to drill on property for oil or gas, the title must be investigated to assure ownership. The title opinion is the attorney's document spelling out to the client how current title stands and what needs to be done to correct any errors or "glitches" that occur in the chain of title. This document is often drafted by the paralegal. Both creating the chain of title and drafting the title opinion are steps that a home-based paralegal who is well-versed in title work can easily perform. You can produce the results on hard copy or on disk, or dictate them, and then return them to the attorney.

This work requires a thorough background in the fields of real estate and oil and gas law, as well as meticulous attention to detail. For a home-based paralegal this work has the advantage that it can be done at any hour of the day; you can work it around your baby's schedule, for example, because it does not require contact with outside agencies who might have restricted hours for phone calls.

Judith Current, a longtime highly experienced paralegal in Denver, has worked in these areas, as well as in probate and corporate law. She has worked at home on chain of title and title opinions (an opinion an attorney issues when title to certain property, usually mineral interests, must be verified). In these cases, Judith takes home the entire abstract of title, a document produced by a title company that shows each document of record ever filed on that property. She reviews the abstract from the first filing forward to the present day, and charts out the chain of title, showing each transaction throughout the history of the property and its mineral interests, culminating in a conclusion that the current holder has proper title, or if not, where the "glitches" are. That chain is then used to produce a title opinion for the client.

Real estate and oil and gas are currently slow areas for the lawyers and paralegals because of the poor economy. However, the work can be combined with other paralegal work in a freelance business.

Foreclosures

Foreclosure work is another area where paralegals abound. Although very few have home-based or freelance practices in this area, the work is very systematized and could be done from a home office. Foreclosures take place when someone has not paid a debt that is secured by real property, and the creditor or note holder decides to foreclose on his interest, i.e., take the security for the loan, the real property. The practice is very structured, based on state statutes and regulations, and the procedures involve a lot of paperwork, notices, and court filings, and are routine and repetitious—good paralegal work.

Other legal practice areas

There is actually a huge array of other practice areas in which paralegals work, and we list nearly 50 of them in Table 3-1. Here is a brief view of four major areas:

Environmental law   Environmental law encompasses all the legislation on clean air and water, and regulations that affect businesses at all levels. It particularly involves litigation over who is responsible for cleanup of toxic waste sites. Paralegals working in this area, besides doing the tasks involved in litigation as detailed in chapter 2, also do research in state and federal statutes, case law, regulations, and sometimes law review articles on questions of environmental law and policy. They obtain and review maps and records in government offices, contact government officials, and develop research notebooks on topics in the environmental area. They monitor changes in regulations and policy that might affect the practice of clients in the natural resources industries, and they write memos and summaries of their findings. They might also attend hearings of federal and state legislative committees and summarize the proceedings.

Environmental law paralegals might also do a lot of writing, such as creating draft histories of legislation, and memos on the impact of administrative and court rulings, or on the substantive and technical differences between drafts of legislation and/or results of amendments. Some help attorneys prepare speeches and articles in the environmental law area.

Many legal assistants in this area have undergraduate or graduate degrees in biology, natural sciences, environmental sciences, or land management as well as their paralegal training.

Water law   Water law is very similar to environmental law, and is a busy practice area in the dry southwest states like Colorado, Utah, Wyoming, Nevada, Arizona, and California. In these areas, there is a lot of litigation over water rights, and in some states there are special courts for proceedings involving water rights with special court rules and calendars. Paralegals do the standard litigation tasks, and also do much investigation on statutes and regulations regarding water issues. They perform research at the Bureau of Land Management and state land and water offices. They might review maps and prepare reports regarding the historic use of certain plots of land. They also perform title searches in county clerk and recorder's offices and review client records regarding the use of water throughout the history of the property. Legal assistants might prepare applications for well permits or change of water use, or coordinate and monitor the well permitting and drilling process.

Trademark & **intellectual** **property**   The intellectual property areas of law govern the use by companies or individuals of such things as trademarks, service marks, patents, and copyrighted materials. The statement you see at the end of videotaped movies and movies in theaters saying that the use of the product is protected, etc., was drafted by an intellectual property law attorney (or paralegal). Paralegals in this area learn the intricate procedures for registering and reserving trademarks and patents. Like the attorneys who work in this area, paralegals can become highly specialized as they learn the administrative maze of the U.S. Patent and Trademark Office. They prepare applications, conduct factual investigation using magazines and trade publications, and help guide clients through the processes involved in reserving their rights to their creations. They keep track of due dates, conduct searches of existing trademarks and patents, and draft simple licenses and agreements regarding proprietary information and technology. Today, computer science is an excellent academic background for a paralegal in this area, as high-technology intellectual property is an expanding area in this field.

This is not a big practice area for paralegals, but many do work in public defenders' offices, in district attorney offices, and for private criminal defense attorneys. Most of the work done by criminal law paralegals involves investigation, obtaining background information regarding the accused or the circumstances of the crime, and interviewing witnesses. They try to verify information, review written reports, and conduct legal research. Many of the typical litigation steps are involved in trial preparation, including reviewing the list of proposed jury members to identify desirable and undesirable jury members for a specific trial, and assisting in preparing questions for direct and cross examinations of witnesses.

Criminal law

Table 3-1
Law practice areas for paralegals

Administrative law	Communications & media
Admiralty & maritime law	Computers & software
Advertising & marketing	Consitutional law
Aging	Construction law
Agricultural law	Consumer law
Alternative dispute resolution	Contracts
Animal law	Copyright law
Antitrust & trade regulation	Corporate law
Arson, fires, & explosions	Criminal law
Appellate practice	Disabilities
Art law	Domestic relations
Aviation & aerospace	Drugs & narcotics
Bankruptcy	Election, campaign, & political law
Banks & banking	Energy
Biotechnology	Entertainment law
Broadcasting	Environmental law
Business law	Equipment
Casinos & gambling	Federal tax
Chemicals	Fidelity & surety
Child custody & support	Finance
Civil practice	Franchises & franchising
Civil rights	Fraud
Class actions	General practice
Commercial law	Health care
Commodities	Highways

Table 3-1   Continued

Hospitals	Personal injury
Immigration & naturalization	Probate
Indians & native populations	Product liability
Insurance	Professional liability
Intellectual property	Public law
International	Railroads
Labor & employment	Real estate
Law enforcement	Real property
Leases	Resorts & leisure
Libel & slander	Securities
Litigation	Taxation
Marriage & family	Technology & science
Medical malpractice	Telecommunications
Medicare	Torts
Mergers & acquisitions	Trade & professional associations
Military law	Trademarks
Mortgages	Transportation
Natural resources	Trucking
Negligence	Trusts & estates
Nonprofits	Wills
Patents	Zoning & land use

Deciding to specialize

The variety of paralegal work available offers opportunities for people with interests and aspirations of all kinds. Consider the following questions to help you identify your preferences:

- Is there a specific field that has always attracted you, in which you have always been inclined to work?
- Do you feel strongly about any issues?
- Do you currently belong to any organizations or donate to any causes that you believe in?
- Do you know people or have friends who have specialized in paralegal work?
- Is there a school or an institution in your area that is known for specializing in a specific area of law?
- Is there a lawyer you admire for whom you'd like to work in order to specialize in the same area he or she does?
- Do you feel you have a gift in any particular area, in the sense that you have always found it easy to understand that subject?
- Is your goal to make the most money possible or to find a specialization that you enjoy?
- Do you think that the specialization you have selected will continue to be a viable career option five years from now?
- What do you think you can add to or bring to the field if you were to work in the area of specialization that you like most?

We hope you are provoked by these questions and that they help you come closer to deciding what areas of the law you might wish to work in the most. Take into account that specializing in an area (the ones we've covered or an area of your choice) has its own advantages and disadvantages. Specializing can make you valuable, because you become well-versed in an area of law that few people know, including lawyers. This can improve your chances for work, and also might allow you to charge more. In chapter 6, for example, we look at several "niche" careers for paralegal consultants who specialize in such area as asbestos consulting and medical consulting.

On the other hand, specialists must be able to generate enough jobs in their specialty to keep working and earning. If you have too narrow a focus, and cannot do other paralegal work (or do not like other areas), you might limit your own earning potential and inadvertently close doors to future work.

If you are just beginning to think about a paralegal career, your first step is to obtain the paralegal training we described in chapter 1. If you are already in school, you will need to plan your strategy to obtain a job in a law firm, a corporation, an agency, a department of government, or elsewhere, as we described in chapter 2. Getting that first job can be a first step to finding out which area(s) you particularly enjoy and what opportunities might lie in your community. Some students are able to obtain a nonpaying internship as part of their training in order to gather more experience while looking for a paying position. Also, some temporary positions are available to new graduates through placement services and legal temporary services for work in specialized areas. Although in some cases these positions are open only to experienced persons, some might be available to you if you have undergraduate experience in that specialization or if you are willing to combine paralegal and secretarial work in one position.

Getting started

It used to be that paralegals would not accept positions that involved any typing at all; in the early days of the profession it was important to avoid confusion between the work of legal secretaries and that of paralegals. However, computers are now a necessary fixture in most paralegal positions, and keyboard facility is virtually a requirement. Depending on how difficult it might be to get that first experience, you might decide to accept a combination position in order to get paralegal work. If you are inclined to do this, be sure that there is some substantive paralegal work involved in the position, so it will provide you with what you need to move on in your paralegal career.

As for paralegals who have already been working and are considering freelance work, establishing your business in a specialty area is perhaps the best direction to take as long as you are willing to take on other work until you are able to build a regular clientele in your specialized area. If you haven't already, read the last section of chapter 2 about three ways to become self-employed, and the practice tip containing special information on ethics and the independent practice of law. Finally, chapter 7 contains more details about establishing your business.

4 Court reporters & scopists

Most people know what a court reporter is—in every courtroom scene on television or in the movies, whether fictional or real, a reporter is part of the picture, seated somewhere in front of the judge, tapping away on a recording machine. However, most people who have not worked in the profession have no idea what the reporter is actually "tapping" into that machine (it sort of looks like a typewriter but it is not) and few people know what happens after the trial or hearing is over when a person called a *scopist* might take over. Scopists help with the process of converting what comes out of the machine into sensible English.

In fact, what the reporter is doing is making a record of exactly what is said in the courtroom or deposition room—questions as well as answers, instructions of the judge, objections and other comments of attorneys. Believe it or not, court reporters have been doing what they do, in some form or other, for nearly 2,000 years. However, the note takers recording Roman orators could not have imagined what technology would do to their profession in the 1990s.

This chapter explains the career path of court reporters and outlines the background and preparation you need for this interesting field. We also look at the closely affiliated profession of scopist, a person who helps translate and edit the court reporter's notes. For both professions, we discuss the job outlook, the earning potential, and how to obtain training for them. Throughout the chapter, we provide profiles of some individuals currently working as reporters or scopists.

What court reporters do

Understanding the job of court reporter is actually best done by looking at the history of shorthand and the growing computerization of the field. According to the National Court Reporters Association (NCRA), the use of shorthand for recording speech goes back to ancient times when a form of it was used to record the great Roman orators. Shorthand evolved over the centuries into an increasingly formal system, and training in shorthand became a skill.

Modern court reporting took a giant step forward with the introduction of the stenotype machine in 1913. The machine, which has 24 keys comprising letters and numerals, records a phonetic code to capture the words of a speaker. The machine output—called *notes*—are printed on a narrow paper tape. Today they are also recorded on a computer disk. The notes made by the court reporter represent a phonetic code made by combining letters. Some letters mean themselves, some mean other sounds, and some combinations mean whole phrases or sentences that are especially common in courtrooms. For example, a few strokes might always mean "Is that correct?" so the reporter doesn't need to repeat the full phrase every time. The machine is set up so that more than one key is pressed at a time; more like a piano than a typewriter (see Fig. 4-1). At each stroke the paper advances, and each stroke is usually one syllable or word. (See Fig. 4-2.)

In the "old" days, after a trial or deposition, court reporters typed their notes into transcripts on manual typewriters, using carbon paper for extra copies. Later, when belt-operated dictating systems became available, some reporters dictated their transcripts to typists. Later, more sophisticated dictation systems evolved, including reel-to-reel and then cassette tape recorders.

Computer-assisted transcription (CAT)

In the late 1970s the first generation of computer-assisted transcription (CAT) became available. In these early CAT systems, the reporter's writing machine captured phonetic symbols on a disk or on magnetic cassette tape or internal memory unit, in addition to the printed symbols on the paper tape. The symbols on the computer disk or internal memory unit were then loaded into a computer that translated them into readable English. The computer contained a dictionary to match the stenographic symbols with the English words and letters they represent. Of course, there were always some unrecognizable symbols the computer could not transcribe; these appeared on the computer screen in the form of raw stenotype notes that the person had to translate manually.

The first CAT systems utilized mainframe computers, bulky and expensive. The reporter used a cassette that fit into her stenotype machine. After the deposition, the reporter removed the cassette from the machine and took it into an office that had a mainframe computer. (Obviously, mainframes were too expensive for individual freelance reporters; most were located in agency offices, so freelance reporters had to work for agencies.) The computer received the cassette, and also the reporter's personal dictionary of terms,

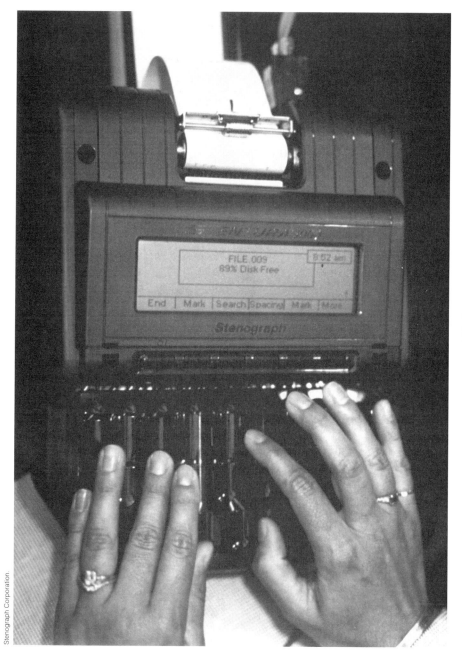

4-1
Stentura 8000 Stenograph Writing Machine.

and translated the codes that were recorded on the cassette, matching them against the reporter's dictionary—a sort of combination "spellcheck" and "search and replace" in today's word-processing terms. The mainframe output was then recorded onto a floppy disk that the reporter took home, where she or he had an editing station on a hard drive, and did the editing, correcting the symbols the computer had not been able to translate, adding

```
TKPW    O   F          >  Govenor
T P H   O     R           Roy
        R O EU            Roy
        R O E   P L     >  Romer
              E  R
                  R B G S   (comma)
TK          E    PB       Denver
   P H A  EU R            Mayor
      W      E      LG  >  Wellington
T           O    PB
      W      E     B      Webb
               R B G S    (comma)
         A       PB       and
S K      O   E  R     S   scores
               F          of
         O   E  R         other
         O*            >  officials
T P         EU R BL  S
      W          R        were
S        AO           D   sued
T    H      U R      S    Thursday
   PW      EU             by
         A                a
TKPW RAO        P         group
S        AO E      B G  >  seeking
                   G
T        O                to
      R O   FR            recover
T        A       B G S >  taxpayer
   P     A  EU R          money
   P H  O E   PB          money
S  P        E   PB   T    spent
  TK          U R    G    during
   P     O E    P         Pope
S K W R O       PB        John
      P  A    U     L     Paul
   2                 8    II's
S        R   EU      S  >  visit
             EU      T
   T P H                  in
         A    U     G     August
           F  P L T       (period)
```

4-2
Coding example Created by a Stenograph Writing Machine.

punctuation, and formatting. That setup cost the reporting agency $100,000 for the mainframe, and the reporter roughly $8000 for the equipment used at the deposition and at home to edit.

As you might guess, this system was cumbersome, and a "second-generation" system developed, although it was still before PCs became popular. This smaller system was more reliable than the first-generation equipment, and less expensive—perhaps $75,000 for the office equipment, $6000 for the reporter's.

Finally, with the growth of PCs, we now have a "third-generation" system that includes a new writing machine, which translates the reporter's notes to English as they are being written. As the notes come out on paper tape, they are also recorded to a 3½" diskette and/or to a hard disk. The reporter can read back the notes as the work is being done, either on a small screen on the machine, or from a screen on a notebook computer connected to the machine. This way, reading as he or she goes, the reporter can quickly spot if the symbols used are not creating the word or phrase intended, and can try to remedy it while still at the deposition or in court. Even better, the reporter's laptop can be also be cabled to the attorneys' laptops if they wish to be able to read what is being recorded at the moment. (In order to do this, the attorney's laptop must have appropriate software, which costs about $500, plus a cable.)

After the deposition, the reporter puts the disk into a PC, on which either the reporter or a scopist can do additional correcting and editing. These third-generation systems cost the reporting agency about $60,000 and the reporter $10,000 to $12,000. The recording or writing machine and software systems that reporters must buy are made by many companies, but are basically the same and are comparably priced. The most popular brands used appear to be Stenograph, StenoCAT, ProCAT, and XScribe. Of course, the reporter's writing machine must be compatible with his or her PC. (If the reporter works for an agency, the machine must also be compatible with their equipment, so that the reporter can modem the transcript to the company for proofing.)

The newest CAT technology: Real-time reporting

In the very newest CAT systems, which use what is called real-time reporting, reporters can provide instantaneous translation of the testimony from the stenotype machine onto a computer screen, in written English, within seconds of when the testimony is given. Reporters who have real-time skills have learned to exercise much more detail and accuracy in their writing, so that the computer-translated transcript is much more complete and accurate than that of other systems. At present, only a small minority of court reporters have this level of skill, but those who do are more valuable. The newest systems are already being utilized by attorneys or judges during the process of the trial, hearing, or deposition. One use is when a hearing-impaired person in the court room needs to know what is being said. (In fact, the same real-time reporting skill is used in captioning, such as when written script is instantaneously needed for events and for television for the hearing impaired.)

The other major use of instantaneously available transcripts is by attorneys, who can do word-searches when they want to go back in testimony to find any names, dates, or key terms that came up. In the future, the technology is moving towards integrating the testimony currently being transcribed with that of all prior depositions in the same case, so that the attorneys can search all testimony at the same time using the same terms. When real-time reporting is being utilized, there are also occasions in which a reporter is writing and a scopist is editing simultaneously, so by the time the deposition is over, a transcript is ready to go.

The implications of real-time technology on trial preparation procedures are hard to imagine. Changes have been happening so fast in the court-reporting profession that people who are still in the peak of their reporting careers can remember dictating from their notes onto a belt dictation system, or typing up their notes using carbon paper to get copies. These same people are now writing in real-time format, using modems to send transcripts to and from scopists or to and from agencies for proofreading; and are providing captioning for television stations, making programs available to the hearing impaired. As technology is changing the way reporters are used, it is also providing more and more uses for their skills.

A day in the life of a typical court reporter

Now that you understand the basic technology, here's a sense of a typical day for a court reporter. Assume that the reporter has an appointment to record a deposition. He or she appears at the location of the deposition well in advance to set up the writing machine and other materials, load the paper into the machine, and have everything ready. When it is time for the deposition to start, the reporter swears in the deponent, and the questions and answers begin. The reporter listens intently, and captures every word spoken by tapping in the phonetic codes on the writing machine, attributing the words to the appropriate speaker, and recording every spoken word as precisely as possible. According to NCRA, in a six-hour day, a reporter writes approximately 72,000 words, sometimes at speeds of up to 300 words per minute.

Occasionally during the course of the testimony someone will ask the reporter to "Read that back, please." The reporter then goes to the appropriate passage on the paper where the notes have been recorded, and repeats the testimony word for word. This is not as easy as it sounds. The "notes" are in a phonetic code; and although reporters learn to read directly from the notes in school, with the advent of CAT systems, many reporters do not have the regular practice they used to have at reading the notes directly from the paper tape. On the other hand, more and more reporters now have real-time equipment that translates immediately, and uses a monitor or is connected to a laptop computer, so they can see the translation. In those cases the reporter can read real English words from the display or laptop screen.

During the course of the deposition the reporter is also responsible for labeling and keeping track of exhibits that have been used in the examination, which he or she will later provide along with the deposition transcript. At the end of the deposition, the reporter packs up all the equipment and exhibits and leaves, taking the notes on paper or on computer disk. In many cases, but not all, the notes must be subsequently transcribed to form a full English transcription; this means the notes will be "scoped" and edited, then proofread into a complete, accurate, and readable transcript. (Details about scopists are discussed later in this chapter.)

Most court reporters then have two weeks to deliver the transcript to the client, although there are some who will provide expedited delivery at an extra charge. (Those reporters who work through an agency must give the transcript to the agency in enough advance time for the agency to copy or print it, then bind it for delivery to the client.)

Court reporter Jamie Vance

Business profile

Jamie Vance has been a court reporter in Denver for about three years, and before that she spent several years as a legal secretary. When she realized she wanted to work from home, she went to court reporter school, and then got offers from three different agencies that handle court reporters. She currently works for just one agency.

To find out about her assignments, the agency calls her, or she checks in by about 4:30 every afternoon for a message about where her assignment is for the next day. Sometimes she reports to the agency office, sometimes directly to the location. Typically the assignment is a deposition, or it might be an arbitration to settle a dispute. She takes the deposition, then goes home and scopes and edits it herself. She then turns the transcript over to a proofreader to read it and get it back to her for corrections before copies are made.

For Jamie, there have been considerable benefits to being a reporter, as compared to her former work as a legal secretary. She feels more professional, and she finds that attorneys seem to have much more respect for reporters than they do for secretaries. She says that although you only deal with them briefly, you are an important part of their case. They know they have to treat the reporter well to get the deposition transcript when they need it. Nevertheless, Jamie found she had to get over being intimidated by lawyers. She was terrified early on as a secretary, and found she took on a "slave" attitude to handle her fears. As a reporter she had to assert her professionalism, and insist on what she needed to do her job.

The disadvantages? Jamie says "The work is hard, sometimes grueling, in depositions. Most attorneys will be nice, and will ask if you need breaks, etc. There are some that act like you're a doormat, but for the most part you are treated like a professional."

Jamie gets new clients by talking to attorneys and by doing her best at depositions where opposing counsel are impressed. She typically gives out her business card to everyone at the deposition so they know who she is and to get her name known. All in all, Jamie is very happy with her profession.

What is a scopist?

Not all court recordings need to be transcribed into English; some simply stay in "note" form on paper tape and computer disk. However, whenever a written transcript of a proceeding is needed, the court reporter's notes must be translated and "scoped" or edited. As we explained previously, most reporters these days use computer-assisted transcription (CAT) that translates their notes into text, sometimes instantly. Nevertheless, the transcript must be cleaned up. Enter the scopist, a career that originated about 15 years ago when CAT systems first became available. (The term *notereader* was also used at one time, referring to someone who read the reporter's notes.) Many reporters do their own scoping, but many others hire scopists regularly or on occasion.

In effect, CAT systems translate only about 60 percent of what the reporter has done. They do not add punctuation, for example, unless the reporter strokes it into her notes. They do not resolve errors, mis-strokes, or sound-alike words. Depending on the level of sophistication of the software used by the reporter, and on the level of complexity of the strokes made by the reporter, the computer might not know the difference between various homonyms; for example, "there," "their," or "they're," and might mistake other symbols in the transcript.

As a result, a scopist is needed to make sure the transcript is in proper English and complete. The scopist puts the disk containing the reporter's notes into a computer, and cleans it up. He or she corrects the "un-translates," (symbols the computer could not translate such as homonyms, proper nouns, or mis-strokes); then edits, perfecting the punctuation, adding the title page and other standard format items. Finally, the scopist reviews the transcript for consistency and sense. In case the transcript has a passage that makes no sense at all, the scopist can switch over and bring up on the computer screen the notes—the phonetic symbols keyed in by the reporter. The scopist can then see how the notes were taken, and attempt a more meaningful translation.

The economics of scoping are clear. A reporter who employs a scopist frees herself to attend and record another hearing instead of spending time or energy scoping the transcript from the previous hearing. Reporters earn much more money attending the hearing or deposition than in completing the scoping part of the job. For the scopist, too, the arrangement pays off. A scopist might be able to learn the skill without attending the entire court reporter training, which is lengthy and expensive. While the scopist's income is not as great as the reporter's, the scopist can perform the work entirely at home and on computer, and enjoys a more flexible schedule.

Scopist Jodie Hughes

Business profile

Jodie Hughes does scoping out of her home in Mound, Minnesota. Jodie learned about the scoping field from a pamphlet she saw featured in a career column in the *Minneapolis Star & Tribune*. She was pregnant at the time and thinking about changing jobs as well, so the pamphlet on home-based careers really appealed to her. Jodie's background was in personnel benefits, work that had given her an extensive medical vocabulary. After reading the pamphlet on scopists, she enrolled in correspondence training offered by At Home Professions (the program is no longer offered by this company). That course took her about eight or nine months to complete, and then she began to check out the local court reporter and scopist community in her area. She met some scopists and attended a local convention of the Minnesota Freelance Court Reporters Association, where she found herself sitting next to a reporter who needed a scopist. Jodie had her first client.

Scoping turned out to be different from what Jodie expected. She was under the impression that reporters had such fast computers, they did not need scopists any more. In fact, however, there is still a great need, in her opinion. A reporter would need a phenomenal dictionary—perhaps 80,000 words—built up in order for her software to translate so perfectly that scoping was unnecessary. Most reporters start with a 15,000- to 20,000-word dictionary. Jodie has calculated that for every hour of reporter's writing, it takes a scopist about two hours to scope and edit. A half-day deposition would be 100–125 pages, or about three hours of reporting; this would require six hours of scoping and editing.

Jodie has also expanded her business by becoming certified as a trainer for Stenograph for their Premier Power software. Her personnel background prepared her well for the training work.

Court reporters work either as employed or official reporters, or as freelancers working alone or with an agency. Scopists usually work independently or for agencies. The following sections explain the various options.

Employed as official reporter   Employed reporters typically work for the courts as official reporters, although other jobs are available; for example, recording legislative proceedings, United Nations sessions, or recording administrative hearings for government agencies. Wherever they work, employed reporters are generally in the same setting day after day.

The job market for reporters & scopists

Court reporter work options

The advantages of working as an employed reporter include, of course, the usual advantages of employment: guaranteed income, health insurance and other benefits, and the stability and camaraderie of returning day after to day to the company of known coworkers. Those working for courts do not automatically transcribe every trial and hearing; some reports are done at the request of one party or another, and then the reporter earns an extra fee for the transcription. Transcripts are needed, for example, if a case is going to be appealed in order to document accurately what took place during the trial. Because of this, and because official reporters are generally paid less than freelance reporters, not as many official reporters have purchased CAT equipment; some still dictate their transcripts.

Freelance reporters Some freelance reporters work through agencies and some work independently, having their own business and obtaining their own clients. Freelancers work on a job-by-job basis, usually serving at depositions, for example, but also occasionally at arbitrations, administrative hearings, corporate meetings, or other occasions where a formal record of speech is needed. Depositions can be held at a variety of locations, so the freelance reporter must travel to the proceeding.

Deposition reports are almost always transcribed, usually as soon as possible after the deposition, and generally no later than two weeks afterwards. According to the NCRA, two-thirds of current court reporters are freelancers who either have their own business or work for a freelance reporting firm.

Scopist options

It is rare for a scopist to be employed, as reporters are, in an official court position. Since not all trials and hearings are transcribed, and the reporter earns extra compensation for producing a transcript, an official reporter can arrange to hire a freelance scopist if assistance is needed. Most scopists must therefore work freelance, providing services to court reporters who call on them for projects. This seems to vary by area, though; for example, in California and on the East Coast most scopists are independent; in Colorado, most work through agencies. The scopists who work at home have their own CAT software; those working at agencies use the agency's software.

Reporters usually have one or two scopists they use regularly, and whose software is compatible with the reporter's. The reporter can deliver a disk to the scopist, or send the transcript by modem to the scopist's computer. There is usually a short turnaround time for the work, since the reporter has no more than two weeks for the entire transcription process (and often much less, if the transcript is needed on an expedited basis). Following the scoping work, proofreading remains to be done. The scopist probably will have no more than two or three days to complete one transcript.

Like the freelance paralegals discussed in chapter 2, reporters and scopists find advantages and disadvantages both in working alone and in aligning themselves with an agency. The agency obtains the jobs for you, so you do not have to do any promotion of your own business. The agency might provide technical support, scopist and proofreading services, and access to printing and copy machines for a fee.

The agency can probably afford a higher level of technology than you can in your own freelance business, so they are able to attract deposition work from lawyers and law firms who handle large litigation cases and prefer a variety of electronic options in their transcripts. For example, many attorneys prefer transcripts delivered on disks in ASCII format or with a full-text management/indexing program such as Discovery ZX or CAT-Links. An agency is also more accessible to clients; for example, the agency is available to provide an immediate response to a client's call, whereas a home-based reporter must rely on an answering machine or answering service, and a client with an immediate need might have to take the business elsewhere. Agencies can offer other amenities to clients as well, such as a conference room for scheduling depositions when a neutral location is required. The agency can also handle sudden large projects when work pours in and a lot of transcripts are needed in very short time. A sole practitioner might have trouble with time conflicts unless backup arrangements are made between two such reporters or scopists.

Some freelance reporters recommend that you work only for agencies that allow you to sign up with more than one agency, rather than insisting that you work for one agency exclusively. This enables you, as an independent contractor, to increase your opportunities for obtaining good work. On the other hand, Eileen Hyatt's company, Hyatt Court Reporting & Video in Denver, uses employee reporters rather than independent contractors. Eileen provides training, mentoring, and employee benefits. The employees do most of their work at home, but they are employees of her company.

Some independent contractor reporters who work for agencies begin to pick up some of their own clients while working for an agency, which is acceptable so long as you do not take away any of that agency's clients! This is one way to begin to build your own client base while still working for an agency.

On the other hand, the greatest advantage of being a home-based freelancer (and the corresponding disadvantage of working through an agency), at least for reporters, is that the agency takes a cut of the freelancer's fee. For reporters, the agency's typical commission can range from 15 to 50 percent. Working as a home-based reporter, you are able to keep the entire fee.

As a sole practitioner you can establish a closer client-reporter relationship— scopists with their reporters, and reporters with certain attorneys or law firms—a situation that benefits the freelancer and the client alike. Lawyers often get used to a good reporter and want to be able to use that reporter repeatedly, especially when there are a number of related depositions on the same case. If the law firm is working through an agency, they are sometimes unable to get a requested reporter. The service element is not as personal, as the agency will send an unknown replacement. (If a sole practitioner is unable to appear when a client asks, at least she can offer to arrange for a replacement, and the personal contact element of the reporter/client relationship is not lost.) Freelance scopists usually arrange to work for two to four reporters, depending on how much work the reporter has. The reporters and scopists are accustomed to each other's working style and work quality.

Once independent reporters have an established clientele, they might be able to get more work through their own business than working for an agency. In some communities, however, there are too many reporters, and consequently neither independent freelancers nor those working through an agency get enough assignments to provide full-time equivalent income.

There are other subtle problems in relying on an agency to obtain your work for you. Sometimes the agency will favor its long-term reporters over newer hires, who are relegated to a lower preference and thus get fewer jobs. Also, if you do want part-time work you might be passed over for the better assignments that go to those who want to work longer hours. It is a risk at-home reporters take. Similar problems can arise for agency-connected scopists as well.

According to the reporters and scopists we interviewed, there are wonderful benefits to freelance work, whether you work through an agency or have your own business. Jamie Vance, who gets her freelance reporting work through a Denver agency, loves the flexibility in her schedule that enables her to be with her son. She enjoys the variety of going to a different place or type of proceeding every day, and the depositions are varied—some are interesting, some are awful, or sad, and some are "just OK."

Independent reporters and scopists have a lot of control of their schedules. You work when you want to, to get transcripts out—you can work at night, or at four in the morning, during quiet times in the day, in the evenings or on weekends.

Business profile   Scopist Debra Schiff

If there is an expert in this field, it is probably Debra Schiff, a scopist in Philadelphia, Pennsylvania, and the editor of the monthly "Scopists' Workshop" column in the *Journal of Court Reporting*. Debra says that while most scopists are former court reporters or court-reporting students, she is an exception to the rule because she was a former editor and proofreader, backgrounds she feels are excellent for scopists. Debra had seen an ad from the Court Reporting Institute in Philadelphia describing the scopist as an "Editor/Transcriber," which appealed to her. Once she learned to read the stenograph codes she had an easier time than other scopists picking up the skill.

Debra is very happy about the money she earns as a scopist and the flexibility she has in her at-home work schedule. She gets scoping work from three reporters, and it provides her with full-time work. One reporter gives Debra all her transcripts, and does not do any of her own scoping. That reporter keeps Debra informed of her schedule all along, so Debra can monitor her workload and schedule accordingly. Debra's other clients can do their own scoping, so if Debra cannot take their work because she is too busy, they have the option of scoping their own. Debra tries not to keep anything longer than two or three days, and tells reporters if she sees she can't get to their work in that time.

Debra says it took a long time to get to the point of having regular clients and full-time work. It takes most scopists some time to get a client base. On the other hand, she advises new scopists, "Don't go out and get too many clients. If they all get expedited transcripts at the same time, you are really up a creek."

Debra takes pride in her work and would not want to have to subcontract out her work, so she monitors her workload carefully. However, she does advise scopists, especially new ones just acquiring client bases and not sure of their workload capacity, to make arrangements with other scopists to share overload work. In areas where most scopists use a popular or common software system, it is possible for them to exchange work that way. (Not all CAT software systems are mutually compatible. The scopist's software must be compatible with the reporter's, of course, and with that of any scopist with whom she shares work.) Which software is most popular varies depending on the area of the country.

Debra has written a book entitled *The Scoop on Scoping* that was due to be published in late 1993. It will be advertised in the *Journal of Court Reporting*.

Earning potential for reporters & scopists
Court reporters earnings

One of the reasons many people decide to pursue a court reporting or scopist career is that the profession can produce an excellent income once you are established. Here are the earnings potential on each profession.

Marshall Jorpeland, Director of Communications for NCRA, explains that there have not been any nationwide salary surveys of court reporters in recent years. Most reporters work independently, and many prefer part-time—both of which make surveys hard to obtain, and annual salary figures not very meaningful. Some people in the field estimate that an average annual income approximates $45,000; Mr. Jorpeland suggests it ranges anywhere from $17,000 to $80,000 depending on geographical area and how much the reporter wants to work. Eileen Hyatt estimates that people willing to work full-time, very hard, will earn between the $35,000 and $70,000 in the Denver area. The range varies depending on the reporter's efficiency, flexibility and availability for a variety of jobs, and how well the person fits with a variety of personalities—some are good with tense attorneys, for example, and some are not.

How reporters charge   As explained earlier in this chapter, official reporters, employed by the court, do not transcribe every trial or hearing; transcripts usually are ordered only when a case or decision is being appealed, and then the reporter charges the party ordering the transcript a fee for producing it. Those fees are approximately $2.50 per page for the original and one copy of the transcript, and 50 cents per page for each additional copy.

Freelance reporters charge for appearing at the deposition or hearing, and also by the page for transcripts. The appearance fee at depositions and other noncourt proceedings ranges from $25 or $30 up to $50 for a half-day appearance; hearings might be $100 to $150 per day plus the transcript fees—more than a deposition because they last all day and are intense. Sometimes no transcript is ordered, so in those cases, the appearance fee is higher (rarely the case for depositions—99 percent of depositions are transcribed, and in the other 1 percent of cases, reporters will sometimes double the appearance fee if no transcript is ordered).

As for transcript fees, the freelancer also asks for $2.50 to $3.25 per page for the original transcript and one copy, and anywhere from $1.35 to $1.75 per page for an additional, second copy. For extremely difficult subject matter, such as hearings on contaminated waste cleanup for a specific site (something *very* technical), reporters often charge more. There might be a higher per page charge for a shorter turnaround time, such as $5 to $6 per page for overnight delivery.

As an example, say a reporter has a 90-page transcript from a two-and-a-half-hour deposition, and the parties order the original and two copies of the deposition. Including the appearance fee, and with the usual turnaround time, the reporter's fee will be between $400 and $450 dollars, but if overnight delivery is expected, the amount increases to $650–$700. (Don't forget the reporter might need to pay some of this fee to a scopist or take extra time doing the scoping herself.)

Fees vary with the competition in the local geographic area. As Jamie Vance points out, the work is difficult and reporters are well-trained, but they can only charge what is an acceptable rate in the community.

There are a lot of variables that go into how much scopists earn, depending on the area of the country and the community where they work, what the competition charges, whether the work is done through an agency or directly for a freelance reporter, or is subcontract work for an official reporter. According to Debra Schiff, although some agencies pay by the hour, most scopists work by the page; so it depends on how fast you work; an average is 70–80 cents a page, the range is 60 cents to $1. On a good day a good scopist can do 150 pages on the work of a good reporter; some do more. Fast typists do manage more work per hour than others, but you still have to read every word you are scoping, so there are limits on how much can be accomplished in one day. Scopists, like reporters, can charge more for expedited jobs. In addition, they might make more on a transcript if they do the "recorrections" after proofreading, a step usually performed by the reporter.

Jodie Hughes finds that some reporters in the upper Midwest area use audiotapes at the depositions they record, for backup and for filling in missing portions of the transcript. Since the audio tapes slow up the scoping, she charges $1 a page for transcripts with an audio tape. She uses a transcribing machine with a speed adjustment, and listens to the tape as quickly as she can, until she gets to a portion that needs clarification. Then she uses the tape to help her comprehend the material. The need for this depends both on the reporter and the speaker—how hard it was for the reporter to get the speech accurately. Some of the better reporters will use tapes only for expert witnesses, to confirm medical and technical terms (these terms can be so similar it takes careful listening in order to be accurate).

If the scopists must do any printing—such as a rough draft to get the reporter's corrections—the charge averages $1.25 per page (depending on the writing skills of the reporter, and what the market will bear).

Skills, knowledge, & aptitude requirements

Both reporters and scopists must be very intelligent and enjoy a broad range of knowledge. They must possess large vocabularies and have outstanding English language and grammar skills, because they are making their living in an occupation where linguistic accuracy is paramount. The outcome of a legal proceeding can be dramatically affected by the condition of the legal transcript, so there is no room for sloppy grammar, diction, usage, or vocabulary. Obviously, reporters also must have excellent listening skills.

Because of the highly technical nature of the reporting profession, and the speed with which that technology is advancing, anyone going into it now must be comfortable with computers, and preferably adept at the keyboard. Both the keyboard (and the writing machine for reporters) require manual dexterity as well.

Finally, reporters, and to a lesser degree scopists, need to be familiar with the entire legal process, not only to understand how their work fits into the entire litigation scheme, but because a lot of language in trial transcripts and even in depositions (in verbal exchanges among attorneys) comprises legal terminology. To a lesser degree, some general knowledge in a variety of fields of study is extremely helpful to the reporter and scopist, since they will be trying to make sense of testimony from many fields of knowledge.

Although a high school education is usually the minimum requirement for reporter training schools, many agencies require at least some college in the background of their reporters. They say that high school graduates (without college) will often do very well in their writing machine speed skills, partly because their manual dexterity and keyboard facility are good; but also because they are mentally unfettered by any involvement in what they are transcribing, or by any reaction to the material. However, they are not as good when it comes to transcription, editing, and proofreading—recent high school graduates often lack the English grammar and language skills necessary to be a good reporter. When they are in a reporting situation, for example, a lot of words sound alike, and if they do not have enough life experience or education to recognize the context of what is being said, they frequently misunderstand and make errors in their reporting.

Young and inexperienced people with little life experience, often have not developed interpersonal skills and are at a disadvantage dealing in a deposition situation with high-powered professionals. For example, a reporter who went to reporter school directly from high school could not possibly be equipped to handle either the personalities or the level of subject matter in most sophisticated depositions.

Janet Shadeix, of the court reporting business Shadeix and Associates in Minneapolis, puts it another way. In her hiring of independent contractor reporters, a college degree carries a lot of weight. As Janet puts it, "You need to be very worldly, you need a good vocabulary, you need to be able to do a lot of research, and you need to be someone willing to put in extra time and do homework. If you take a metallurgic engineer deposition one day, and an orthopedist the next day, you need to be able to research what the words mean—you could have sound-alike words, and it changes everything in the transcript."

Personality traits of reporters & scopists

Eileen Hyatt believes it is hard to find the right combination of characteristics in potential court reporters. She feels intelligence is the most important quality for a good court reporter. On the other hand, people with sufficient intelligence to make good court reporters are typically people who are not content to play a passive role; they would rather be involved in the action, as a member of the team. Instead, they find themselves, as reporters, in positions where they have no input as an individual into what is going on.

Perfectionism in most people is viewed by mental health professionals as unhealthy in the sense that the person exhibiting that tendency has excessively high expectations of himself and of the people around him, perhaps to a destructive degree. However, many court reporters cite a healthy perfectionism as a necessary trait—meaning the need to produce a perfect work product, as well as having high expectations of oneself. A good reporter is meticulous, in a recording session, about capturing every syllable uttered; and in transcribing, about verifying every term, name, or expression in a transcript for absolute accuracy. A finished transcript, before being delivered, must be proofread very carefully.

In a February 1992 article in the *Journal of Court Reporting*, "Reporters and the Perfectionist Personality," Barbara Barnett discusses the good and bad points of perfectionism. For example, she says, perfectionists have difficulty asking for help or admitting they need help. She adds, however, that perfectionists make great reporters, because "they are very responsible, self-disciplined, love autonomy, and are dependable."

Denise L. Doucette in the "Students' Section" of the *Journal of Court Reporting* March 1992 issue, mentions the desire to please as another trait of good court reporters. That trait leads the reporter to put the clients' needs first, often resulting in a sacrifice of personal life in the interests of producing what the clients need when they need it. Denise also mentions her respect for the judicial system and enjoyment of the formality of the courtroom proceedings as helpful attributes in her career.

Other traits are also important. Jamie Vance says, "To do the job well, you need to be outgoing because you meet different lawyers and people every day. You can't be afraid to walk into different situations. Even if your client is familiar, the opposing counsel is different. You must be able to assert yourself, to tell them to slow down, or get the attorneys to stop yelling at each other so you can get the information down."

Besides lawyers, you are likely to be dealing with a lot of doctors, who can be harder to report than lawyers. They are getting paid a lot to give a deposition but they talk fast, and they don't have the time to give you what you need. Jan Burnham agrees good people skills are valuable, pointing out how easy it can be to lose a client when an attorney gets a new secretary who wants to call someone she knows or prefers when a reporter is needed. You must be able to stay on good terms with attorneys and their support staff to stay in business.

Reporters also need the resilience to be comfortable working in a lot of different situations. As a freelancer, you frequent a variety of settings, typically attorneys' or doctors' offices. It might be a small space with a number of people together, so you can't always get comfortable and spread out as you might want to. Jan Burnham feels strongly that you have to be self-motivated. "You need to be able to meet deadlines whether you want to or not, and you have to be almost a workaholic—the work demands a lot they don't tell you about in school, like you go to a job and they need the transcript the next day. So you work all night, and have to cancel dinner plans and any plans for sleep. Sometimes you work weekends to get the job out. You can take a day's hearing and they might need it really fast for the next hearing. Orders are almost always a crisis, and then when you get one you get three, so it's feast or famine. You must be willing to do whatever it takes to get it out."

Training for court reporters & scopists

According to the NCRA, court reporting is taught at more than 400 schools all over the United States. Some programs are offered by community colleges or business schools, but many schools exclusively teach court reporting. Some colleges give an associate or bachelor degree coupled with court reporting instruction. Some programs are approved by the NCRA, and a list of these NCRA-approved court reporter training programs appears in appendix C.

Most reporter training programs are two or three years in length, although the time involved varies according to the student's speed and performance in mastering the machine writing technique. The cost varies a lot; some community college programs, which might offer an associate degree with court reporter studies, are relatively inexpensive; private programs can cost as much as $15,000. A high school diploma is required as well as the skills mentioned in the previous section. Prior college education is extremely helpful for the advanced English skills, the vocabulary, and the broad range of knowledge acquired in four years of college. However, many students enter court reporting school without a college background.

Courses in a typical court reporting training program include, in addition to shorthand theory, machine shorthand, dictation sessions, (practice developing speed on the stenotype machine using live or taped dictation), court reporter procedures, CAT technology, English grammar, vocabulary and composition, legal terminology, medical terminology, anatomy, physiology, technical terminology, and applied law. Students also learn how to read and transcribe notes, and prepare transcripts.

Look for a court reporter training program that has been approved by NCRA. However, there are many good programs that have not received such approval but meet the NCRA's guidelines. Programs should include the courses listed previously. There should also be an internship where the student interns with a working reporter, during which the student spends at least 40 hours writing. The school should have a library and well-credentialed teachers.

You should be aware that there as a high dropout rate in court reporter training programs, as much as 50 to 90 percent. This dropout rate is due, in part, to the requirement for students to pass successive speed tests in order to graduate from the program. Some students get disheartened when they hit a speed plateau and cannot increase their speed sufficiently to pass the tests when other classmates are passing and graduating.

Who succeeds at court reporting schools? Students who ranked high in their high school classes and have very good English skills have the best chance of succeeding, according to Pauletta Morse in the article "Who Will Finish Reporting School?" in the March 1990 *National Shorthand Reporter* (*NSR*), (predecessor to current NCRA *Journal of Court Reporting*). Court reporter training requires a lot of effort, persistence, and hard work. Court reporters who succeed are strongly goal-oriented and take pride in their achievements and in the quality of their work product.

NCRA is the professional association for both court reporters and scopists. It was established in 1899 and currently has approximately 30,000 members, including 17,000 working reporter members as well as students, retired reporters, honorary and associate members (including scopists and proofreaders). It is an information resource, and provides numerous services to its members, and to court reporters everywhere. Dues are $135 per year for U.S. court reporters, $70 a year for scopists and other nonreporters, $45 a year for students.

National Court Reporters Association (NCRA)

NCRA publishes the monthly magazine, the *Journal of Court Reporting* (*JCR*), and puts on annual conventions and midyear seminars offering continuing training opportunities for members. In addition, NCRA provides its members with a membership directory, group insurance plans, a legislative monitoring service, employment referral service, reference books, scholarship programs, and loans. Other consumer benefits are also available to members.

NCRA offers a clearinghouse of information, the National Court Reporting Resource Center, on the technologies affecting the court reporting profession. They also conduct workshops in videotape recording and offer a certification in that area as well, Certified Legal Video Specialist. NCRA also offers an Employment Referral Service and has adopted a Code of Professional Conduct for members.

Training for scopists

Scopists also need some specific and thorough training in order to be able to work efficiently with the reporter's notes and the CAT software programs used. However, the knowledge needed by scopists is limited. They don't need to learn how to use the stenotype machine; they just learn how stenotype is formatted, how it is written, and the sounds. Like reporters, they must also learn legal and medical terminology, since so many court cases are related to medical situations. They learn to read those terms in stenotype, also; and they also spend time typing up actual sets of notes.

Some scopists are reporting students who have taken most of the course work at court reporting school but are still working to increase their reporting speed. During the interim, they might accept work as scopists. Some students become disenchanted with trying to perfect their stenotype speed, leave court reporting school, and go into scoping work instead. In a few cases, scopists train just for that work and never intended to be reporters.

Only three court reporting schools we could find offer in-school scopist programs: The Court Reporting Institute in Philadelphia; the Denver Academy of Court Reporting, and Wisconsin Indianhead Technical College in New Richmond, Wisconsin. The training costs approximately $4000, plus equipment, and takes about 9 months. (We do not recommend the program from At-Home Professions called Legal Transcriptionist, in which you learn to read court reporters' notes but do not learn current CAT systems. The program might appear to be teaching you scoping, but it is not a complete scoping education that would enable you to get a job as a scopist.)

Debra Schiff recommends that potential students try to get in touch with past graduates of a training program through the CompuServe CRFORUM, and ask how satisfied they were with the program and the availability of jobs.

Business profile

Court reporter Jan Burnham

Jan Burnham works as an independent freelance court reporter, recording depositions and hearings for the Colorado State Compensation Insurance Fund, and also for the Colorado State Board of Equalization (for which she had to become a part-time state employee). Jan does her own editing and scoping full time; if she gets extremely behind, she hires a proofreader.

Jan finished court reporting school and got her first job in 1978. She worked as an official reporter in court for four years, leaving in 1982 to spend more time with her five-year-old son and one-year-old daughter. She decided at that point to leave the world of regular employment, do only fill-in work in court, and to try to get work of her own. She put her name in at the courts in various counties around the Denver area. She found some work through friends from school: one was working for the Colorado Division of Labor as a reporter part time, and needed help taking depositions for workers' compensation. In addition to that work, she got an offer to work for a freelance firm part time, which she did along with depositions and hearings.

Jan says finding jobs back when she was starting was easier than it is now. There seem to be a number of graduates from training schools in Colorado competing for the few new positions available in the area. However, some other states are crying for them, for example, she believes Montana and the Southern states are good locations right now.

Jan has gotten most of her new clients by word of mouth, but attorneys and firms can be very fickle. An attorney who's been using you might get a new secretary, who in turn will call her own contacts, and the loss of business to you has nothing to do with the quality of your work.

Jan's lessons from experience: "Ask questions over and over, ask, ask, ask—even stupid questions; don't not know something; get names' spelling immediately—don't assume you can get them later; people and exhibits all disappear; you can sweat blood trying to get things later. Get reference materials for language, medical dictionaries, engineering books, and look up everything. Assume nothing—every occupation has its own lingo and trying to take it down is hard. Also, be willing to take advice from people. The biggest mistake reporters make is to be unaccommodating to a judge or a court clerk. Be willing to work as team, and get your jobs out on time—nothing makes people angrier than tardiness in the work."

Jan is looking forward to the variety of technological changes that are affecting the reporting world. With real-time and computer-integrated courtrooms the work continues to be constantly interesting and challenging.

Advantages & disadvantages of court reporting

The freelance court reporters we interviewed thoroughly enjoyed the freedom of setting their own schedules. Some have small children and can work their schedules so that they spend occasional days with the children, and use evenings for transcribing and scoping work. Many court reporters are also very satisfied with the income their profession has provided for them. Despite the initial costs of schooling and equipment, the financial return has been more than sufficient for the following years.

Jamie Vance enjoys being a professional and being treated like a professional. "It's better than being a legal secretary; I pack up my machine when it's over and I am treated better." Jan Burnham enjoys the satisfaction that comes from hard work and a job well done. As with so many reporters, she takes great pride in a timely and perfect work product.

On the other hand, Jamie Vance finds only a couple of real disadvantages to court reporting: "There are depositions when you hear some awful things, and doctors can be jerks or you can't understand them." Others mentioned that subject matter is occasionally boring. However, this is often balanced by assignments where the testimony is delivered by celebrities, the cases are high profile, or the subject matter is very interesting.

In some geographic areas, the profession is currently glutted and job opportunities are slim. Some reporters who would like full-time work cannot find that much.

Finally, although there are few drawbacks once you have achieved the status of reporter, many students in court reporter schools become disillusioned early on. Some have had difficulty achieving sufficient speed to finish the programs, and others have found the course work tedious.

Jamie Vance suggests someone considering becoming a court reporter first go and sit in on some classes, because the commitment is so substantial—school is expensive to attend. You can also contact a court reporting firm and see if you can sit in on a deposition—they take students along sometimes, to get an idea what it's like. Some people find it boring.

It is always a good idea to talk to people who are working in your chosen profession. Most professionals are more than willing to be open about the joys and disappointments of their work. Since court reporting involves such a large initial financial outlay (detailed later), such advance research would be time well spent. Most people enjoy talking about their jobs and love to give advice, so you can learn a lot. Also, the court reporting community is a small one, and once you start to get active, your name will become known.

Maybe you would prefer to be a scopist?

Although there are a lot of similarities between court reporters and scopists—in fact, the scopist is doing one piece of the reporter's work—the differences between the professions are significant.

Scopists, like reporters, can earn a good living provided they are fast at what they do and provided they can garner enough work as freelancers to stay busy. This varies by geographic area and community, so you need to survey the local need to see whether this work is possible for you. Talk to some working reporters, and to a freelance agency in your area, to get an idea of the demand for scopists. Larger cities, the Northeast area, Chicago, and the West Coast are probably good areas for scopists. The work is catching on more slowly in the middle areas of the country. However, with modems and software for CAT systems, which have communications built into them, work can be sent across the country.

There is far less financial investment in scopist work than in court reporting; the scopist must have training and editing software, as well as a computer. The risk is less than that for investing in a court-reporting career.

Scopists enjoy great flexibility in their schedule and can do all of their work at a home computer, so if you want to work at home, this can be an excellent option. For people who enjoy working with words and language and want a home-based career, scoping can be an enjoyable and fulfilling way to spend time and earn good money!

Unfortunately, there are very few places to obtain training for scopist work. You can attend a court-reporting school, but that can be expensive, and you might end up learning a lot more than you need, and spending a lot of time. Much of court-reporting training involves developing speed on the stenotype machine, which you do not need as a scopist. Jodie Hughes warns potential scopists: "This is very much a deadline-driven industry; not your type of job if you want a nine-to-five structured work schedule." You never know when work will appear, and when it does you have to have a fast turnaround time; it might mean working all night or weekends and evenings.

There is a sizable monetary investment, even for scopists: training will cost between $2500 and $5000; you need a good-capacity IBM compatible computer—probably $1000 at the minimum; and software costing approximately $4000 for what is called the *edit station*.

Scopists do not actually attend depositions, so they are not in a position to experience the excitement of live hearings, trials or depositions—they only see the computer screen account of what took place, and work in isolation nearly all of the time.

Despite these disadvantages, however, the scopists we interviewed enjoyed the work very much, and were enthusiastic about being part of the court reporting community. If you are still interested in scoping—or if court reporting sounds like a better idea—read on to learn what you will need to invest in terms of training and equipment to set up your court reporting or scopist business. Minneapolis scopist, Jodie Hughes, recommends that someone considering the work try to communicate with other scopists, either through the CRFORUM on CompuServe, or by reading advertisements in the NCRA *JCR*. Scopists should also consult with other scopists in the area to see how scopists are used and with court reporters to see if they need or use scopists, and what they look for in them. Jodie Hughes wishes she had checked out the local scene before she finished her course work. Sometimes a reporter is willing to take you under her wing and help you learn.

If you are considering either reporting or scopist work, review the following questions to see if they help you make up your mind.

Deciding if this business is for you

_____ Do you enjoy playing word games?
_____ Are you a good speller?
_____ Were you in the top 25 percent of your high school class academically?
_____ Do you consider yourself a perfectionist?
_____ Do you get satisfaction from working hard?
_____ Do you love reading?
_____ Are you content to be a silent observer rather than have a part in the action?
_____ Do you enjoy working alone?
_____ Are you confident dealing with other professionals?
_____ Are you outgoing? Assertive?

If you have not answered yes to most of these questions, you will probably not enjoy being a court reporter or scopist.

Getting started

Establishing a home office for reporters and scopists includes many complex issues, from equipment and marketing to being aware of the ethics and professionalism of this field. Here is an overview of these issues.

Equipment

You'll need the usual basic office equipment—an answering machine, a desk, a comfortable place to work, and a computer. However, the special hardware for this profession is a significant investment. Some reporters can use an older model stenograph machine, especially those working in small communities, and get by with WordPerfect for transcription of their paper notes. In fact, often small firm attorneys in small communities would rather not pay the premium to have higher technology available to them; a word-processed hard copy deposition transcript does very nicely, thank you. However, for reporters working in communities of any size, a CAT program is becoming more and more of a necessity, and that involves a sizable financial investment up front. The total cost will be between $10,000 to $15,000, including a new writing machine ($3000 to $4000), that most students buy when they begin working at high speeds, or when they are getting their first job; a personal computer ($1000 to $1500); the CAT software ($4000); a laser printer ($1000 to $1500); and a modem ($150 to $200).

If you begin by working through a freelance company, they might have computers you can use at a price (they might charge you for computer time); or they might buy the equipment and ask you to pay so much per page, or they lease it to you (and take commission from you for the job, of course). Scopists have less overhead. They do not need a writing machine, but they do need the computer and editing station software.

Jodie Hughes says a scopist needs an IBM compatible PC (she recommends no less than a 386 with 4MB RAM and a hard drive greater than 100MB), and recommends a modem once you get the CAT software. The software will run $3000 for the edit station alone.

In addition, as a home-based business, a reporter might want to have a system that offers calendaring and billing functions (it is possible to get that in a program with the other reporting software).

Reference materials

Both reporters and scopists need extensive libraries of reference material for confirming spellings and correct terminology from depositions. Janet Shadeix recommends a good generic dictionary, medical and industrial dictionaries, sound-alike word references, English guidebooks for punctuation and grammar, and whatever dictionaries there are for the practice areas in which you do most of your work. Her office also finds lots of use for old telephone books, when deponents refer to old companies, for example.

Freelance reporters should arrange for liability insurance to cover their equipment as well as any notes and exhibits that might be in their possession. Jan Burnham, like many freelance reporters, carries liability insurance through NCRA because she knew a reporter whose car was stolen. If it had had files and notes in it, the insurance would have picked up the costs of having to redo the hearing. Also, if someone broke into her home, and she had taken home the deposition notes or exhibits, the insurance would have helped with the liability.

Insurance issues

Before reporters can expect to be hired for regular employment, they should obtain a certification, either through NCRA or through a state examination process, or both. NCRA sponsors two certification programs—Registered Professional Reporter (RPR) certification and a Certificate of Merit (CM) program. Both programs involve passing an examination, including dictations at speeds of up to 225 words per minute for RPR and 260 words per minute for the CM. In addition, many states have statutory requirements for certification of reporters.

Certification

In her August 1993 Student's Corner column in *JCR*, Denise Doucette says certification is the most important factor in a reporting candidate. "With the present market conditions, agency owners and court administrators have the luxury of being very selective. Because of that, you should do everything within your power to set yourself apart from the crowd and distinguish yourself as an exceptional candidate. One way to do that is to obtain higher certification." She recommends that reporters pursue NCRA's Certificate of Merit examination, and other certifications that reflect extra achievement.

Agencies often look for candidates with the RPR certification, which represents the basic level of achievement. In addition, they might encourage people to earn the CM designation, not only because it represents a higher level of skill, but because it instills a sense of confidence, with which the reporter is better equipped to handle some of the critical situations that arise in a deposition setting. A reporter with that level of achievement will know "If anyone can handle this, I should be able to," and it raises her expectations of her own performance.

As with paralegals, there is something of a "catch 22" for a reporter looking for a first job. There is sometimes strong competition for reporting jobs, especially in certain popular urban communities. That situation has fluctuated over the past five years, and will continue to do so. In some places, local county courts have changed from using live reporters to using audio tape recording. This has been an unfortunate development for new reporters, who used to get their beginning experience in those courts. Many now get small jobs through agencies, to get started.

Getting a first job

Some beginners take court substituting jobs, since there's more need for that. However, there are some drawbacks to that route. According to Jan Burnham, "Substituting in court is a terrible hassle. You substitute for a day, and afterwards you have to leave your notes (they are the property of the state, as are the exhibits). If you get a transcript order, you will need the exhibits to do the transcript, so you need an order from the judge to get the notes and exhibits, and it is murder to get access to the exhibits to use for transcription."

For substitutes, payment per page is not as high as freelance so you don't make as much. The court reporters already there have a full-time job with benefits, have access to free paper and the use of the copier, etc.; even if paid at the same rates as the regular reporter, the freelance substitute is getting less. Finally, whoever calls you in (usually the regular court reporter) also takes a percentage before they pay you out of their pay.

Another disadvantage to the temporary court assignments is that you don't know people, and you're the *only* one who doesn't know everyone. This can cause problems when, for example, the district attorney, or some other regular participant, is not used to pronouncing carefully; and judges have their own idiosyncrasies. You are on your own to cover those problems.

On the other hand, such "dues-paying" work can pay off since most official positions are filled by word of mouth. Denise Doucette writes in her August 1993 column "For those interested in working in court as officials, cultivate relationships with local officials. Intern in their courtrooms as frequently as possible, far in excess of the minimum requirements specified by your school." Not only does the experience serve you well but the relationships that develop through that contact can be very helpful, as the court personnel have a chance to size up your capabilities. Sometimes temporary assignments become available and they might think of you. She adds "Officialships are often filled from the ranks of pro tem reporters who have 'paid their dues' by accepting sporadic, part-time assignments."

Getting agency work

Many reporters start out with an agency working on smaller cases. Eileen Hyatt, owner of a Denver agency, recognizes the problem of asking for experience from candidates who are trying to get the experience everyone is asking for. However, she suggests students not try to start at an agency that handles highly sophisticated cases, but instead try agencies that work for attorneys doing small cases. Scopist Debra Schiff started out at an agency using their equipment for two years, which she recommends as a good way to start, because the software is expensive.

The importance of networking

Just as with paralegals, networking is by far the most effective way to find first, second, or third court reporter or scopist positions, and to find clients. Freelance court reporters make contacts through associations, as well as maintaining the contacts they made during their class work in court reporting school. Those contacts are the sources of most of the clients the reporters acquire and keep through the years. (Networking also helps in case you get double-booked—if you have no contacts you lose the job entirely.)

Through her local association, scopist Jodie Hughes got to be friends with other scopists who all have their own clients; they pool their resources for advertising and they go together on a booth at the convention; they put a joint advertisement in the association's membership directory, and are working on one for the newsletter, and they keep in touch in case the workload gets heavy. "If people call us who aren't on the same system we are, we will know someone else who is, so we put them in touch."

One network available to court reporters is an online information network, the Court Reporters' Forum on CompuServe "CRFORUM." It is a bulletin board information exchange program, and an opportunity to engage in E-mail conversation with reporters from all over the country. For example, if you want advice on a certain type of equipment, you can type in a question and you will receive, in turn, messages from reporters around the country, giving you hints on which brand is the best. Reporters and scopists also list information on their services on the Forum, so it operates as an additional route for finding work. The Forum is also another place to turn for current information about the professions of court reporter and scopist. It provides on-line access to NCRA and its *Journal of Court Reporting*.

Using CompuServe's CRFORUM

The Court Reporters Forum was initiated on December of 1992 with 162 members and as of May 10, 1993 had 1,400 members, according to Richard Sherman in his "Forum Life" column in the August 1993 *Journal of Court Reporting*. (For information on joining CompuServe and the CRFORUM call (800) 872-4768.)

There is clearly competition for reporter jobs, especially in some communities. Besides being willing to relocate to where opportunities might be more promising, there are a number of things you can do to give yourself an edge in the competition. One step is to continue to progress, obtaining further certifications to show your dedication and your skills. Technical innovations will probably continue to be made, and the more proficient you are (e.g., being able to offer real-time and captioning), the more you will be set apart in communities where there is use for those technologies. (In smaller or more rural areas, clients might prefer to pay lower fees since the technical advancements might not be of use, and might even be intimidating.) Developing a specialty area of expertise for yourself might help you in competing for work in those areas; for example, medical areas, construction or engineering, water or natural resources, or other highly technical areas of study. Not only will you develop a reputation for knowing the area, you might find the subject matter of the deposition more interesting.

Staying ahead of the competition

Professionalism

Court reporters, like other professionals in the legal arena, pride themselves on their professionalism. This is demonstrated in their dedication to putting the client's needs first. The need for dedication and hard work is mentioned several times in this chapter, because the work of a reporter requires that level of effort. In addition, the following techniques help reporters maintain their professionalism:

- Present a business-like appearance whenever you record a proceeding. Agency directors list a neat, professional appearance high on their list of important qualities in the freelancers they want to use.
- Retain membership in a professional association, in order to stay current on developments, especially technological changes that affect reporters. Membership in a state association, or the NCRA, or both should be part of the standard equipment for any reporter or scopist. Janet Shadeix strongly recommends association membership, not only for people in urban communities but particularly for the more isolated reporter. Scopists would also find much of interest in either associate membership in, or subscription to, the periodicals of their state associations. Scopists also need to keep up with rules changes, and have support to help share workload and provide company in their solitary work situations.
- Pursue continuing education credits. To remain Registered Professional Reporters (the NCRA-sponsored certification), reporters must earn at least 30 continuing education credits every three years in NCRA-approved programs. Workshops, seminars, and courses are offered for reporters (scopists might also attend most of them); NCRA's *Journal of Court Reporting* provides a comprehensive list of scheduled programs.

Ethical standards

There are also ethical considerations for court reporters on the scene at the deposition, and afterwards. First, all information to which a reporter becomes privy, whether through testimony or through exhibits, must be kept strictly confidential at all times. Just as important, both at and after a deposition, a reporter must retain total impartiality, and must avoid even the appearance of impropriety. For example, at the scene one attorney might want to go "off the record" and another will want to stay "on the record." This is particularly sensitive if the attorney who hired the reporter is the one wanting to go off the record. Most reporters' policies are that as long as one attorney wants to remain on the record, they stay on the record and the reporter continues to record.

For another example, at a deposition but during a break, an attorney might ask the reporter her opinion of what is going on in the deposition. The reporter must maintain the status of impartiality, and should not comment on the case, or suggest further questions for the attorney to ask. The reporter can remind the attorney that he or she knows nothing about the case except what has gone on in the deposition room, and so is not prepared to give an opinion on the case. The reporter can also give a candid opinion about the witness as a witness; for example, if they seem to present themselves well.

After the deposition other ethical situations can arise. Attorneys might call believing there is an error in the transcript. Eileen Hyatt's policy in this situation is the same for the client as it is for the attorney on the other side of the case. There are three ways a transcript can be amended. First, the deponent always gets an opportunity to read the transcript and make notations of any errors in his testimony on a special appended page at the end. Second, any attorney whose words are part of the transcript might also make similar notes on an appended page—but only with respect to his own comments. Third, someone brings to the reporter's attention an error in which he or she misinterpreted the speaker's comments, or the dictionary was inadequate and did not correctly translate some words. In all three cases, any suggested changes do not get put into the transcript itself, but are added at the end of the transcript on additional pages, and everyone involved who orders a copy of the transcript receives a copy of each added page.

The outlook for court reporters & scopists

People who have been in the court reporting field for years are encouraged about the outlook for the future. Eileen Hyatt believes that the outlook for court reporters continues to be good. "Court reporting has been threatened with extinction for the past 30 years," she says, pointing out that it hasn't happened yet. Perhaps, the industry is currently under more challenge than ever, with some courts beginning to use audio and video taping instead of live, certified reporters, in order to save money. However, Eileen points out the savings is short-term; if the recorded proceeding needs to be transcribed for any reason, it is much more time-consuming and expensive to transcribe from audiotape or videotape, and those transcriptions cannot be expected to be nearly as accurate as they would be had a reporter been present to be sure everything was accurately and completely captured. A number of things can interfere with audiotape: overlapping conversation, chairs scraping or other noises, a mumbling witness, etc. Without a reporter present to ask for clarification those comments will be lost.

Eileen points out, in addition, that attorneys' need for accuracy in deposition and trial transcripts is getting more acute, rather than less. Litigants and their attorneys are nit-picking to a greater degree, and jumping on inaccuracies or uncertainties in testimony.

Challenges to the industry, more than audio- or videotaping, might come from the public's demand for litigation reform, which could result in changes to the discovery or trial processes. If there is more conflict resolution through mediation or arbitration, for example, the need for reporters might diminish.

It is likely, however, that as long as litigation continues to be a popular form of resolving problems in our culture, the need for both court reporters and scopists will probably continue. Courts must have a way of keeping an accurate record of the proceedings in each courtroom, and as discussed in the following chapter, "Deposition Summarizers," the need for written versions of the evidence gathered in pretrial stages of litigation provides considerable demand for court reporters to record and transcribe depositions.

The considerable technical changes in other fields are also working in reporters' favor. There is growing use of captioning to record television programs and certain proceedings (civic meetings, school classes) to allow hearing-impaired individuals to participate by reading, on a screen, an immediately available transcript. The opportunities for reporters who are adept at real-time reporting and can operate captioning equipment are therefore growing very quickly. Reporters who want to maintain an edge over their competitors will hone their technological skills as much as possible, and learn these techniques to add to their reporting skills.

As for scopists, the reporters we spoke with were also confident that, although a number of people are becoming so well-versed with their real-time equipment that they don't need much scoping work, they are a small minority in the court-reporting community. Most reporters will continue to need scoping for their transcripts, and the opportunities for scopists, at least for the near future, appear to be growing as well.

5 Deposition summarizers

Deposition summarizers are not really a separate profession from paralegals—most of them are or were legal assistants who wished to specialize. We devote a separate chapter to them because there are so many people summarizing depositions as a freelance business, and because, unlike most freelance paralegals, a large number of deposition summarizers work at home.

This chapter explains how deposition summaries are used, why they provide good work either at a law firm or an at-home business, how the summarizing work is done, and what summaries look like. We discuss how summarizers get work, the background, skills, and traits necessary for the career, what the income potential is, and the equipment and materials necessary. We also profile several people who are currently deposition summarizers.

What a deposition summarizer does

In the information-laden world of law practice, particularly in the litigation field, the discovery phase is critical to evaluating a case and gathering evidence. Much of this evidence is information that is not on paper, but in the stories people have to tell. And those stories often amount to thousands of pages of documents that must be translated into something that can be studied, analyzed and evaluated by attorneys on both sides of the law suit.

One format for collecting information and interviewing witnesses is a deposition in the presence of a court reporter. Here, the sworn oral testimony by someone (called the deponent) whose story has some bearing on the case is taken. The testimony is given in answers to questions asked by any number of attorneys. Typically, each of the parties and most witnesses must appear at such a deposition. After it is over, the court reporter transcribes everything that was said and provides it to the attorneys, either in hard copy or on disk.

Depositions go on for hours, and the transcript is sometimes hundreds of pages long. Multiply that by at least two parties and many potential witnesses, and you have a lot of paper for lawyers or paralegals to read. In the frantic period of trial preparation, a deposition summary provides a more useful tool than a full transcript.

The deposition summarizer is the person who prepares the summary from the full transcript. To do this, you have to be able to read and quickly analyze text and distill it into a few succinct phrases that do not change its meaning. The summary must be accurate, succinct, and helpful to the attorney. (Actually, summarizing is also applied to the full text of transcripts from many trials and hearings, but to simplify our discussion, we refer only to the deposition for now, since it is by far the more common assignment.)

The use of deposition summaries

Good summarizers must have some idea of how deposition summaries are used in trial preparation. The most obvious purpose of a summary is for someone (usually the attorney) to be able to read a brief document and quickly get an accurate impression of what the deponent said, in a format that facilitates finding specific testimony. The paralegal and attorney preparing for trial use the summary for the following tasks.

- Find specific testimony on an issue or subject, or get information verifying a fact that is critical and germane to the case.
- Pinpoint facts or information that need further verification or clarification to understanding the case.
- Identify areas that might be helpful or harmful to the case.
- Prepare for examination of the deponent at the trial and evaluate his conduct as a witness.
- Get a feel for how the issues will take shape at trial.
- Identify the role of certain exhibits to be used in trial.
- Formulate questions for future depositions of other witnesses.
- Compare testimony of two or more deponents on the same issue or event.

In addition, the summary is used for clients and other attorneys working on the case, whether or not they were in attendance at the deposition itself. Expert witnesses might also have a need to read a deposition summary or portions of a transcript in order to learn some history of the case.

After a summary has been made, it is important to know about one additional item that is commonly prepared from the summary: indexes. An index can be as complete or as small as the lawyer wants. It might be made by noting the page number of key words that are obviously important in the case (e.g., names, dates, or specific "issue" words relevant to the case such as fire, accident, vehicle, car, injury, etc.), or it can be made using every single word in the transcript, which can be useful if the attorney or paralegal want to see what types of terms have been used in order to pick out the key words.

Good work for a home-based business

Deposition summarizing has traditionally been paralegal work, but most paralegals say they detest doing it. Because it's miserable work? Not really, but because it takes a block of time and concentration to do it efficiently and correctly, and legal assistants in an office situation can rarely shut themselves off long enough at a time to do a summary uninterrupted. This condition is aggravated because deposition transcripts often come in while other trial preparation work is increasing at a dramatic pace. If the staff at a law firm has to work weekends or evenings to complete deposition summaries in a short time, clients can find themselves charged high overtime fees. Nevertheless, the summaries must be done, and the deposition transcripts can sit there, in a pile on the floor of the paralegal's office, a silent reminder of work that is not getting done.

Enter outside freelance summarizers! The same factors that make depositions summaries hard for in-house legal assistants makes them perfect for work-at-home freelancers. A home-based summarizer doesn't have to find a place to hide out in order not to be interrupted by other aspects of the case or by attorneys. He or she can concentrate on what needs to get done, often completing summaries more quickly than the paralegal at the office can—especially today, when summaries can be done on a computer using one of several new sophisticated software packages.

Many law firms find it cost-effective to have the depositions digested or summarized by freelance paralegals or by services who employ freelance paralegals to do it. It is cost-effective not to use paralegals in the firm, because they often need to dictate the summary, then get it proofread, revised, and indexed—a process involving the paralegal, a word processor, and perhaps a paralegal supervisor, all of whom have other trial-related tasks building up. Instead, a transcript sent out for summarizing can be quickly summarized, indexed, and delivered in hard copy and on disk, saving the firm time and money (in personnel time).

In an article in the *National Paralegal Reporter* (Spring 1992) called "Computerized Digesting: A Time-Saver for Cost-Conscious Law Firms," paralegal Lyn Hill estimates that "For most firms, the manpower costs for digesting services [within the firm] run from $6 to $8 per page. For firms where the system involves longhand writing, word processing, an individual proofreader, and a paralegal supervisor, the cost can be much greater." That compares to an average of $1 to $1.75 per page for summaries done outside (although rush jobs from outside can also cost as much as $3 per page).

One disadvantage to the law firm when a deposition transcript is sent out of house for summarizing is the paralegal on the trial team, not having done the summary, will not be as familiar with the testimony given. This drawback must be weighed against the benefit of the more efficient production of the summary. Of course, the in-house paralegal can familiarize herself with the deposition testimony in a small fraction of the time it would take to do the summarizing.

The process of summarizing

Deposition transcripts can arrive in hard copy, on disk, or via modem from the court reporter. Then, the paralegal case manager determines how the summaries should be done, what format is desired, when the job must be done, and other pertinent details regarding the summary. The summarizer needs to know a number of things about the assignment in order to do the most useful summary for the law firm. Ideally the summarizer will be told:

- The time frame for the assignment.
- The desired format for the summary (page/line sequence, topic organization, chronology, etc.).
- The preferred style (e.g., first or third person narrative, and whether indexes are desired).
- The facts of the case and the issues to look for.
- Who the deponent is (an expert witness, other witness, or a party).
- Terms to use consistently throughout (accepted abbreviations, key words and phrases, format for names, etc.).
- Whether the summary is desired in hard copy, on disk, or both.
- How the attorney will use the deposition summaries.

Sometimes the only person using the summary is the attorney who attended the deposition. In this case, the summary can be a little more abbreviated than if it were to be used by another attorney who did not attend the deposition but is preparing the case for trial. Sometimes the summary is sent on to the attorney's client; sometimes it is used to fill in an expert witness on the story of the case. In this case, the summary needs more detail than it would if the only person using it were the attorney.

The better informed the summarizer is, the better job she can do of producing a summary that meets the needs of the lawyers. Someone who knows the attorneys and has worked with them before will have a sense for how they use summaries and their preferred style and format. It is hard for a person at a service getting the assignment to be able to get those questions answered. By the time a law firm calls a service or a summarizer for help, they are often severely pressed for time. The attorney rarely makes the call; such details are left to paralegals or other staff who do not have answers to the questions about format, issues, etc. In fact, summarizers say in the real world you will be lucky to get anything more than the time frame spelled out clearly to you.

Representatives from good deposition summarizing services do their best to obtain the necessary information from attorneys or law firms before assigning the work to a summarizer. Nick Norman of Templeton and Associates in Minneapolis talks with the client to learn how the summaries will be used, whether the client has computer capabilities (and if so, whether the client will use the deposition transcript or the summary in a database), how inclusive they want the summary to be, and whether the client has any special computer needs. He finds, however, that clients generally still want hard copy summaries.

Nick says most of their work has a turnaround time of five business days, although they occasionally get requests for same day service, which is always done in the Templeton and Associates office.

The whole idea is for the summary to be shorter than the original transcript without losing any of its substance; to capture the flavor of the testimony and the precise evidence and facts without editorializing or comment. This takes practice.

How the process starts

Before computers, the traditional method of creating deposition summaries, especially in law firms, was for the paralegal or junior attorney to read the hard copy transcript while dictating a summary, which was then transcribed, proofread, revised, proofread again, and manually indexed (i.e., re-reading every page and physically noting which key words appear on which page; a time-consuming task). Surprisingly, a number of outside summarizers and even law firm attorneys still work that way, sending the dictation tape to a service or legal secretary.

For instance, Joanna Hughbanks, owner of Paralegal Associates of Denver, has freelance summarizers who dictate instead of using word processing. She has the dictated summaries delivered to a legal transcriptionist, Miriam "Sam" Moretz, who types and proofs the summaries. The one benefit of this is that Sam is highly experienced in the legal area, and she provides Joanna with feedback on the quality of the summary dictation, which helps with the quality control necessary for a service like Joanna's. She proofs for consistency, for example, makes sure names are spelled the same way throughout, and provides other quality control. (You can read more about this field in the chapter 6 section on legal transcriptionists.) Of course, since the service must pay for transcription of dictated tapes, summarizers who dictate do not earn as much as those who create and finalize their summaries using word processing on a home computer.

Nick Norman at Templeton and Associates uses summarizers in the office as well as some who work at home, all of whom work on WordPerfect 5.1. He calls home-based workers before sending them work, to be sure they have time to complete it. He then provides them with a disk that he has set up for the desired format for the summary (which means that he sets up the disk to automatically include critical items like title page, identifying headers and footers, and case caption). He also might provide any special instructions regarding the assignment or the specific case on an instruction sheet that summarizers need to follow. Templeton and Associates also provides careful quality control for their clients, and has a system for letting summarizers know what changes might have been necessary to their work. The quality control person in their office also generates an index to the summary, indexing all topic headings. Then the summary with its index is sent back to the client. Most of Templeton's summarizers have been doing it for years, and the company has minimal employee turnover.

Most summaries done by freelancers or services are created by the summarizer directly on a PC using a word processing package, usually WordPerfect. This approach eliminates the dictating, proofing, revising and re-proofing; all this can be done on screen. Word processing also permits the summarizer to go back to an earlier place in the summary and revise it if he or she notices that testimony is later contradicted or supplemented on a specific item, or make a note to the lawyer such as "Note that this is clarified below at page 25."

Some summarizers receive the transcript on disk and use the WordPerfect option that allows the screen to be to split into separate windows. The transcript is in one window, and the summary they are writing in the other. This way they can read and summarize simultaneously, without looking away at a hard copy transcript. In some cases, they use full-text management software such as CAT-Links, Discovery ZX, and Summation II, as described in chapter 2 in the section on computers and litigation.

Formats for deposition summaries

The following are several ways to organize and produce the summary.
- Page/line summary—simple
- Page/line and topic summary
- Chronology
- Narrative
- Summary by issue or topic
- Highlighted transcript

The summarizer rarely has the opportunity to choose the organizational format of the summary. In most cases, the attorney or law firm has a standard format they prefer, which they provide to the freelancer as a template. Some services, like Templeton and Associates, provide the summarizers with a disk with the desired format prepared on it. The summarizer need only follow the format set out on the disk. Here is an explanation of the various styles. Figure 5-1 shows a hypothetical transcript for which we show a few summaries in the following styles.

```
                    P R O C E E D I N G S
                       EXAMINATION
BY MR. JONES:
1    Q      Do you understand that upon discharge home, that Mr.
2 Smith at that point in time had residual permanent brain injury?
3    A      Yes, sir.
4    Q      Did you understand that from that residual permanent
5 brain injury, he was unable to carry out his normal activities
6 in an independent fashion?
7    A      Yes, sir.
8    Q      And was unable to continue with his employment?
9    A      Yes, sir.
10   Q      Now, correct me if I'm wrong, but if I understand your
11 testimony, you have concluded that this was a minor insult, to
12 use your language, because there was no apparent loss of
13 consciousness. Is that correct?
14   A      Let me explain that a little bit more. A head injury
15 can be assessed as mild, moderate or severe based upon a number
16 of things that occur with the patient at the time of the
17 injury.
18          If a patient has no significant loss of consciousness,
19 is conversant and walking around even though confused, one does
20 not consider that a severe head injury unless the patient were
21 to develop later some complications of that injury.
22   Q      Well, did this patient later develop complications
23 from that injury?
24   A      Yes, sir, he apparently did.
25   Q      Okay. What complications did he develop from that
26 injury, as you understand it?
27   A      After what appeared to be a relatively lucid
28 interval, he progressively got worse in terms of developing a
29 language disturbance, developing probably weakness on the right
30 side and developing seizures.
31   Q      And based on everything you know, do you have an
32 opinion as to what sections or lobes or areas of the brain were
33 involved?
34   A      Yes, sir.
35   Q      Which ones?
36   A      From his language disturbance, in spite of the fact
37 that he's left-handed, we would assume he had left brain
38 injury. That was suggested later and documented by EEGs which
39 suggested left brain injury.

                       Page 15
```

5-1

Sample transcript from which a digester works.

Page-line format—simple Page-line is the most commonly used format, with page numbers (and often line numbers) of the transcript in columns on the left side of the page, and a broad right-hand column containing the summary of the testimony from that place in the transcript (see Fig. 5-2).

A page-line summary is useful to the attorney who conducted the deposition and who might have some recollection of the order of questioning. The numbers are important in case the attorney wants to point out contradictory

```
                        Page Summary (Simple)
Summary of Dr. Francis Franklin Deposition
September 25, 1990
Smith v. Highpower Motor Company

Page                     Summary
15                       His understanding is, from residual permanent brain
                         injury, Mr. Smith is unable to carry out normal activities
                         or employment.

15                       Without significant loss of consciousness, injury is not
                         severe unless patient later develops complications.

15-16                    Smith apparently later developed complications. After
                         lucid interval, he got worse, developed language
                         disturbance, and probable weakness on right side,
                         seizures. Assumes Smith had left brain injury and EEGs
                         suggested the same.

17-18                    Also, there is possible anterior quadrant injury, per
                         EEGs, and his problems with comprehension of speech and
                         language.
```

5-2
Page summary (simple).

testimony or refer to the full-text transcript to support an argument by turning quickly to the actual page and line where the testimony appears. This type of summary proceeds in page number order from the beginning to the end of the transcript (often resulting in the same subject or event appearing multiple times at different places in the summary). This format permits the attorney or paralegal to locate the testimony precisely, and it provides the assurance that all testimony is covered in the summary.

The disadvantages of page-line summaries are they are not necessarily in a logical or chronological sequence to the material. Topics might be jumbled in mixed order throughout the summary, as they are in the deposition transcript itself.

Page-line with topic headings   The page-line format with topic headings is the same as the page-line format except another column has been added to include words or phrases identifying the topic under discussion (see Fig. 5-3). Some summarizers use a headline-type statement instead of an added column (see Fig. 5-4).

This format permits the attorney to scan down the topic column and find all the places where a certain topic or event is discussed. Topics are easily located in a summary formatted this way—the topic headings and terms jump out clearly—but the material might still be jumbled in order. If the summary is word processed on a computer, the terms in the topic headings can be searched and even moved around in blocks until they are grouped together, creating a more logical listing with all summary items with identical topic headings together.

```
                    Page/Line/Topic Summary

Summary of Dr. Francis Franklin Deposition
September 25, 1990
Smith v. Highpower Motor Company

=======================================================================
Page/Line          Topic                Summary
15/4               RESIDUAL INJURY      His understanding is, from the
                                        residual permanent brain injury,
                                        Mr. Smith is unable to carry out
                                        normal activities or employment.

15/20              EXPLAINS SEVERITY    With no significant loss of
                                        consciousness, injury is not
                                        severe unless patient later
                                        develops complications.

15/26-16/14        LEFT BRAIN INJURY    Smith apparently later developed
                                        complications. After a lucid
                                        interval, he got worse, developed
                                        language disturbance, and
                                        probable weakness on right side,
                                        seizures. Assumes Smith had left
                                        brain injury and EEGs suggested
                                        the same.

17-18              LEFT BRAIN INJURY    Also, there is possible anterior
                                        quadrant injury, per EEGs, and
                                        his problems with comprehension
                                        of speech and language.
```

5-3
Page/line/topic summary.

Chronology format   This format puts the summarized testimony in order by the chronological sequence of the events being described, with a column of dates or time periods along the left side of the page, and a summary of the testimony with respect to the time period on the right. It is useful for cases in which a time line of events is helpful for comparing recollections of various witnesses. This type of format is particularly useful in cases where the sequence and timing of events is critical, such as a case involving fraud or one which rests on when which parties knew what information.

Summary by topic   This format organizes the testimony by topic or issue so that all information on one topic appears together in the summary.

It is especially useful when the deposition consists of several volumes, covers questioning by several attorneys, or in cases where just one attorney has done all the questioning but has jumped in and out of a variety of issues, so that the same issue is covered in a number of places in the transcript. However, this type is a difficult and time-consuming summary to create without a computerized system.

A summarizer using a computer and a transcript on disk can create this type of summary using the search capabilities of word processors to search the

5-4

Page summary with "headline" topic.

```
                    Page Summary With "Headline" Topic

Summary of Dr. Francis Franklin Deposition
September 25, 1990
Smith v. Highpower Motor Company
_____
Page                    Summary
15                      RESIDUAL INJURY
                        His understanding is, from residual permanent brain
                        injury, Mr. Smith is unable to carry out normal activities
                        or employment.

15                      EXPLAINS SEVERITY
                        Without significant loss of consciousness, injury is not
                        severe unless patient later develops complications.

15-16                   LEFT BRAIN INJURY
                        Smith apparently later developed complications. After
                        lucid interval, he got worse, developed language
                        disturbance, and probable weakness on right side,
                        seizures. Assumes Smith had left brain injury and EEGs
                        suggested the same.

17-18                   LEFT BRAIN INJURY
                        Also, there is possible anterior quadrant injury, per
                        EEGs, and his problems with comprehension of speech and
                        language.
```

transcript for key terms, and with a split screen, can search the transcript on one screen and create the summary at the same time on the other. Some full-text management systems help perform this function efficiently, provided the same key words or phrases are used in the transcript to identify the issue. Frequently, however, the summarizer must read the transcript to confirm that the issues have been thoroughly identified, or to find places where the issue might have been discussed using other language. Another potential disadvantage to this format is that material that does not fit neatly into one category or another might be left out of the summary.

Narrative format   This summary format is useful for providing the attorney with more of a feeling for what occurred at the deposition, or for a report to an expert witness who only needs a basic understanding of the deponent's testimony. Included is a general description of the deponent, what took place at the deposition, and the gist of the testimony on the issues discussed. It is organized by topic, not by the order of the testimony, is written in full sentences and paragraphs, and might be only a couple of pages in length. Rather than a genuine summary or digest, this product is more a memo on what took place. This is not the format usually expected of a freelance paralegal. More likely, it is dictated by the attorney or a paralegal who attended the deposition or by the in-house paralegal working on the trial.

Highlighting on condensed transcripts   Some court reporters provide condensed transcripts, an additional form of summary more useful than lengthy multipage transcripts. A condensed transcript page includes all the testimony in the transcript but is produced in condensed format so that 5–7 pages of transcript appear on one page. Min-U-Script from Scribeware, available from some court reporters, condenses transcripts this way. For example, a 225-page single-sided document can be put onto 15 double-sided pages, in clear, readable newspaper column style (see Fig. 5-5).

Case Name Description	Three Column Format	Witness Name December 14, 1989

Page 1

IN THE COURT OF COMMON PLEAS OF PHILADELPHIA COUNTY
FIRST JUDICIAL DISTRICT OF PENNSYLVANIA
ADELINE GOODRICH : DECEMBER TERM, 1986
V.
High Rise Associates, et al. NO. 1761
Friday, December 14, 1989
Philadelphia, Pennsylvania
Transcript of videotaped trial examination of RAYMOND JOINTDEXTER, M.D. taken at the offices of WILBUR STONEWALL, Federation Building, Philadelphia, Pennsylvania beginning at 9:00 a.m. on the above date before Joy Johnson, a Court Reporter and Notary Public in and for the Commonwealth of Pennsylvania and Jim Berger Video Technician.
Generic Reporting Service
254 Common Street
Philadelphia, PA 19103
(215) 988-9500

Page 2

APPEARANCES:
WILBUR STONEWALL, ESQUIRE
Suite 800
Federation Building
Philadelphia, Pennsylvania
Counsel for Plaintiff
JOHN Q. STAR, ESQUIRE
Figglethorpe and Baker
7 Liberty Place
Philadelphia, Pennsylvania
Counsel for Robert Tilston
JANE M. STANLEY, ESQUIRE
Stanley and Stanley
7 Hope Lane
Media, Pennsylvania
Counsel for Greenview Partnership

Page 3

[1] BY MR. STONEWALL:
[2] Q: Dr. Jointdexter, are you a duly licensed [3] physician in the State of Pennsylvania?
[4] A: Yes, I am.
[5] Q: What undergraduate education did you [6] receive?
[7] A: I graduated from Harvard University in 1969 [8] with a degree in biology.
[9] Q: And what medical school did you attend?
[10] A: I graduated from Harvard Medical college [11] in 1973.
[12] Q: Did you pursue any postgraduate studies [13] after your graduation from Harvard Medical [14] College?
[15] A: Yes. I spent a year of surgical internship [16] at the Hospital of the University of Washington, [17] and I spent four years of orthopedic surgery [18] residency at City Hospital, [19] and after being in the Navy for two years, I spent [20] an additional year of hand surgery fellowship, six [21] months at Iowa State University, and six [22] months at the University of Texas.
[23] Q: And do you pursue any specific specialty in [24] the field of orthopedics?

Page 4

[1] A: Yes. I limit my practice to hand surgery.
[2] Q: Doctor, have you been — have you received [3] your Board certification?
[4] A: Yes. I'm board certified in orthopedic [5] surgery.

[6] Q: And when was that?
[7] A: That was in 1979.
[8] Q: And would you tell His Honor and the [9] members of the jury what is necessary in order to [10] receive a board certification?
[11] A: In orthopedic surgery, a four year [12] residency at an approved hospital is the first [13] requirement.
[14] Then after the completion of the [15] residency, after being in practice for two years, [16] oral and written examinations are given in [17] Chicago, and upon successful completion of these [18] tests, board certification is conferred.
[19] Q: Who gives these — these tests?
[20] A: The American Board of Orthopedic Surgery.
[21] Q: Have you had any academic appointments [22] since your graduation from medical school and your [23] finishing your residency?
[24] A: Yes. I teach orthopedic surgery at City

Page 5

[1] University Hospital.
[2] Q: And you're teaching the medical students [3] there; aren't you?
[4] A: Medical students, residents, and hand [5] fellows, yes.
[6] Q: I see, and what hospital appointments have [7] you had?
[8] A: Oh. I'm on staff at City [9] University Hospital, the Adams Eye Hospital, [10] Beaver Hospital, Broad St. Hospital, [11] Holbrook Hospital, Mt. Jordan Hospital, and [12] I'm hand surgery consultant at the Navy [13] Hospital in Wilmington, Delaware.
[14] Q: And what, if any, professional [15] organizations do you belong to?
[16] A: I belong to the American Medical [17] Association, the American Board of Orthopedic [18] Surgery, the American Academy of Orthopedic [19] Surgery, and the local medical associations and [20] orthopedic societies.
[21] Q: Have you done any research in the field [22] of — what, if any, research have you done, [23] medical research?
[24] A: Yes. I've done research with regard to

Page 6

[1] hand surgery, basically with regard to artificial [2] tendons, absorbable wires to fix fractures, and [3] also research in pain syndromes in the upper [4] extremity.
[5] Q: Have you written any articles concerning [6] the hand orthopedic surgery in the — with [7] relationship to the hand?
[8] A: Yes. I've written about twenty-five [9] articles and chapters.

[10] Q: I see. Doctor, have you, in addition to [11] that, have you made some scientific presentations?
[12] A: Yes. I've made a number of presentations [13] with regard to the research that I've done, with [14] regard to the tendons, the K wires, and the pain [15] syndrome.
[16] Q: Would you tell us who are these scientific [17] presentations made to?
[18] A: These are made to other physicians, and are [19] either part of presentations to discuss research [20] that's been done, or educational programs for [21] other physicians.
[22] Q: Do you have any idea how many of those [23] presentations you've made?
[24] A: I don't know the exact number. It would be

Page 7

[1] more than fifty.
[2] Q: Now, in the course of your practice as a [3] hand surgeon, Doctor, did you have occasion to [4] treat a patient by the name of Adeline Goodrich?
[5] A: Yes, I have.
[6] Q: And when — would you look at your records, [7] Doctor?
[8] A: Uh-huh.
[9] Q: And when and where did you first see her?
[10] A: The first time I saw her was on April the [11] 22nd 1986
[12] Q: And when you saw her on that date, was it [13] necessary for you to obtain a history as to what [14] she was there to see you about?
[15] A: Yes, it was.
[16] Q: And would you tell us about that history?
[17] A: Yes. At the time I first saw her she was [18] fifty-six years old, and she had explained to me [19] that she had injured her right thumb when it was [20] caught in a window, and showed that the thumb had [21] been out of place, and that she required reduction [22] of the dislocation, and casting for six weeks.
[23] When the cast was removed, there [24] was still a great deal of swelling about the MP

Page 8

[1] joint, which is the joint at the base of the [2] thumb.
[3] MR. STONEWALL: Doctor, before we go [4] any further, Doctor, would you mark this as [5] an exhibit?
[6] MR. STAR: Could I see what [7] you're referring to, please?
[8] Q: Doctor —
[9] MR. STONEWALL: Would you mark this? [10] First mark this. Mark it on the back, [11] please.

A. L. T., Inc. (215) 546-0998 — Min-U-Script® — Page 1 - Page 8

5-5

Eight pages of condensed transcript. Min-U-Script is a registered trademark of Automated Litigation Technologies, Inc.

Formats for deposition summaries **135**

A summarizer who works from a condensed transcript highlights the pertinent portions of testimony on the condensed format pages so that the attorney can gather the gist of the testimony by reviewing only the highlighted sections. This format is easier for an attorney to scan than a full transcript would be and makes the page/line summary less necessary, especially if the original transcript was 100 pages and the highlighted condensed version only 15 to 20 pages.

There are several advantages to this format: it is quick to produce, does not require typing, proofing, etc., and—should the attorney wish to consult the full text of the transcript after reading the highlighted portions—it is all there, he or she does not have to reach for a second volume.

On the other hand, a highlighted summary is not as readable as a typed summary. There are no topic headings, and the information still has not been put into chronological order as with the other types of summaries. Also, the product does not look as neat, which might be important if the client wants to see the summary.

Indexes In addition to the summary itself, the attorney might also want indexes prepared showing, for example, which exhibits were discussed during the deposition and where they appear in the transcript. Court reporters often attach a computer-generated index to the transcript, in which case the summarizer need not add it. But other indices might list names of individuals and page numbers where they appeared, or topics and the pages where each is discussed. As you might imagine, an index can be an important supplement to a page-line summary. Figure 5-6 shows an example of a subject index.

```
           INDEX TO DEPOSITION OF JOE SWANSON

       Subject                              Pages

       Circumstances of Accident

              Location and time             4-7, 15

              Description of accident        4-7, 16-18, 21

       His Injuries                         10-11, 24-26

       Medical Treatment                    24-26, 31-34
```

5-6
Example of an index.

Many services that use freelance summarizers have standard formats that must be followed, and most attorneys seem to have their strong preferences for one organizing format or another, depending on how they prepare for trial and the types of cases they usually handle. A summarizer might have a preference, but unless the summarizer is consulted for a recommendation, the format that must be used is the one the service requires or the one an attorney wants. However, summarizers who are familiar with a variety of formats can do their clients a service occasionally by recommending a format that would be more appropriate or useful for their purposes than the traditional format.

Which format should be used?

The summary should have as few words as possible without varying the meaning of the testimony, so summarizers learn how to abbreviate their style in effective ways. For example, it is usually acceptable to leave out of the summary the deponent's name, as well as pronouns that refer to the deponent, since he is the only person testifying. For example, the transcript might read:

Style suggestions

Q: Were you in Milwaukee at any time during August of that year, ah, 1988?
A: Yes, I recall that I was there.

Q: When was that, exactly?
A: It was on the 25th of August.

Q: And did you meet with Mr. Jones and, ah or, Mr. Smith while you were there?
A: Yes, I did.

Q: Did you meet with one or . . . which one? Or was it both of them?
A: I met with both of them.

Q: Together, or at separate occasions?
A: The meetings were separate.

Here are two examples of a summary:

Correct:

"He met with each R. Smith and W. Jones in Milwaukee on 8/25/88"

Incorrect:

"The Deponent says he was in Milwaukee on August 25th, 1988, and he met with Roger Smith and Wilbur Jones, at separate meetings"

However, the emphasis in summarizing is not simply to arrive at a collection of short phrases. The summary should convey information, and bad writing style can be incomprehensible. Most summarizers are careful to use complete sentences and to produce a summary that flows smoothly and is easy to read.

Some services and some summarizers set an expected guideline for percentage of reduction. For example, ten pages of testimony should be reduced to one page of summary. Others do not find it a good idea to follow such a formula religiously—the purpose of a summary is to reflect the substantive information in helpfully condensed form. Some deponents run on for minutes and say very little; others can fit a lot of testimony into few words, so the size of the summary can vary according to the talking habits of the deponent or the depth of the information being conveyed.

When the testimony in the transcript is completely opaque it might be necessary for the summarizer to quote it word for word in the summary, rather than take a stab at very vague comments and possibly be misleading.

Some material need not even be mentioned in the summary. For example, a lot of interchange among the attorneys at the deposition is transcribed by the court reporter but it is not pertinent to summarize unless there is a substantive objection (as opposed to objections as to form or procedure); in those cases it might be appropriate to make a brief comment in brackets, but it should be clear that those words do not reflect testimony of the deponent.

Condensed language is not necessarily rephrased or reworded language. Summarizers do not put the testimony into their words, they put the deponent's words into condensed form, repeating, whenever possible, the deponent's actual words.

A good summarizer is sure to reread the summary before it is delivered, to be sure the summary itself makes sense. If anything sounds unclear to the summarizer, it will not be useful to the attorney or paralegal it is delivered to and needs clarification. If this sounds too obvious to mention, remember that the topic of the deposition might be an extremely boring one, and the summarizer has already read and thought more about it than she ever wanted to. One last re-reading of the summary might seem to be too tedious to tolerate. This is when the summarizer needs to get a breath of fresh air, then do one last careful reading, pretending he or she knows nothing about the deposition to ensure the summary makes complete sense.

Computerized summarizing & indexing

As we mentioned in chapter 2 on litigation support software, the new generation of full-text transcript management software is also changing the digesting process. New software such as CAT-Links, Discovery ZX, and Summation II allow a transcript to be viewed over a split screen so that a summary can be created in one window while reading the transcript in the other window. Many programs also have a "bookmark" or electronic "post-it" feature that lets the summarizer or paralegal add annotations to the transcript right on screen to act as reminders of questions they might have or inconsistencies in the witness's testimony; for example, "See also page 55, further detail provided," or "This passage contradicted by Mr. Jones in his deposition, page 25." Some software automatically inserts the page and line location while creating the summary.

In addition, rather than traditional summaries, several new full-text programs can print reports made from the electronic notes to take to other depositions or to court. The reports can be created for viewing on screen, for copying to disk to take to court on a laptop, or for printing out in a variety of ways. The summarizer can indicate which information the report should include, and arrange the columns in any preferred order (by topic, page, date, etc.). One can even limit the items in the report to those meeting a certain definition; for example, those including a certain word or phrase or those identified as relating to an identified issue, or those notes entered by a certain summarizer or operator. One unique feature of some packages is that the summarizer or coder can flag dates in the transcript or summary, and then automatically produce a chronology of every event using the comments that each person made. Similar reports can be created covering a number of depositions in the same case.

However, there are drawbacks to using a full-text management system for creating summaries. Most attorneys are familiar with only the common page/line summary and find it most useful for their purposes, rather than the sort of "new-fangled" type of summary that can be compiled using a full-text document manager. A lot of attorneys aren't comfortable yet with computers; and among those who are, not many are likely to carry a laptop computer to a deposition or use database searches on the spot to try to find testimony from an earlier deposition while a new deposition is taking place. Instead, most attorneys simply prefer to review and flag pages of a deposition summary hard copy, and bring that with them to make notes as the new deposition proceeds. It is a format attorneys know and are comfortable with.

As attorneys and paralegals become more familiar with the versatility and power of computerized summarizing and indexing, they might become more universally used. It is possible that in the future, as more and more attorneys use PCs themselves, or become familiar with the enhanced capabilities computerized summaries offer, they will want to use computerized systems more in their trial preparation, in which case the work of the deposition summarizer will benefit from the potential that already exists with the new software.

The job market for summarizers

Despite the development of computer programs for transcripts that provide a variety of systems for indexing and identifying issues in transcripts, most attorneys still seem to prefer the traditional, manually summarized transcript for their trial preparation work, and that means that the demand for summarizers remains strong.

Because much summarizing is done outside the office, it is an excellent area for paralegals and others with training who want to work from home. Those paralegals who found depositions a miserable pain in the law firm might be surprised to find them enjoyable work in the home office. For those paralegals who enjoy learning new computer applications, in particular, the opportunity to handle lengthy transcripts and make them more useful to attorneys will continue to be available for a long time.

Business profile

Elizabeth Burda
Deposition Summarizer

Elizabeth Burda summarizes depositions and raises cattle near Yorktown, a town of about 2100 people in a farm and ranch community in south Texas. Elizabeth says of Yorktown that there are not a lot of law firms to work for: "There's not too much litigation here since all the banks have been closed, though there was a rumor that a fist fight took place downtown."

Elizabeth was a family law paralegal for 14 years. When she decided to relocate, she bought an old house, and now she is able to combine her country life with deposition summary work. She has an arrangement with one law firm in Austin that ships deposition transcripts to her. She dictates the summaries, which the firm then transcribes and returns to her for editing (all by overnight courier, since she is not close enough to pick up and deliver).

Elizabeth remembers that when she was a paralegal in the office, depositions were the hardest thing to do, but at her home she likes it. It's all she has to do, so she is not worried about other paralegal tasks waiting to be done. The depositions get done quicker, and she's much more efficient at home, where there are fewer interruptions.

Elizabeth, like other deposition summarizers we interviewed, believes hands-on paralegal work is virtually required as background for this work, because deposition testimony is not easy to consolidate accurately. When she was doing family law, she was always looking for the nuance that might clue you in to an answer hiding behind a comment. That background—especially her background in family law—helps her to find a recurring theme in a deponent's testimony.

Summarizers need to be sensitive to the issues, and since they don't get much of an outline of the case with their assignments, they have to figure a lot of it out themselves. That's where a paralegal background helps a lot. As Elizabeth says, "I could guess when I read the comments of a particular lawyer over and over in one complicated suit, what his axes-to-grind really were."

Elizabeth gets her work from the paralegals at one large firm; they have a coordinator who puts the word out at the firm that Elizabeth has time to help, and someone usually has a deposition for her to work on. She tries to keep in voice contact with the paralegals and the coordinator who know her, to keep reminding them of her availability—and she sends them baked goods at Christmas with a note that this delicious bonus was theirs because she was able to be working at home (a cute marketing tactic)!

Elizabeth's advice to potential new summarizers is to get in your solid work experience first, before trying this from home, and if you decide to accept work through a service, negotiate a good hourly rate for yourself, commensurate with your years of paralegal experience.

Working for temporary or deposition digesting services

Many summarizers get work from a paralegal temporary service or a deposition summarizing service. Although some services use people with little experience, most of them seek experienced paralegals for deposition summarizing work.

Laurel Davies of Gibson Arnold and Associates' Denver office maintains a file of qualified, experienced and available freelance deposition summarizers. She obtains the names for her file from word of mouth. Laurel spent many years as a litigation paralegal and was active in the Rocky Mountain Legal Assistant Association and the National Federation of Paralegal Associations, a fact that has given her credibility among and access to most of the good experienced paralegals in the Denver area.

Today, Laurel has a broad base of talent on which to draw for the assignments that come into her service. Occasionally she places ads for deposition summarizers, as well as for freelance paralegals for other positions. She conducts a thorough interview so she can be comfortable that the summarizers she uses will be thorough, detailed, accurate, and efficient. Laurel is in the process of putting together tests for deposition summarizer applicants—a proofreading test and a case analysis test, requiring the applicant to summarize issues and facts—to help her evaluate applicants.

In hiring summarizers, Nick Norman of Templeton and Associates looks for legal assistants with at least two years experience (but most of his summarizers have more). Special skills are also helpful; they had one summarizer with six years of paralegal experience who also was an accountant, which is helpful in working on depositions from financial expert witnesses. Environmental, medical, or other specialty background areas can prove helpful. The more experience a paralegal has the more she can cover a broad variety of subject areas in summarizing.

Mary Sue Bach

Mary Sue Bach has been a deposition summarizer for Templeton and Associates for four years. Before that she was a paralegal working in litigation and corporate law. During her years in a law firm she had done many deposition summaries. At that time, Mary Sue looked on deposition summarizing as ". . . the pits of the work. I avoided it like the plague. But during the last three months before I left the firm, the computer people taught me word processing and I knew it before I left."

When she went off on her own, she contacted placement agencies planning to sign on to do summarizing work at home. One company wanted only people who would work on the premises, but she signed on with Templeton. Templeton paid the same as she would have gotten from her firm, and Mary Sue has been happy getting all her work through the service.

Mary Sue recommends that a summarizer have five or more years of experience working in a law office. Some come out of paralegal school and can do it without a lot of experience, but it helps to know what lawyers are going to do with the summary—which is hard to do from a service.

Mary Sue does not miss going to the office at all, but she does miss the little conversations with people you interact with at the office, "when you ask about their families, and so on. You have to be ready to give that up or fill it up in other ways." Mary Sue's secret to being called repeatedly and being paid well: "You have to behave as if you were a perfectionist, produce an accurate product."

Earning potential & income

Compensation for summarizing work varies according to geographic area, and sometimes depends on the summarizer's level of experience. Most summarizers determine what to ask for based on their knowledge of the going rate in their community, and by talking to others at paralegal association meetings. We did not find a standard rate from the summarizers we interviewed, but those for services earn about $12–$15 an hour for dictating summaries, with the understanding that the summarizer will cover no fewer than 20–25 pages of transcript per hour (although they might proceed more slowly if the subject matter is highly technical). This comes out to about $.50 per transcript page for dictating. The summarizer who types or word processes is usually paid more, often half again the amount of the dictation, or a total of $.75 per original transcript page.

A summarizer working directly for an attorney or law firm, without the middleman of the service company, often earns about $20–$35 an hour (based on $1 to $1.75 a page) but in turn must pay her own FICA and withhold her own income taxes.

Good deposition summarizers have a thorough background in paralegal work, probably at least some litigation work. Their English skills have to be excellent. They should know how depositions are used in the discovery stage of litigation and how attorneys use deposition summaries to cross-check witnesses' stories against one another or to get a feel for the type of witness each deponent makes. Understanding legal terminology is also helpful for recognizing the types of interchange that take place among the various attorneys at a deposition. Anyone specializing in a particular area, such as the medical area for personal injury or medical malpractice cases, needs an understanding of that area's terminology. Knowledge of word processing, particularly WordPerfect, is necessary. An understanding of how the computerized indexing systems operate (e.g., Discovery ZX, Summation II, and CATLinks) can be very helpful and provides flexibility if law firms begin to utilize these programs more broadly. The more knowledge summarizers have in a broad variety of areas that are frequently litigated, the better job they can do, and the more work they will get.

A combination of analytical skill and succinct writing ability is probably the most important skill for this line of work, along with the ability to understand what is being read and say it absolutely accurately in a very few words. The summarizer cannot try to write creatively and must resist the temptation to improve on the deponent's words. The gist of the testimony must be exactly the same in the summary as it is in the transcript.

Proofreading skills are also critical. The summarizer must double-check the accuracy and completeness of the summary content as well as complete sentences, spelling, and punctuation. Since the summary material might be less than tantalizing, the temptation to skip this step is real, but it must be overcome. A summary with any inaccuracies is much less useful, if not harmful, to the attorney's case. A single error in a date or a number or even the spelling of a name could be critical.

Many paralegals comment that they encounter summaries in which the language does not make any sense by itself, and so they must consult the original transcript to figure out what happened. This obviously defeats the purpose of the summary. The summarizer has to be able to read the summary and tell whether or not it makes sense or if it is best to quote certain passages exactly from the transcript.

Many of the skills needed by summarizers are best developed with experience as a paralegal in a law firm setting. In order to be able to exercise judgment, determine which information in a deposition is critical and which isn't, it helps to have worked with discovery, trial preparation, and evidence. As a result, someone with paralegal litigation experience has the most valuable experience of all.

Traits & personality Home-based deposition summarizers, like home-based paralegals, must be able to work alone, sometimes for very long hours, on one project and to concentrate on one thing for an extended period of time. They must be able to question the terms of the assignment and get information about the case and the type of summary being requested. Since there is little or no contact with other workers in an office setting, the summarizer must be able to arrange for her social needs to be met in other ways, outside work.

Patience is also a virtue in summarizing work. Otherwise, a summary statement might be rushed despite the fact that the testimony being reviewed does not make sense at that particular point. A more patient person might be able to scan ahead and review several pages to decide whether or not ambiguity is resolved later before creating the summary statements for the ambiguous material. This particular skill is a valuable one and a difficult one to conjure when the timeframe for the assignment is drawing short and the work to be done is still heavy.

Summarizing work also requires judgment. There are many steps along the way where choices must be made: Should this item be quoted exactly? Is this an error by the reporter that should not be in the deposition? Is there a particular tone to this person's language that should be noted in an aside? Summarizing, like paralegal work, seems to involve a share of ambiguity—what exactly does the lawyer want in this summary?

The paralegal requirement for integrity carries over into this line of work as well. The material handled by the summarizer is every bit as confidential as the work paralegals and attorneys handle in their regular jobs. Integrity also covers the issue of not permitting a conflict of interest in the work. Summarizers who work for services often will have their work screened by the service to prevent the possibility of one person working on matters that might create a conflict with a prior client. However, for summarizers working on their own, the responsibility for screening possible conflicts remains a personal obligation. (See appendix B for information on ethics and conflict of interest.)

Finally, summarizers must respect deadlines—absolutely. Often, there is little turnaround time. Any summarizer who shows the least disrespect for deadlines will probably not have another opportunity to work for the same client.

Training There are no training programs specifically for deposition summarizers outside of paralegal training programs (see the section on paralegal training programs in chapter 1). However, there are some ways for a paralegal to learn deposition summarizing techniques before leaving a regular job for a home-based business.

Paralegals working in a law firm can learn a lot about deposition summaries. Even if they are not working in the litigation area, paralegals will probably be glad to share some standard summary formats with someone who might be available to take the summarizing work off their hands. They will probably also share hints they have learned in their use of other's summaries.

On-the-job training

Several articles in *Legal Assistant Today* magazine, NFPA's *National Paralegal Reporter*, and NALA's *Facts and Findings* are helpful in understanding more about the deposition digesting process. To mention only a few:

Publications

"Deposition Summaries; a Basic Format" by Lillian B. Hardwick, *Legal Assistant Today*, Nov/Dec 1986; provides some good hints on writing style.

"Computerized Digesting: A Time-Saver for Cost-Conscious Law Firms" by Lyn Hill, *National Paralegal Reporter*, Spring 1992; explains how a deposition digesting service operates.

"5 Ways to Digest a Deposition" by Cynthia Tokumitsu, *Legal Assistant Today*, March/April 1992; outlines the format options, discusses software, and even lists some tips on what not to do.

"The Art of Summarizing Depositions" by Lana J. Clark, CLA, *Legal Assistant Today*, September/October 1993; explains how some of the computerized systems work.

Compared to in-house or freelance paralegal work, deposition summarizers can concentrate on a deposition transcript and complete it more efficiently and productively because they don't have the distractions of other trial preparation work. The summarizer learns a lot about the witness and the case from the deposition, and it can be very interesting work depending on the subject of the case and whether the same summarizer is able to work on a series of depositions in the same case over a period of time.

Advantages & disadvantages of deposition summarizing

For someone wanting to work at home, deposition summarizing has many advantages. Deposition transcripts are very portable, and there is very low overhead involved—the summarizer needs only the transcript and the summarizing equipment, either a computer equipped with WordPerfect word processing or a dictating machine. The summarizer's schedule can be very flexible, responsive to needs of the family or other involvements and interests.

Jane Bourgoin, after a number of years as a law firm and in-house corporate paralegal, enjoys working on deposition summaries at home for a change. She can take a short break and spend a little time with her cats or put on a pot of beans to cook for the day, things she can't do from the office. In fact, Jane enjoys working at home so much that when she was sent by the service to what was to have been an in-house assignment and discovered that it involved summarizing depositions in the office, she convinced the law firm to let her take the work home to complete, explaining that she would be much more efficient and productive in that setting.

Most summarizers admit that a number of deposition transcripts they work on are tediously boring in content. This is a hazard of the work, but is not always the case. Often the opposite is true, just don't count on a constant supply of fascinating cases to read about.

Litigation work is notoriously unbalanced in the workload department, which affects paralegals in law firms, service companies doing litigation support, and freelance deposition summarizers. There will be dry times and there will be times when the work is so heavy that the summarizer's personal life is put on temporary hold. Good summarizers work their lives around the fluctuations. Mary Sue Bach is relieved that the workload seems to be slow every summer, because she and her family enjoy their Minnesota lake cabin during those times.

One of the unsatisfying disadvantages to this work is that the summarizers rarely hear the outcomes of the cases they have worked on, and that can be a disappointment. If the work has come from a former employer, the summarizer probably has personal friends in the firm who will let her know at the end of the case whether or not the client came out ahead. But for those who work through services, the stories are often left without an end.

Business profile

Jean King

Jean King, who lives in Castle Rock, Colorado, has been summarizing depositions for her former employer, the law firm Montgomery, Little, Young, Campbell & McGrew in Denver, since she has been home with her new baby. Now she feels she has the best of both worlds.

In early 1992, Jean left the firm to have her baby, and after a few months was planning on working as a freelance paralegal when the firm called her to do deposition summaries at home. Jean believes deposition summaries gives her the best of both worlds; she works as much or as little as she wants; she can schedule the work around her baby's schedule; and she doesn't have to worry about transportation of transcripts—a secretary from the firm lives near Jean and she delivers transcripts and tapes. Jean is currently dictating summaries, but if the volume increases, the firm will provide her with a modem. The firm's word processing department currently transcribes her tapes, and Jean gets the summaries back for proofing.

Jean appreciates being on a payroll (she is paid hourly, an amount based on her last salary at the firm); she doesn't have to pay her own taxes or social security.

Jean does not find the work boring at all, and she does not miss being in the firm with all the stress and the deadlines, or coping with the personalities of attorneys on opposing sides of the cases she worked on.

Jean recommends a potential summarizer be experienced, probably at least three years. At the law firm she worked for, she learned that new paralegal school graduates do not know how to summarize, their summaries were too long and mentioned the wrong things. You need to know what items are important to pull it out of the testimony.

Deciding if this business is for you

Perhaps deposition summarizing is beginning to sound attractive and feasible to you. Take a few moments to think about these questions. They might help you to decide whether this would be an occupation you would enjoy and one at which you would be successful:

_____ Are you good with language, i.e., was English one of your best classes?

_____ Do you enjoy concentrating on one task or one subject over a long period of time?

_____ Are you a good, concise writer?

_____ Do you enjoy putting a story together in your mind, from reading a series of jumbled comments?

_____ Do you enjoy working with computers?

_____ Can you work with a high level of ambiguity?

_____ Do you enjoy working alone?

_____ Do you have, or are you interested in acquiring, considerable paralegal experience?

_____ Do you know law firms or attorneys who will give you summarizing work?

_____ Are there paralegal service companies or deposition service companies in your area where you can look for summarizing work?

Getting started

Getting started as a deposition summarizer requires attention to a few particular issues.

Equipment

While most deposition summarizers get by with very low overhead in their home businesses, there is some equipment and supplies that are necessary to the business. Most summarizers have a computer to prepare the summaries that they then deliver in hard copy or on disk, or both, depending on the preferences of the client. Some use only a hand-held dictating machine, delivering the dictation tape to the client's office where it is transcribed. In this case, little or no office equipment is required, except a computer desk and a comfortable place to work.

The more entrepreneurial might decide to provide more options, depending on how much you anticipate working, your need to attract more clients, and the needs of your clients. A good, fast fax and a laser printer might allow you to provide faster service in both receiving the transcript and transmitting the summary. In addition, an internal fax/modem in your computer can permit you to receive a deposition transcript via modem and to transmit the summary to the law firm instantly, a particularly good feature if you are located a distance from the law firm or transportation or parking make hand delivery a difficult option.

Reference materials

All summarizers should have a good, thorough dictionary, unabridged if possible, to consult for spelling and for clarifying words in the deposition transcript. Although court reporters are meticulous about spelling and accuracy, there might be occasions when the words might not be spelled exactly. In addition, summarizers who specialize in certain areas such as medical practice areas will want to have reference books available for similar clarification of terms.

Transportation

The summarizer should have an efficient method of picking up or obtaining the transcripts and delivering or transmitting the deposition summary when it has been completed. Although the law firm or service might arrange for this, the summarizer should be prepared to meet the client's specific need in a way that takes the work off the client's hands. Open an account with a courier service so you can offer swift, convenient pickup and delivery services when they are needed.

Self-discipline

A home-based deposition summarizer must have enough discipline to structure the summarizing time into the day without outside supervision or suggestion. The summarizers we interviewed did not have problems getting the work done, although there were times when the volume of work was so heavy that personal interests had to be set aside for a day or a few days.

Relationships

You cannot do summarizing with the expectation of getting a full-time job out of a temporary assignment. Some people begin to love a firm and want to work there, which can interfere with their relationship as a summarizer. It can cause friction between a freelancer and paralegals who work regularly at the firm if they see you as a competitor for an in-house position. If a freelance summarizer is trying to get a foot in the door, it can make regular employees uncomfortable.

Cash flow

Many home-based summarizers have only part-time work from this occupation. To someone looking for full-time income from deposition summarizing, this might be problematic. A full-time summarizer might have to put more effort into marketing than those who are finding sufficient part-time work without any marketing effort.

Good summarizers who want to attract more work keep in touch with the paralegals and attorneys who know them and the quality of their work. As with freelance paralegal work, contacts in the paralegal community are invaluable, as are membership in a local paralegal association. Working on an association's committees keeps the summarizer's name and specialty familiar to a number of lawyers and paralegals.

Some summarizers set up a nationwide business, advertising for business in national paralegal or legal publications. We did not interview any home-based summarizers who worked with that broad a geographical client base; however, it is quite feasible. Lawyers frequently must schedule depositions in foreign cities and might want to call on someone outside their own area for summarizing. However, the risks of uneven work flow suggest that such entrepreneurs have available sufficient capital to maintain themselves over the early stages of the business or have sufficient local clientele to be assured of steady work during the transition from local to national client base. In addition, an attorney calling on an out of town service for summarizing probably has a monumental summarizing task to be completed in very short time and it would be important to have additional summarizers available to help fulfill the immediate critical need.

Marketing & networking

Marketing your business through national advertising

Richard Meyers

Business profile

Richard Meyers is a busy man. His life is currently split between running a deposition summarizing business, working at a legal software company (Summation) as a customer service representative and trainer, and earning a teaching credential in American History in order to pursue his current goal of becoming a high school teacher. Richard is nevertheless a good example of the freedom and flexibility that a deposition summarizing business can enjoy.

Richard runs The Depo Collective, formerly an independent group of summarizers that included several people but now is a partnership between Richard and one other individual. Although he did not attend a paralegal program, Richard learned the business while he was in college and was working part-time for a law firm where he learned summarizing, indexing, and coding of depositions. With his experience, he has been able to develop his skills, and now he works for a few major clients in the San Francisco area.

Richard generally uses WordPerfect since most of his clients want him to prepare his summaries in an informal conversational tone that gives them more a feeling for the deponent and what was said rather than a tight but cryptic summary. He also uses Summation for other types of summaries and when preparing indices. Richard charges by the page for summaries, generally $1.75 per original page although he knows other firms in the Bay area that charge as high as $3 and some that charge as low as $1.50.

One of the things Richard points out about freelance work is that you have to be prepared to handle a big job when it comes in, so he maintains a list of people he can rely on to take his overflow as a sub-contractor when he and his partner get overloaded. In general, he says business is more steady than not, although he and his partner continue to seek bigger clients and more work.

Richard believes deposition summarizing is a great business and that there is plenty of opportunity for others. He likes being his own boss and the flexibility of the work. As he says, "If you want to play golf on Thursday afternoon, you go play golf." But it's hard to imagine that Richard has time for golf, given the number of jobs he performs and energy he puts into them.

6 Specialized legal businesses

In addition to the careers and businesses presented so far, an increasing number of niche businesses are available for people with legal experience. Work trends indicate that, as the world becomes more and more service and information oriented, there is a corresponding increase in the specialization of work. For example, years ago, a computer consultant might do many types of work, while today consultants specialize in very focused areas of hardware or software. This is because the amount of knowledge required to truly understand a specialized field has grown exponentially. The same is true of legal, medical, or financial services.

Accordingly, we found many businesses in the legal field that demonstrate opportunities to specialize. This chapter highlights a number of highly focused businesses we believe represent good potential for others. (Our philosophy is that if a business can be successful in one location, it can be equally successful in another.)

This chapter describes the following legal business ideas:

- asbestos abatement consulting
- computer consultant
- consultant to start-up law firms
- corporate service company
- demonstrative evidence specialist
- independent professional law librarian
- mediation service

- multimedia/video specialist
- nurse/paralegal consultant
- proofreader
- Social Security claimant representative
- transcriptionist

Asbestos abatement consultant

Lots of paralegals become experts in the area of law where they work, but few have gone on to develop consulting careers in those specialty areas. As you read the following profile, bear in mind that similar consulting businesses could be developed in a variety of areas, especially for paralegals or other people who have developed an expertise in any type of federal regulations. Federal regulations are constantly changing and it takes considerable expertise to keep up with them. The person who is able to do so becomes quite valuable to a law firm, thereby increasing the opportunity for highly paid contract work.

Business profile

Mary Griffith

As a legal assistant for a law firm in Wisconsin, Mary Griffith's clients included school districts dealing with asbestos in their school buildings. She helped them comply with EPA regulations for asbestos in schools and in doing so she became a "mini-expert" in EPA asbestos rules. She saw the opportunity for a specialized career when she learned, in the EPA regulations, that schools were required to hire someone who was not an abatement contractor (who would have a vested interest in doing removal) to do inspections and draw up a management plan for the school.

After leaving the law firm, Mary obtained EPA training and was almost immediately hired, not just by the firm's clients but by a whole district of clients. She was meeting a need that was mandated by the EPA.

One of the benefits of becoming an expert in an area like EPA regulations is that once people see you in that role, you have a ready client base without doing much marketing to get your business started. Mary's Griffith Consulting Service did one mass mailing after she got her accreditation, and the next day she had clients.

The EPA work involves inspecting buildings and taking samples to test for asbestos. Because the required plan varies according to the building's age and construction type, Mary hired architecture and engineering students to help her with that information. She writes a management plan that instructs the district to remove the asbestos, maintain it, or treat it. Once the plan is ready, the consultant meets with the school administrator to explain what the plan means.

There are many ways consultants such as Mary help clients who have no familiarity with government regulations, and no time to spend studying them. Depending on the plan she wrote for the school, Mary helped the district get abatement contractors to do whatever was required, and helped the schools prepare programs for informing staff and parents of the situation. She also trained their custodial staffs to deal with the asbestos condition in the building.

Becoming an expert can snowball into additional work. Mary found herself being hired to consult with law firms representing construction companies that could be liable for the asbestos condition. She explained the EPA regulations to the attorneys so they could explain them to their clients. At other times, she served as an intermediary between a law firm and the EPA during negotiations.

Mary feels this area is still a promising one, especially for paralegals with asbestos experience. She acquired a partner and they hired four other employees and two secretaries—still working out of their homes. She and her company inspected more than 200 buildings during the two years she did it (she left her business recently to attend law school). Business continues to be good—schools must conduct a review every three years and produce another management plan at that time.

Mary's paralegal experience contributed the most to her consulting work, which resembled the work she did during the discovery stage of a law suit: reviewing records, inspecting evidence, and drawing conclusions from what the test results revealed about the building. It was a logical next step in a paralegal career. Besides paralegal training and experience, Mary had an undergraduate degree in science education, which undoubtedly helped her with some of the technical aspects of the work.

There are no particular requirements for this consulting work aside from the required EPA training and subsequent examination. Mary recommends you have a strong knowledge of EPA asbestos rules; a basic understanding of construction contracts, how things get bid out and how specifications are written; and current information on the new technologies for asbestos abatement procedures and methods. In her case, this knowledge all came from her paralegal work.

If you are interested in the EPA asbestos area, research the EPA books about asbestos and school rules. The best way to learn about it, however, is to go to a local school. Ask to see the management plan that was written for that school and talk to the head of maintenance about how the management plan was written and what he thinks of the whole process. (The plan is public record, they have to show it to anyone who comes in and asks to see it.)

Mary priced by trial and error in this new work. She kept track of time and tried to decide whether she was making money on the work. She took into consideration the age of the buildings and other complicating factors and charged on a square footage basis. She even called schools that had used other consultants to see what bids they had accepted.

Whether you are a paralegal now or are considering a career in that area, think about specialization. Many areas could lead to the rewards of independent consulting work.

Computer consultant

As this book suggests, the computerization of the legal field is happening rapidly, which means many jobs and careers will open to people who understand both computers and law. If you have a good background in these areas, consider working as a computer consultant or even as a salesperson for a software company specializing in legal software. Here are a few examples of jobs in the the computer area that show how it is feasible to build a business for yourself.

Business profiles

Shirley Jantz, Cory Levenberg, and Laura Woodrow

Shirley Jantz of Jantz Small Law Office Specialties in the Denver area and Cory Levenberg of Third Wave Consulting in Berkeley, California, have both been in business for just under two years, but they are finding a booming career setting up law offices with computers and teaching lawyers to work with them.

Shirley was a paralegal for several years, having gone back to school for her paralegal certificate after a previous career. She discovered that a growing number of lawyers want to use computers to automate their offices, so Shirley started her own company to meet this need. As she says, "The business evolved without my even trying."

Shirley does a number of things for her clients. First, she works directly with independent lawyers and small firms—a larger market in recessionary times, particularly in the Denver area where many large law firms have cut staff. For these lawyers, Shirley teaches a range of things, from the basics of DOS and how to use a word processor such as WordPerfect to more advanced software such as dBASE and Lotus 1-2-3. She also teaches independent lawyers to use special legal software such as Summation. She sets up offices to do their time-keeping and invoicing on programs like TimeSlips. With Shirley's growing computer knowledge, she occasionally gets a contract to help a lawyer decide which hardware to purchase.

She also works directly for a few law offices doing their billing, primarily for solo lawyers who haven't time to do their own billing. Shirley examines the files and time records, and using TimeSlips, prepares invoices and mails out the bills.

Shirley also does an assortment of other computer-related tasks for independent attorneys. She might do personal tutoring on computer skills, physical hardware upkeep (such as defragmenting a hard disk), and backing up data. She even helped one attorney prepare his own marketing materials, creating brochures and announcements. For this work, she uses desktop publishing programs and stationery from Paper Direct, a supplier of prefolded blank brochures and business cards that you can use in your own laser printer for a professional look (call 1-800-A-PAPERS for a free catalog).

Finally, Shirley handles paralegal research for several attorneys, using Lexis and Westlaw as well as Dialog Information Services.

When we spoke, Shirley said she had about 10 clients, most of whom used her services on a monthly basis. Shirley said she was looking for 15–20 clients per month to keep her busy and possibly allow her to hire one person for assistance with her own administrative matters. For her company, Shirley maintains three computers (a notebook computer, a 386, and a 486) that she networks together using LANtastic so that she can share her HPIIP+ laser printer and her HP550C Color Printer.

Shirley's advice for setting up a legal computer consulting business is to be prepared to do a lot of marketing, because many attorneys are afraid of computers and are not yet fully aware of how much they can help their practice. This includes doing a personal presentation to a lawyer. In her experience, sending your own brochure to a mailing list of attorney's names is often a waste, because many lists have wrong addresses and attorneys get too much to read already. She also advertises occasionally in a local legal directory.

Shirley charges slightly different rates depending on the nature of work. For computer consulting, she charges around $35 per hour. For research and other paralegal work, her fees go as high as $40 per hour, of which she requests half up front to cover her database access fees when she uses Dialog. (For Lexis and Westlaw, she goes to the Supreme Court library in Denver where she pays $5 per minute connect time, since the fee to have your own connection is $10,000.) To do billing for an attorney, she charges only $25 per hour, provided the work is routine, and her clients hire her on a more regular basis to do the billing.

Cory Levenberg commands $85 per hour (soon to be $110 per hour) in the San Francisco Bay area to provide hardware expertise and software recommendations to independent attorneys and small law firms. Cory says he finds no problem getting business—lawyers are starving for help and want to spend their time doing law, not learning about computers.

Cory gets his clients through word of mouth from satisfied customers and by speaking extensively at local bar associations on computers and the law. He expects to soon become accepted by the California Bar Association as a certified provider of minimum continuing legal education (MCLE) courses, which entitles him to give his own seminars and collect profits.

Cory backs his business with strong hardware knowledge, obtained from his undergraduate years as the manager of the PC computer center at the University of California, Berkeley. (He doesn't feel you always need to be a hardware guru, though; you simply need to know a fair amount.) He is a certified Value Added Reseller (VAR) for IBM products, Apple, and Compaq, which means he can sell hardware directly to lawyers. (He says becoming a VAR is quite simple for most companies except Apple, whose application is lengthy and complex.)

For the single-lawyer firm, which makes up the bulk of his business, Cory consults on the purchase of new hardware, modems, and basic general software. Because Cory does not have a paralegal background, he does not consult on specialized legal software but on off-the-shelf software such as word processors, spread sheets, and database programs. Cory also specializes in installing networked computers in small companies.

Cory's advice is straightforward. "This market is huge and largely untapped. I would say that you need a niche to specialize in. The best marketing is word of mouth, although giving seminars is a great way to get your name out there. You get a concentrated group of people who think you are an expert, even if you aren't. The reason consulting to lawyers is so good is that they are educated in one area and they've spent a tremendous amount of money on it, and they are willing to spend to learn about another area. It drives them crazy not to know about computers, and they understand that your hourly rate is below theirs, so it doesn't matter to them."

Laura Woodrow typifies a paralegal using her skills and knowledge of the legal process to obtain a position with a software company specializing in software for lawyers, called CAT-Links. Laura worked for three years with one of the largest New York law firms. After moving to California to join her husband and work with another law firm, the case she was working on was transferred to Arizona. Since her husband couldn't move, Laura decided to move on and went looking for a job. She saw an ad in the paper one day announcing a job for a paralegal and discovered that the position was actually not paralegal work per se, but rather selling litigation support software. As Laura says, "I looked at the software and thought to myself that I should have been using this for years."

Laura loves her work and knows her skills and background in paralegal work have helped her in her new career. She is committed to her product, about which she says, "I felt that it was important to help other paralegals and make them aware of this product. After all, litigation often relies on thousands of documents and you never know which piece of paper could make or break the trial. One document could make a difference, and this software lets you find it within seconds. When I went to school, we had only a one day seminar about computers and it wasn't even hands on! I can see a day in the future when everyone will be using computers in legal work, and every paralegal will be automated. It might even become a criteria for becoming a lawyer."

Although selling software most likely means working a real job rather than a home-based business, we included it because it is quite possible that, like many sales positions, you can work extensively from your home.

As you can see, all three of these jobs can be exciting, highly profitable careers that someone with either a computer background or paralegal background can exploit. As mentioned in chapter 2, the more you know about computers today, the greater your opportunities. The legal world becomes your oyster.

Many people have legal administration experience, combining training in law office administration, marketing, contracts, hiring, and so on. These individuals have excellent accounting, finance, and marketing expertise. Using these skills to assist attorneys in a start-up setting is good contract work because many attorneys lack administrative experience. The following is a profile of one individual who has been able to turn her experience into money.

Consultant to start-up law firms

Eileen Brown

Business profile

When Eileen Brown left her job of many years as legal department administrator with Manville Corporation in Denver, she was looking for new ways to use her many years of experience as a legal administrator and paralegal. While in the process of completing the course work for her Diplomate Certificate in the MSLA (Masters of Science in Legal Administration) program at the University of Denver College of Law, she became acquainted with a fellow student who was an attorney. He had been working for a company that left the area and was in the midst of starting his own small law firm. Eileen became his start-up consultant and contract administrator.

Eileen used her knowledge to equip his office with the initial necessities— arranging for and setting up office space, finding good prices on furnishings and equipment, setting up a library, a filing system, and a records retention system. The attorney already had his own computer but needed software. Because computers are not her specialty area, Eileen subcontracted the acquisition of appropriate software to a computer consultant who set him up with software, such as the Timeslips billing program.

Eileen's administrative experience equipped her well to interview and hire the attorney's initial support staff (one secretary), and set up an initial job description for that position, (although he had already selected someone for that position). Using her contacts in the legal community, Eileen assisted the attorney in finding contract law clerks to take on some special projects in corporate law and bankruptcy. She also put together a marketing plan for him and taught the two attorneys in the firm how to effectively use paralegals and the secretary.

Eileen was the first paralegal at Manville Corporation and, consequently, was allowed to do a broad variety of things. She got great experience, working on acquisitions and mergers, investments, and in corporate and real estate law. Later, she was made the manager of the paralegals then manager of the legal department at Manville. When the corporation was coming out of its Chapter 11 bankruptcy, Eileen found a replacement for herself so she could work on reorganizing the entire legal department, then left the company to find new opportunities for her many skills and talents.

Today, Eileen is pursuing a different, nonlegal business, but she feels strongly that there is a niche for legal administrators interested in helping small firms get on their feet. As with any entrepreneurial effort, developing this sort of a consulting specialty would take considerable marketing. Eileen recommends several marketing steps: advertising in legal publications, especially bar journals; becoming vigorously active in the legal arena by joining and volunteering time to bar association committees (most have a law office management committee, for example); and offering your services for panel discussions or seminars on management issues. These activities go a long way toward familiarizing the legal community with your special expertise.

Attend a lot of seminars and stay in touch with who's attending and why they are there. How-to seminars are particularly good. For example, people might be there to learn how to upgrade some of their systems in the law firm or because they are leaving the protected status of a large firm to starting up their own. Bar luncheons are also good, because you can meet and chat with people and let them know what you do. She also recommends staying on top of what the other consultants in the community are doing. You may want to use them as subcontractors in areas where you need extra expertise, such as computer consulting.

Attorneys know all about practicing law, but getting a business started draws away their energy. They realize they are most profitable when they are billing their time to clients, hour by hour, minute by minute. An administrative or management consultant can save them many hours. With the consultant doing the footwork and organizing, the attorney can be billing his time, bringing in money. Most attorneys recognize that management is not their greatest strength, and if they are offered what is clearly a cost-effective way to deal with all the nuts and bolts details of setting up the office, they'll jump at it.

Paralegals working in the corporate area develop a full Rolodex of resources to help them in their work. Among the many services they draw on are corporate service companies who can be called upon to do any of the following tasks.

Corporate service company

- Retrieve public documents from a variety of government offices.
- File papers in those offices.
- Search records in secretary of state or county records offices to determine whether liens exist that are held by certain people or entities or against the assets of certain people or entities.
- Search database records to determine if certain individuals appear as officers or directors of corporations or as owners of real estate.
- File papers to incorporate companies, to change incorporation documents, to qualify corporations in other states, and to withdraw corporations from certain states.
- Reserve or register trade or business names in various jurisdictions.
- Obtain verification that corporations are in good standing in various states.
- File papers to form limited partnerships, to change partnership documents, to qualify limited partnerships in other states, and to withdraw them from certain states.

All these services are things paralegals in corporate law know how to do themselves, but it makes sense to have a service company do them for several reasons. First is cost. Paralegal rates can be as high as, or exceed, $60–$70 an hour in some areas. Even if the firm is located near the secretary of state's office, for example, it would probably cost a client $60 to have the law firm's paralegal make a trip over to the secretary of state to do a filing or a search. It is more cost effective to have a service company do the running around. They can do several such errands on one trip for about $25 each. The law firm's client saves money and the paralegal can stay at the office doing more substantive work.

Another advantage of law firms using a service is the time and distance factor, especially if the agency is in another city. While obtaining records or filing papers individually is always feasible, it is often cumbersome. Many offices require payment in advance, even though the fee might not be definite. It takes a long time to write for documents and wait for them to come in the mail. Much corporate transactional work these days is done in a very short time frame. Attorneys want a document dated today for a closing scheduled for tomorrow, or even today. The only way to get documents instantly is to have someone representing you at the agency's counter to pick up the document and fax it or send it to you by courier. Services do that, and many also have access to the agency's computer database (some agencies sell their database access to service companies), and can print the document in their office (and fax or courier it). They will advance the fee as needed and bill the law firm. The convenience factor is obvious.

The third reason to use a service company is that filing services understand well what they do most, so they know the details of costs, timing, filing requirements, etc., for a number of government agencies. A law firm paralegal might know these details for one or two offices, but cannot be an expert in as many situations as the service company can.

The following profile shows you how someone can make a complete business out of service work.

Business profile

Carolyn McKown

Carolyn McKown had years of experience as a corporate paralegal and as a former officer of Corporation Service Company. She used her expertise to build a business doing corporate service work—CorpAmerica, Inc. in Dover, Delaware. As Carolyn says, "Anytime you have any expertise, whatever you are in, someone will pay for what you know."

Law firms and corporations pay her to help companies incorporate, act as a registered agent for out-of-state companies, and do the other corporate services we mentioned previously. She obtains document copies or does filings at the Delaware Secretary of State office at rates that are highly competitive with larger service companies. In addition, she is a consultant to new businesses.

State laws require a corporation incorporated in, or qualified to do business in, that state to have some sort of office there to receive mailings from the secretary of state and service of process—usually called a *registered office* where a *registered agent* is located. Many corporations incorporate where the law is favorable (e.g., Delaware) even though their operations are elsewhere. Corporate service companies offer to serve as a registered agent for a fee of about $120 a year per corporation. Individuals can also provide this service—it amounts to maintaining an address for the company and forwarding mail from the secretary of state or service of process that might be delivered for the company.

If you have corporate paralegal experience, this could be a career option for you. Delaware is a particularly busy state because the corporation law there is designed to attract business incorporations. According to Carolyn, there are other individuals in Delaware who also provide corporate services from home-based businesses. Legal assistants in other states have set up similar independent businesses, particularly if they are located in the state capitol where most such agencies are located. For example, Capitol Filing Service, Inc., in Nashville, Tennessee, is a home-based corporate service company providing services in that area. Former corporate paralegal Ruth Harriston has had her corporate document filing and retrieval business in Columbus, Ohio, for more than 10 years.

To get started, you need basic office equipment, including a typewriter for filling in forms, computer with word processing and, if possible, a modem to access databases, transportation to get to the agencies, and of course, a potential client base—law firms and corporations who know your capabilities in the corporate area. It is particularly important to have contacts or reciprocal arrangements with someone like Carolyn in other state capitols so you can arrange for service if your client needs it.

You can market your service through corporate paralegals you know in paralegal associations to which you belong, as well as among attorneys. As corporate paralegals have learned, law firm clients have become extremely cost conscious, and smaller service companies have low overhead and can compete successfully with larger companies, especially in certain areas of service. Consequently, more can be done all the time using modem communications, and the possibilities in this area can only grow.

Demonstrative evidence specialist

It is commonly said that people remember only 10 percent of what they read, 20 percent of what they hear, 30 percent of what they see, but 50 percent of what they see and hear. This fact reflects the trend that, particularly in today's world of television and film, we are a visually oriented society. Regardless of learning style, people are more adept at learning and understanding with the help of images rather than through reading the printed word or listening to a voice alone.

This is not a function of the brain per se. Harvard psychologist Howard Gardner has written much about how each of us has one or more learning styles that range from musical to mathematical to kinesthetic and that influence our basic learning mode throughout life. However, our day-to-day information has become too complex for most of us to absorb simply by reading. We absorb information better when it is presented to us in other ways, such as aurally or—even better—in a combination of visual and aural presentations.

Think about how you would prefer to learn about, say, the division of corporate revenues and profits in a company that has 15 departments. Would you rather read a list of numbers, hear a person reading off the numbers, or see a pie chart that visually portrays the various groupings of numbers into color-coded segments? Would you rather see a diagram of an injured knee or hear a doctor describe the muscles and ligaments, or read about it in a dry medical book?

The answers to these questions are obvious, and trial lawyers are slowly taking note. More and more of them are recognizing that visuals go a long way in winning a case. Here are a few reasons that justify the use of visual evidence:

- Visuals quickly clarify the relationships between things or people. Think of an organizational chart for a company, or a family tree.
- Visuals simplify a complex issue. Think of a diagram of a jet engine or a time line showing the exact sequence of events leading up to a disaster.
- Visuals add drama and pizzazz. Think of a photo of an accident scene, or the actual output from an EKG showing a failing heartbeat.
- Visuals add certainty. Think of a blown-up contract showing a definitive signature at the bottom.
- Visuals help us to imagine. Think of a drawing of an explosion suggesting how the pieces might have skyrocketed away.
- Visuals add understanding. Think of an illustration of a new product that you've never seen before showing how to wire it together.

For all these reasons, there are growing small and home-based businesses producing graphics and artwork for lawyers, usually using computers to assist in creating the visuals. This material has come to be called *demonstrative evidence,* and it includes many types of things:

- blow ups of documents, with or without highlighted sections
- medical and technical illustrations
- charts, graphs, and maps
- chronologies and time lines
- photos
- lists of bulleted ideas on huge posters
- computer-generated images

According to Shelley English, owner of LegalArts, a demonstrative evidence company in Santa Barbara, California, just about anything can be turned into a piece of demonstrative evidence with the right skills. Shelley is one of the growing legion of people who came into this field with visual or fine arts degrees, medical illustration experience, or a legal background. These businesses are sometimes home-based and sometimes located in offices near the law firms in major cities (in order to service them faster).

One small business we visited is Executive Presentations in Los Angeles, founded and owned by Rick Kraemer. Rick felt that in some cases, it would be difficult to be a home-based business in this area because attorneys need to feel they are working with a dependable company that will come through for them. He pointed out that home artists might get sick or not finish the job, and the attorney would certainly not use them again. Rick also felt that solo artists would face cash flow problems; even his firm had trouble collecting sometimes when they worked for law firms that were also waiting to get paid on their contingency cases.

Finally, Rick pointed out how much equipment is sometimes needed: a quick tour of his offices revealed a dozen computers, two oversized plotters to make blow ups and posters, and plenty of tables for pasting and mounting. All total, about $30,000 worth of equipment.

However, Rick encourages others who want to get into the business. He cautioned that it is better not to go after the high-end market because, "Attorneys don't need great artwork. The evidence is purely temporal; it has to be functional and a high enough quality to impress a jury or opponent, but it doesn't need to be Leonardo da Vinci."

We found that Rick was right. The home-based field is actually growing rapidly, and there is even now a national association for demonstrative evidence people, DESA, which stands for Demonstrative Evidence Specialist Association. Founded by Susan Whaley, owner of Litigation Graphics in Spokane, Washington, DESA currently has about 150 members. The following profile contains several examples of small demonstrative evidence businesses.

Shelley English and Debra Bozanic Schechter

Business profiles

Shelley English and Debra Bozanic Schechter came into the demonstrative evidence business from two opposite directions, but both are highly charged about the opportunities for themselves and others.

Shelley formerly worked for a large Los Angeles trial consulting company, where she used her strong graphic arts background from her previous work in videos to produce demonstrative evidence. Because of changes in the company, Shelley decided to open her own shop, LegalArts, which she runs out of her home as well as sharing an office in Van Nuys, California, with a friend who does trial consulting. Shelley specializes in what she says is the wave of the future: getting in early on a case and working with the lawyer to prepare a comprehensive strategy that includes visuals and demonstrative evidence.

Not surprising, Shelley considers herself a consultant, and she aims to help lawyers understand which pieces of evidence can be made even stronger through graphics. Shelley can blow up a calendar, for example, and color code dates so that a pattern emerges, such as in a wrongful termination case. (The pattern might show, for example, a huge preponderance of shaded dates on an employee's record when vacation, sick time, absenteeism, and missed work are all combined together, thus heightening an employer's defense.) Or she can create a chronological time line on a magnetic board so that the lawyer can move around the magnets showing the many different versions of a story the defendant has claimed. The essential point, she says, is to "put yourself in the jury's shoes. If you don't understand what the lawyer is saying, the jury won't."

Shelley believes that when it comes to finding clients, many lawyers are completely untapped. Although she says that graphic work can be very high-priced, she feels it's better to focus on the lower end of the market because many lawyers aren't willing to pay big money for fancy graphics. Shelley gets her clients by giving presentations at law firms, networking among the paralegals (who can suggest hiring her), and word of mouth. She also does some pro bono work to get her name around. At the moment, Shelley charges $80 per hour for her consulting work.

On the other end of the spectrum, Debra Schechter was a pre-med student with a minor in art. She was doing medical research for a physician who noticed her art talent and recommended her for a job with a small company doing visuals. After a few years, Debra went solo, and now she works out of her home specializing in medical illustration.

Debra describes the usual sequence of events. A lawyer with a back injury case going to trial will call her. The lawyer usually asks what Debra would recommend, i.e., how many drawings and how much it will cost to render them. Debra then tries to understand the litigation strategy and what they might need as a visual aid. She will then do a large sketch, scan it into her computer, fax it to the doctor who consults on the case, and get corrections or approval for a finished drawing. In some cases, Debra says, the sketch is all the lawyer needs to convince the opponent while in discovery.

Debra confirms what Shelley says about lawyers: they don't think in terms of the graphics that can support their case. For example, Debra recounted how she once had a case where the lawyer had a bunch of statistics about whiplash. Debra knew the statistics were boring, so she created a visual composed of four boards showing how all the information was tied together. One board showed the mechanisms of whiplash; one showed hypertension, one showed hyperflexion; and the last was the statistical board on which she put a little icon for each type of flexion showing the relationships between them all. The boards were convincing and the client won.

Debra is an ambitious marketer. We found two ideas quite interesting: she once went to a law library and put her business card in every book in the demonstrative evidence section, and she once contacted the producer of a famous television show about lawyers to see if she could consult on a show just to get a credit in the end showing her name. More seriously, she also does occasional direct mail to attorneys, and she places ads in local law publications. She especially sends a postcard mailer to clients every other month to remind them that she's around.

The usual job for Debra consists of one large board with two or three illustrations, on which she spends about 10–15 hours, charging hourly. She asks for a 50 percent deposit to be sure that she gets paid, and she says she has no problem collecting her fees. Most of her cases net her about

$1000–$2000 although she once had a case that brought in $6000. Debra feels strongly there is room in the market for other illustrators, particularly those with good drawing skills and special knowledge in an area such as forensics, engineering, or even real estate law.

Both Debra and Shelley use mostly Apple Macintosh computers and software such as Adobe Illustrator, Freehand, Quark Express, and Pagemaker.

Susan Whaley, founder of DESA, says that, in her opinion, the largest number of members fall on the West Coast, but there is plenty of opportunity all over the county, especially in the mid-west and East Coast. To be in the business, she feels you need either real art talent or the ability to hire a good artist to work for you if you are not artistic but provide the technical knowledge in the field (e.g., engineering, aviation, or electronics). One thing that everyone must be aware of, however, is that you must follow both the federal guidelines for Rules of Evidence (available from the U.S. Government Printing Office) and your state guidelines as well. The evidence must not appear to skew the information, and there are sometimes questions on the admissibility of the evidence that the lawyer has to clear up.

Susan recommends reading *Demonstrative Evidence* by Mark Dombrof, *Modern Visual Evidence* by Greg Joseph (Law Journal Seminar Press) and *Tangible Evidence* by Dian Siemer, all of which are available in law libraries. To contact DESA, write or call the current President, Pat Stuart, c/o Trial Arts Inc., 1801 North Lamar, Suite 110, Dallas, TX 75202, (800) 552-DESA.

Independent professional law librarian

A law library is a basic, necessary tool for the practice of law, whether the attorney is working in a law firm, a corporation, or some other organization. Attorneys need dozens of volumes that differ according to practice specialty. The library always includes at least the state's statutes and regulations, case law, encyclopedias of case law, treatises in the practice area, looseleaf services that are regularly updated, and innumerable periodicals. In addition, the attorney uses computers for computerized research and general materials for extended factual research.

Most attorneys collect the notebooks they receive when attending seminars or continuing legal education courses in their practice areas. In addition, they usually acquire innumerable materials for some special case or research. All these materials must be kept organized and updated, and someone must know what is there, which is the best place to find an answer, and how to use a volume.

Large law firms have librarians on their full-time staff, but sole practitioners or very small offices often share a law library in their office building. Between these extremes are many offices large enough to have a library of some size, but not large enough to have a librarian on staff. Enter the contract professional librarian, who comes in on a periodic basis to take care of the library for small firms and solo attorneys sharing a library. This occupation is quite fascinating as the next profile shows.

Business profiles

Librarians Doriana Fontanella and Linda Will

Doriana Fontanella does library maintenance and legal research for several law firms in the Denver area. Her work includes monitoring and routing regular periodicals, filing update pages in looseleaf binders (especially in tax service publications, securities law publications, corporate law binders, etc.); ordering and reviewing new books; doing the library accounting and—of course—reprimanding people who don't sign out books. These services comprise standard "filing service" maintenance, but in Doriana's case, she provides a number of professional services as well, such as performing legal research for attorneys.

Doriana has a law degree from the University of Notre Dame. When she first arrived in Denver in 1982 she worked for a while as a law clerk, and then happened into the law library work when she went to work for another librarian who was doing contract law library work. Eventually, Doriana bought a portion of that business and from that point on she had an established client base. Doriana now serves as part-time librarian for a number of libraries in law firms, in accountants' offices, and in corporations where accountants use many of the same looseleaf services tax attorneys use. The clear benefit for the library's users is that the update filing is done absolutely correctly, by someone who knows how the materials will be used. They have the use of a professionally trained researcher and a specialist in law libraries but need pay for only a few hours every week or two.

Doriana feels it helps to be excessively detail oriented in her work. *Filing* includes putting in replacement update pages in dozens of looseleaf periodical binders, which must be done accurately, because when the volume is consulted for the latest law or regulation, the current information must be there. The librarian must be intelligent and know how to look for mistakes existing in the books, a frequent condition if the volumes have been handled or pages have been removed (for copying or because the user is careless).

Doriana enjoys freelance work. She has a flexible schedule and the opportunity to interact with a variety of people. The total work also represents more than full-time for Doriana—she frequently works six days a week. Working in several different firms enables Doriana to bring to each client the knowledge of how other people do things and how other firms work, so she is gaining library managerial skills that she can offer her clients. Finally, changing offices regularly gives her enough distance from each firm to be able to stay away from office politics—a nice advantage over regular employment. And there are a few extra fringe benefits to working for a number of law firms on a regular basis—"You get to go to a lot of Christmas parties, summer picnics, and have a lot of coffee mugs and T-shirts with firm names on them."

Linda Will of Tampa, Florida, has a library science degree and, like most true librarians, is an information ferret, a media specialist, a professional researcher for legal and nonlegal material, and a lover of books. She is also a business owner, something few librarians are. When Linda saw large law firms beginning to go through an identity crisis in recent years, she saw an opportunity for a law library entrepreneur, someone to help small- and medium-sized law firms compete in the new legal environment by making the most of their information resources, without having to hire full-time professional librarians. Linda is filling these needs for a number of firms in her area, and setting a standard that law librarians around the country can follow.

Linda has a number of clients for whom she provides library and consulting services—very much like what a full-time librarian does in large law firms, but she does it part-time, perhaps 5, 10, or maybe 20 hours a week in each firm, or maybe only once a month, depending on the size of the firm, its practice area and its needs. She starts out with a cost analysis and review of the firm's physical facility, technology, the firm's CLE library, its online services and acquisitions, and what that indicates about where the firm is going. Then she puts together her summary and recommendations in a tabbed presentation. Usually, she recommends a combination of online and hard copy acquisitions, since online is where law firms must be today. After this, Linda hopes that the firm will invite her back to provide part-time library service, such as performing research, helping attorneys and paralegals find answers to their questions, letting them know what new resources are available in hard copy, online, or on CD-ROM.

In fact, the downsizing of many large law firms in urban areas coincided in the early 1990s with an upsurge of available information through new technology—CD ROM. Linda believes that by 1995 or 1996 a large percentage of law library material will be available on CD-ROM and, thus, more accessible and searchable even to solo practitioners.

Linda has considerable advice for any contract professionals hoping to work for law firms, and she has given a lot of thought to the business aspects of such work. In Linda's experience, "Lawyers and librarians have a lot in common—they share a love of books and knowledge, a quest for truth, justice, and the American Way—but they also have no business sense—zero! Same as librarians." Many of her peers have been cut with the downsizing of firms, not because they weren't excellent librarians, but because they don't understand the bottom line, and it has become a dollars-and-cents world. In fact, Linda has done some work for in-house counsel and attorneys employed in corporations and knows how strongly they are urged to control costs by bringing as much legal work as possible in-house away from outside law firms.

Librarians must understand the whole business picture, how their budget fits into the entire scheme of things. Librarians are very service oriented, and library schools fail them by not teaching good business sense. Librarians should be taught how to network within the firm with the marketing director, financial officer, business administrator, etc.

Linda's other business expertise shows up in her creative marketing of herself and her services. She begins by stressing that, in the process of performing her professional library duties, she constantly markets herself to her clients in the variety of services she can do, the range of her expertise, and her contacts from 17 years as a law librarian. Part of her equipment, accompanying her to every job, is a suitcase-sized briefcase containing the latest information on the newest CD-ROM product and her entire Rolodex (directory/collection of phone numbers and personal contacts). Once the firms get her in she finds they become addicted to having a professional librarian coming in regularly and soon have questions waiting for her when she comes in.

Besides marketing through her excellent work performance, Linda gives freely of her experience through her writing—she's been writing for the *Law Library Journal* for five years (a publication of the American Association of Law Librarians (AALL)), as well as doing a column every two months for the journal. That contact provides her with visibility and credibility and a regular supply of newsletters from librarians in other areas of practice, more sources of information.

Linda decided what to charge for her services by taking a consensus from the networking she had done and then calculating how her area compared to the areas she'd surveyed. She charges $100/hour for the cost analysis at the beginning. If they hire her (Linda does not push for a written contract, she has found attorneys very reluctant to put things into writing), she has lower fees for her library work. If she does online research or other professional services she charges $60/hour. For technical services, such as routing periodicals, sending invoices to the accounting department or instructing office assistants on doing filing of looseleaf updates, she charges $17, about what filing services in her area charge. Although Linda does not have a contract, she does need to collect on time. After 30 days, she adds 15 percent per annum interest.

There is no "typical" freelance librarian. Doriana has heard of people with varying backgrounds doing this work. Doriana has a law degree, but some law librarians have special library degrees, some have been paralegals. Law librarians must be able to conduct thorough legal research and assist attorneys in using the law library. The fact that Doriana is a lawyer has helped her gain the respect of attorneys in the firms where she works and has made it easier to develop a camaraderie with them. Linda, however, finds many library-school-trained law librarians ready to meet the growing need for contract library services and provide professional librarianship to law firms, to give small- and medium-sized firms an extra edge at a time when competition for legal business is at an all-time high.

A lot of litigation comes about because someone wants his "day in court," a chance to be heard, maybe even understood and appreciated. An enormous amount of money is spent in that effort and a lot of damage suffered, when in fact there are other routes to an acceptable solution. Alternative dispute resolution (ADR) offers a variety of processes for disputing parties to reach a conclusion, ways that might well become more popular if the "day in court" syndrome, or the psychological need, could also be met.

The most familiar forms of ADR are arbitration and mediation. In arbitration, the parties agree to submit their disputes to a third party who hears both sides and renders a decision, much like a private judge in a less formal process than a courtroom. In mediation, on the other hand, the parties come to their own resolution, assisted or facilitated by a mediator. The resulting agreement becomes binding if and when it is accepted by a judge and made an order of the court.

Mediation defuses the "win-lose" situation. Instead of one person convincing a judge ("winning"), and the other person failing to do so ("losing"), both people work together to pound out a solution each can live with. Consequently, not only is there a result, but both people have probably grown through the effort of thinking the problem through and coming to terms with what the other side finds important, deciding what he can and cannot live with, and then wringing out a mutually acceptable solution. Each person gets heard, and each has an investment in the solution; therefore each will probably work to see the solution succeed. Mediation does meet some of the psychological needs in a conflict situation.

Mediation is harder work for the parties, personally, than standing in front of an all-powerful judge who will determine your future; it is also much more likely to produce an acceptable result. Very few people who have been through a court battle, especially in the family law area, are comfortable with the result handed down by the judge. They think they will be satisfied, but they rarely are.

Mediation is a joint effort that focuses on a solution, not on blame. This is particularly effective in a divorce/custody situation where mediation allows,

Mediation service

even requires, both parents' involvement in the creation of a program where both stay involved as parents in the children's lives. And through the mediation process, antagonistic parents learn to communicate and develop shared responsibility for the children's care and education. When custody has been determined strictly by a judge, there is no practice or training in continued communication, and one parent's voice in the upbringing of the children can be permanently lost.

Many states have established some sort of official dispute resolution procedures, in civil litigation as well as in family law. Some local courts and many family courts even require an attempt at alternative dispute resolution before lawsuits can proceed through the court. Some states require attorneys to inform clients of alternative dispute resolution options. And there are hundreds of nonprofit community alternative dispute resolution programs throughout the United States.

Business profiles

Cathy Schultheis and John Trott

Cathy Schultheis, whom we discussed in chapter 2 on litigation paralegals, combines family law and litigation paralegal work with mediation services in her home office. She meets with clients, usually family law parties, at her spacious dining room table and helps them resolve the issues of custody and visitation, support, and division of family assets, as they mutually plan how their post-divorce lives will work.

Although Colorado law requires attorneys to inform their clients of ADR opportunities, as Cathy says, it might be unfair to ask attorneys to promote mediation—after all, they are taught to get the best result for their client, not to work toward the most equitable solution for all. Nevertheless, Cathy finds her mediation clients through attorneys in the area who know her paralegal work—and so networking for her has been the best route for attracting business. In fact, she and other Boulder area mediators meet in a monthly support group, sharing ideas on promoting mediation and on handling certain quandaries that arise in their practices.

Mediation was also an attractive opportunity for John Trott in Brewer, Maine. He had completed formal paralegal training, had done some freelance paralegal work for attorneys in town, and then accepted a part-time job in the public defender's office for the Penobscot Nation's tribal court in Maine, but was looking for part-time work to fill out his time. Besides formal mediation training, John served eight years as a senior arbitrator with the Better Business Bureau, which added to his credentials in the ADR area. In fact, he recommends the BBB program to paralegals who are considering getting into ADR work; he learned a lot about negotiation and conflict resolution through their program.

John accepts private mediation clients and is also the family law mediator for the Penobscot Nation's tribal court. His fee is $75 per hour for mediation, but both contribute toward it so it's $37.50 per party.

John and Cathy both received formal mediation training and both stay current in family law areas by attending continuing education programs for attorneys in their areas, which also keeps them in touch with potential business sources.

If you are interested in learning ADR and becoming a mediator, look into local opportunities to volunteer in a mediation program. Not only does the BBB use arbitrators and provide training for them, many courts, bar associations, and paralegal associations have programs that provide some mediation training in exchange for a certain number of donated hours.

These programs help you to determine whether this is an attractive career option for you. If so, more formal training would probably be necessary to build your credentials. Most states have mediation associations and there are some national organizations, such as the Academy of Family Mediators. However, there is no requirement that mediators or arbitrators have law degrees or be licensed to practice law. Some credentials are required in some areas, but in most states this area is very accessible to people with backgrounds in mental health or legal fields.

One caution from current mediators: it is still not easy for even the most effective mediators to make a full-time living at this work. Be sure you survey your community well. Talk with practicing mediators and with attorneys who utilize mediators—to find out where the best training is, how mediators find clients, and what attorneys look for in mediators they call in to help their clients. In the meantime, look for a Better Business Bureau or similar program that utilizes volunteer arbitrators and mediators so you can get training and practice in alternative dispute resolution.

Multimedia/video specialist

Multimedia is the buzzword of the year, as we write this. As with demonstrative evidence, lawyers are equally beginning to recognize the value of certain types of multimedia in the courtroom, particularly computer-timed video and computer-generated animation.

The use of video has long been important in the legal field, as many depositions are videotaped, particularly when the deponent will not be available at trial because of time or distance constraints, or because the person is ill and is not likely to survive until trial. As a result, there are already many independent videographers and even some court reporting agencies that send both reporters and videographers to depositions.

However, the world of video is changing in several areas. First, in the litigation support field, there are several software packages such as

Discovery Video^{zx} (Stenograph Legal Services, San Ramon, CA; 800-527-8366) that synchronize the video footage with the court reporter's notes so that an attorney can search a transcript for a word, and call up on the computer screen not just the actual words of the deponent but also the exact place in the videotape to show the deponent's actual demeanor, body language, and voice quality. There is also a growing use of laser disks to store video footage of several depositions together so that several defendants, for example, can be juxtaposed answering the same question in different ways.

In addition, other new video technology from the world of desktop video combines computers, sound boards, and video capture boards in quite sophisticated ways, so that a multimedia specialist can create a completely integrated presentation including stills, video, clipart, sound, speech, music, and computer-generated animation. All of this can of course be edited and enhanced in many permutations with the right equipment and knowledge. Desktop video has already cracked the business and training market, and without doubt, more and more uses will be found in the legal field, including marketing presentations by law firms to potential clients as well as courtroom uses.

Desktop video is efficient and offers many advantages over traditional video methods of editing and post production. It requires special hardware and software in addition to a PC, including a video capture board (to capture analog video frames and turn them into digitized images), a sound board, a CD-ROM drive, and several types of programs such as presentation software, sound-editing software, and video capture and compression software. (There are literally dozens of different programs of each type.)

The fastest growth in desktop video will probably be in the production of animation for simulations. For example, simulations are now being used in litigation over airline and train crashes, environmental disasters, product liability cases, vehicular accidents, construction accidents, and many other areas in which a jury would have a very difficult time imagining what transpired. In most cases, such computer simulations are still quite expensive, on the order of $1000 to $10,000 per finished minute of video, and producing them requires the work of various people with computer skills, graphics experience, and engineering knowledge. As a result, much of this business is more or less beyond the scope of a small home-based business, but the entrepreneurial paralegal or graphic specialist should keep an eye on the potential of multimedia; there is no doubt that it will grow quickly in legal applications. We might expect that within a few years, attorneys will be hiring outside vendors of desktop video services for many applications, including training, animations, and marketing and public relations presentations.

Many lawsuits involve medical matters—personal injury, workers compensation, medical malpractice, and product liability come quickly to mind—with expensive settlements and judgments. As a result, both insurance companies and attorneys are making use of medical and nursing consultants to help reach the most cost-effective solution to the disputes.

For example, in chapter 3, we mentioned Pam Miller who does medical records interpretation as an independent nurse/paralegal. As an outside third party, she might be called upon for an objective review of medical records, to help determine the existence and degree of actual injuries in medical-related lawsuits, combining her skillful reading of medical records with trial preparation experience, and knowledge of court rules and rules of evidence. Pam does this service not only for attorneys representing either plaintiffs or defendants in lawsuits, she also performs the service for insurance companies and attorneys before lawsuits are initiated, to help them determine the extent of a victim's injuries. Pam feels she competes well with companies who perform the same service at a higher cost, and with less personal client attention than she provides.

Here is another profile detailing a related medical consulting business for those with nursing backgrounds.

Deborah Pietrzyk

Deborah Pietrzyk has been a nurse for 11 years, including work in intensive care and the emergency room, and is certified in trauma, flight nurse training, critical care and emergency nursing. She has also worked on transplants and open heart surgery. She learned from some attorney friends that there was a lack of medical expertise in the legal community, so she took paralegal training, finishing it in June of 1992, and decided to try to work as a contract paralegal or a consultant to attorneys in medical areas. She gradually put her business together through advertising in the Colorado Bar Association's monthly journal, *The Colorado Lawyer*, and in brochures sent to attorneys working in personal injury, products liability, and medical malpractice areas, as well as by referrals from doctors who knew her.

Deborah does everything from straight paralegal work, such as organizing medical files, interpretation of data, and deposition summarizing, to case managing, which is acting as the client advocate in dealing with the health care system and insurance companies. For Deborah, the case management is sometimes done for the attorney's client, and sometimes for his client's employee. It might also be done with an insurance company or companies that do case management utilization review—companies, for example, that work to guarantee that a particular patient receives the proper medical procedures in the proper sequence at a good price; that no repetitive testing is done, that lengths of stay in treatment are monitored, whether the treatment is inpatient, outpatient, surgical, or chiropractic.

Case management fees are paid in some cases by a group health plan or an insurance company, and sometimes Deborah works directly for the patients. The need for case management work arises typically in the case of catastrophic injury requiring long-term, expensive patient care. The consultant's role is not just to save money, but to be sure the client is getting the most "bang for his buck." For example, if an automobile victim has no group health and there is a limit on insurance coverage for the injuries after which the patient will be relying on Medicaid for care, it is important to use the insurance funds available first for items Medicaid will not cover. This work requires not only medical knowledge, but also an understanding of how government entitlement programs operate. For example, in one case, Deborah worked with the insurance company that was paying out only $100,000. To prevent wasting the money, she negotiated discounts for hospital and rehabilitation hospital care so the insurance company could use the $100,000 optimally. Insurance companies pay the bills in the order they come in, and then stop paying. Medicaid would pay only a percentage of the costs for durable medical equipment (like a wheelchair and ramp), so she got the rehabilitation hospital to hold off sending their bill until the durable medical equipment had been paid for at 100 percent, then when Medicaid kicked in, the hospital would settle for Medicaid's 70 percent of the hospital care costs. Deborah also coordinated contractors to get a patient's house revamped, talked with the patient's parents, physicians, etc. Then the patient went home and things went very well. Once the $100,000 was used up, Deborah's case management work was over.

Case management consulting can be a one-time shot, giving opinions and recommendations, or the consultant can be actively integrated through the entire case. Deborah says attorneys in such cases need a liaison, a third party, because often when a lawsuit is in the works there exists an antagonistic relationship between the attorney and the medical providers. Deborah can speak legalese, intelligently conversing with both attorneys and physicians.

Deborah does some occasional advertising, and takes a doctor or attorney to lunch sometimes to network. She uses a home computer on which she writes up reports using WordPerfect. Deborah believes anyone wanting to do case management consulting should have heavy duty medical skills from a diverse and clinical background and, she advises, "If you're actively working still in the medical field, even part-time, you are more believable. You need to keep up with the new stuff coming out all of the time. You need to be involved in the networking groups—in nursing, case management, insurance and rehabilitation, nurses groups." And, as

Deborah discovered, beginning paralegal salaries were far below what she was making as a nurse—which provided an incentive for freelance work.

Deborah sees herself as a demanding, driven patient advocate. She enjoys focusing on case orchestration entirely, doing something besides trying to make the most money.

People considering a medical and paralegal combination will want to contact the American Association of Legal Nurse Consultants (AALNC), an organization of registered nurses who do legal consulting work (information in appendix A). The AALNC began in 1989, and by October of 1993 had a membership of 1400. The organization sees medical legal nurse consulting as a separate profession from paralegals, and one involving more expertise than a paralegal's, because of their medical knowledge. AALNC members must maintain an active nurse's license.

Proofreader

In discussing the role of scopists, we mentioned that after the scopist has scoped and edited a court reporter's notes, the document is often proofread for accuracy and correct punctuation and grammar. As a result, there is a body of job opportunities closely related to scopists for professional proofreaders. In some areas in fact, according to Eileen Hyatt of Hyatt Court Reporting in Denver, many more proofreaders than scopists are used in the court reporting industry to edit the final documents produced by court reporters.

As an agency owner, Eileen hires many proofreaders. She indicates that proofreaders usually have at least a 4-year college degree, and many have graduate degrees. Because of their work, they usually love words and language, and adore finding something that isn't quite right in a transcript. Many proofreaders are between jobs or occupations; some are writers, novelists, or journalists who want to work at home. The profession can be difficult to do full-time, however, because it is hard to maintain focus for eight hours a day.

Proofreaders earn between $7.50 and $10.00 an hour, but the best thing about this job is the freedom it allows in someone's schedule. Some proofreaders have medical backgrounds and capitalize on the need for that special knowledge. Proofreading is also a good way to put yourself through court reporter school, building multiple skills at once while developing a network in the reporting community.

Social security claimant representative

The paralegal work described in chapters 1 through 3 involves situations where paralegals work entirely under the supervision of licensed attorneys. Social Security claims is an area where nonlawyers can represent clients directly, without the direct supervision of a licensed attorney, and without running afoul of unauthorized practice of law statutes (see appendix B for information on the unauthorized practice of law).

Most of the problems that arise in Social Security involve the Administration's decisions about who is and is not eligible for disability payments. According to William R. LaVere in an article in the Spring, 1993 issue of the *National Paralegal Reporter*, there is a huge, currently unmet need for people to represent claimants through the appeals process. Social Security Administration Regulations permit nonlawyers to represent claimants if the representative has good character, is capable of giving help to the claimant, is not for any reason disqualified or suspended from doing so by the SSA, and is not prohibited by any law from doing so. The representatives may charge a fee for the representation.

When someone receives a notice that his or her application for disability benefits has been denied, they typically have no idea what the criteria are for eligibility or how to rectify the situation. A disability claim involves complex issues and a definition of disability, as set out by law, that distinguishes many factors, both medical and vocational; and, of course, the regulations that have been prepared to govern the complex law are barely comprehensible to the claimants. Consequently, even those claimants who do succeed at their own appeals take much longer to do so than they would if they were represented by someone specializing in the area.

These factors all go toward making Social Security disability claims an area where someone familiar with the process could be of great help to a number of people. As LaVere says, "The key to proficiency in this area is experience—representing claimants on a regular basis."

If you are interested in this area of work, you might wish to read Mr. LaVere's book, *Social Security Disability: A Comprehensive and Practical Guide to Effective Representation of Claimants*, which is in an expanded second edition (available through LCS Publications, P. O. Box 3470, Arlington, VA 22203). In addition, be sure to investigate whether any sort of liability or malpractice insurance is available to cover your work, since you would not be covered by an attorney's malpractice insurance policy.

There might be a nonprofit center or group assisting the disabled with these appeals in your area. If so, talk to them, or volunteer some time assisting in their cases, to get a feel for whether many such appeals are actually feasible and what sort of fees might be available to the nonlawyer representative in these cases.

Many paralegals yearn to represent clients who really need their help. This is a potential opportunity for gratifying work. The following profile of one company—composed of four paralegals in Bartlesville, Oklahoma—is an example of the business.

Paralegal Support Systems, Inc.

Dan Laird is president of Paralegal Support Systems, Inc., in Bartlesville, Oklahoma, a company that has been in business for six years largely doing Social Security disability claims. Dan's company has four paralegals who work on a contingency fee basis to help people obtain Social Security disability benefits. Some of his clients have been injured in car accidents or have back injuries and others are elderly and ill. Dan gets involved when a person files for benefits and the claim is denied. As Dan says, most people don't know their rights in this area nor do they realize that they can file a request for a hearing in front of a judge. Dan's company therefore prepares briefs and represents the person at the court. His success rate, Dan says, is nearly 80 percent.

It seems there's no end to what people can do who are good on a keyboard and have excellent English skills. Legal transcription is another excellent home-based work opportunity for people who are intelligent, have excellent spelling skills, keyboard accuracy and speed, and familiarity with legal terminology. The following profile illustrates one such business.

Miriam Moretz

Like many legal transcriptionists, Miriam ("Sam") Moretz worked as a word processor in a law firm for many years. When she decided to try working at home, Paralegal Associates of Denver was one of her first clients, and still is today. She types deposition summaries for them from dictation tapes, and also gets some overflow work from a nearby typing service. Paralegal Associates uses Sam because she does more than just typing—she is a part of the paralegal service's quality control program; she reads what she is transcribing and makes sure it is logical and grammatically correct.

Sam says it takes awhile to get an independent legal transcriptionist business going. Don't count on a good income for the first few months, and don't turn down work. She found herself typing math textbooks and editing manuscripts for publishers, for example. The exposure to editing has been very helpful—some of the unexpected work amounted to a paid education.

Sam has minimal overhead. She uses *Black's* legal dictionary, as well as other references for looking up medical and legal terminology. She recommends that you ensure your equipment is compatible with most law firms' systems. According to Sam, WordPerfect is really *the* software to use. She also mentions that you might need an inkjet or laser printer.

What can you charge? Try to find out what word processing services in the area charge—in Sam's area is was $20 an hour. Remember that you will be paying your own Social Security taxes, income taxes, insurance, your own equipment and work space, and your own vacation time. You have to be able to make your own deal and ask for what you need to cover your costs. Don't underbid. If you undercut others in order to get work, you might not realize how many places your money needs to go and find you are unable to cover your costs.

As with some of the other careers we have outlined in this book, it is hard to get this business started without a built-in client base—the best is the law firms or lawyers you have already worked for and who know and trust you. Also, the "feast or famine" syndrome in law practice extends to transcriptionists as well as other legal services. Sam found she was either buried or starved for work much of the time. It is important to have a couple of steady, trusting clients in order to make transcribing work. It also helps to have a network of transcriptionists or word processors to share overload assignments.

Currently, there seems to be a lot of obstacles to this work. As Sam learned when she started her legal transcription business seven or eight years ago, it is very difficult to get attorneys to trust you with their files or materials unless you are well known to them and very fast and convenient. They have confidentiality concerns and they are used to having their support staff very handy and are rarely patient for their work product. If attorneys know you well, that should assuage their concerns about inappropriate disclosures. Sam routinely signs a confidentiality agreement with new clients, promising not to disclose anything she learns from the materials she types.

Communications systems to return a finished product instantly to the law firm via modem might resolve the time and accessibility problems, but increase start-up costs and overhead. Unless you are confident a law firm is eager to keep you despite your move to operate a home-based business, don't invest in the equipment.

The obstacles might be manageable in many cases. Some attorneys have been thoroughly spoiled in recent years when they had enough cash to enjoy instant, excellent support at their fingertips. Since law firms are now struggling with issues of economy, a variety of support solutions might catch on. That situation, combined with technology that can move both dictation and documents instantly across town, might improve opportunities for good transcriptionists.

Selecting your niche

We have profiled here just a few of the many specialized areas that people can create. While the legal field tends to move slowly and maintain its traditional ways, the next decade will see tremendous change because of the increasing specializations of lawyers who will then need increasingly specialized support services. We are also convinced that there are dozens of other, similar opportunities for entrepreneurs to apply some special knowledge to a new need—whether to do something faster, to find a more efficient solution or a clearer explanation, or simply to achieve a more economical way of working so that their clients can increase their profit. You too might have the entrepreneurial spirit to create a niche business. Think it over.

7 The entrepreneurial path

Being your own boss is appealing. Many people working in the legal arena feel they have gone as far as they can in their positions, that there's no place to go on without becoming a lawyer—something not everyone wants. They wonder "what next?" This chapter shows you how you can answer that question for yourself by creating a small business and becoming your own boss. The material in this chapter specifically addresses seven critical steps in establishing your own business:

1. Double-check your decision.
2. Develop a business plan.
3. Organize and plan your financial resources.
4. Attend to business.
5. Resolve working at home issues.
6. Determine your marketing strategy.
7. Pay attention to details.

Step 1: Double-check your decision

Many people want to be in business for themselves, so you are not alone in your goals. Though there are no official figures, recent estimates from LINK Resources show that about 14 million people are self-employed and work from home in full-time businesses of their own, while another 10.5 million moonlight from home while working another job. Small businesses especially are growing, with over 700,000 small business incorporations each year, and additional hundreds of thousands of other sole proprietorships and partnerships. Another statistic of note is that perhaps as much as 70 percent of these small businesses are run by women, with over 300,000 more women trained by the Small Business Administration each year.

However, statistics also show that as many as two out of three businesses fail—usually within the first year. This happens for a variety of reasons, including excessive spending, poor management, cash flow problems, inadequate marketing, and bad service/product. The point is, are you sure you are ready and able to launch your venture? It can be a great help to talk over your plans with someone, preferably someone who knows you and knows what the undertaking will involve. Without being pessimistic, we suggest that you take some time in the initial phase of your exploration to reflect upon the reasons behind your decision.

- Do you want more freedom and flexibility?
- Do you want more opportunity to earn money?
- Do you want to escape from a bad boss or the stress of a difficult job?
- Do you have the personality traits that match the business?
- Are you willing to learn what you don't know?
- How hard can you work to make your business a success?
- How hard will you work?
- Do you have the character to survive the initial start-up phase?

These are all useful questions to answer before you plan your business and future. It can be difficult to get yourself to sit down and answer these personal questions objectively. This explains why so many people fail in new businesses: they just aren't willing to look closely at themselves and ask the right questions.

In fact, a Canadian study found that people who have realistic expectations for themselves and their business have a higher success rate. For example, those who are realistic about how much money they can earn and how long it takes to build a client or customer list are more successful. They don't buy into the "start-a-business" hype that suggests they can quickly make loads of money with little work. They don't think of self-employment as utopia, a solution to all their problems. They realize that building a business income and a new lifestyle takes time and that they will have to invest some money and lots of energy.

Think about what others in your field with a background and experience similar to yours have been able to accomplish, and over what period of time. Looking at the experience of others similar to yourself gives you a baseline for what's realistic. Success is a process that has a schedule of its own, however; if you can see a way to do things more quickly or better, don't limit yourself to what you've seen others do.

We also believe that people often discount their abilities and don't give themselves enough credit for their native talents and skills. Many people can prosper in their own business if they recognize that they truly have the talents, skills, and learning ability to succeed. Knowing yourself deeply allows you to make more meaningful assessments of your skills, abilities, and interests. Don't just jump to conclusions about your decision to start or not start a business. Really think it through, and see if you are minimizing your talents, or perhaps overblowing your immediate knowledge.

Figure 7-1 contains a list of questions for you to consider in double-checking your decision to have your own legal business. Rather than asking you to answer these questions with a simple yes or no, we've included a column for your "qualifying thoughts" in which we suggest that you reflect as deeply as you can about why you said yes or no, and what additional factors you might need to consider to support your conclusion. This column is a kind of "gray area" in which you can write your hesitations and reservations.

Questions	Y	N	Qualifying Thoughts
Personal Questions			
Have you had an interest in running your own business for a long time?			
Do you enjoy technical details, formal systems, and complex terminology?			
Are you willing to learn new things and to work in a profession that requires continual learning?			
Is your enjoying your work more important to you than your income potential?			
Are you independent minded and a self-starter?			
Are you persistent, organized, disciplined, trustworthy, creative, and not easily discouraged—or could you be?			
Are you confident about yourself and comfortable working with professionals such as lawyers, doctors, and business executives?			
Is your family supportive of your interest and effort to start your own business?			

7-1
Questions to ask to double-check your decision.

Questions	Y	N	Qualifying Thoughts
Personal Questions			
Have you had an interest in running your own business for a long time?			
Do you enjoy technical details, formal systems, and complex terminology?			
Are you willing to learn new things and to work in a profession that requires continual learning?			
Business Questions			
Have you had any business training in management, marketing, or sales?			
Do you have many contacts you can use now to get business?			
Have you determined your income needs?			
Do you know how to do bookkeeping and accounting?			
Do you enjoy taking classes on business issues or reading about business issues in newspapers and magazines?			
Do you enjoy working with computers?			
Are you open to learning to use new software in desktop publishing, accounting, and other areas?			
Do you enjoy negotiating?			
Are you willing to do cold calling and selling yourself?			
Are you willing to seek business advice from others and accept suggestions and criticism?			

7-1
Continued.

If you haven't decided firmly to run your own business, you might wish to peruse a few of the resources in the following section.

Working from Home: Everything You Need to Know About Living and Working Under the Same Roof (4th ed.), Paul and Sarah Edwards, Jeremy P. Tarcher/Putnam, 1994.

Finding Your Life Mission, Naomi Walpole, Stillpoint Publishing, 1989.

Running a One-Person Business, Claude Whitmyer, Salli Raspberry, and Michael Philips, Ten Speed Press, 1989.

What Color Is My Parachute?, Richard Bolles, Ten Speed Press, (updated annually).

Live Your Vision, Joyce Chapman, Newcastle Books, 1990.

Resources for double-checking your decision

Support

One last question to consider: Do you have the support of your family and friends? Running your own business will completely change your lifestyle, at least initially, and will be much easier if you have the support of family and friends. Family and loved ones need to be aware of and supportive of the changes that starting your business venture will make in all of your lives. For example, if you are working on your own, you might have to put in longer hours than you had been working in a previous job. Your income might dip at first while you get your business underway. So alert your family and loved ones to all the changes you expect and to the fact that there might be other changes that you can't predict. Then make sure you account in your plans for their concerns and reactions to these changes.

Step 2: Develop a business plan

Given that most businesses that fail do so during the first year, it is in your best interest to do at least some amount of planning before starting your business. Most people do not take the time to write out even the slimmest of business plans, and as a result their business ends up meandering through ups and downs without any true goals. Research sponsored several years ago by the Ford Foundation shows that people who write down specific goals are considerably more likely to achieve them. As an entrepreneur, it's important that you write out a business plan to:

- understand your business and your goals;
- scope out and know your market and your competition;
- determine the best way to target your market;
- define how your business fits into the industry;
- understand pricing and fees in your area.

These issues are all vital to ensuring you have the best advantage when you open your door. The information you get in researching these issues can influence what you name your business, how large a geographic area you should advertise in or do direct mail for, how many clients you might be able to get in your first year until you build up a reputation and a referral base, how long it might take you to break even or have a positive cash flow, and a host of other critical issues that might determine whether or not you remain in business.

Business plans are a map to your destination. A business plan usually begins with a statement of what is called your company "mission," meaning a terse group of phrases that explain your business and stress what you intend to achieve in the eyes of your customers. The mission statement is best viewed as what you would like customers to think about you, so don't include such statements as "I will make $100,000 within two years."

There are many ways to establish goals and a business plan, from the formalized documents you might need to produce if you apply for a business loan to the informal list-making you might do the night you lose your job and decide to start your own company. The following outline is a brief business plan suitable for a home-based business.

I. *OVERVIEW*
  1. *General description of the business.*
  2. *Mission statement.*
  3. *Brief description of your business goals and financial requirements.*
II. *PERSONAL ANALYSIS*
  1. *Strengths and weaknesses analysis.*
  2. *Statement of services you will offer.*
  3. *Technology and resources.*
  4. *Major competitors and competitive positioning.*
  5. *Factors determining success.*
III. *ANALYSIS OF CLIENT COMMUNITY*
  1. *Definition and description of local legal community.*
  2. *Growth rate and changes expected in local legal community.*
  3. *Financial characteristics of the local legal community.*
IV. *MARKET ANALYSIS*
  1. *Size of your total market.*
  2. *Market segmentation.*
  3. *Market barriers to entry.*
  4. *Pricing structure.*
  5. *Marketing mix (advertising, public relations, sales promotions).*
V. *FINANCIAL ANALYSIS*
  1. *Budget projections and pro formas.*
  2. *Financial schedules and statements.*

Each of these sections helps you define in concrete terms your goals, expectations, and policies. The more precisely you can identify and target your responses to these questions, the better you will be able to understand your business and fulfill your objectives. Planning also enables you to weed out faulty thinking, since it forces you to examine your goals as accurately as you can. By writing out your ideas and thoughts, you might discover inconsistencies, as well as gaps you didn't think were there.

Especially if you have a background in the legal field, and think that you know what you are doing, a business plan can prevent you from falling into a common trap: believing that you know your market just because you have been in the business. Working for someone else is still not quite the same thing as working for yourself.

For more information on developing your business plan, many states publish through their Department of Commerce numerous pamphlets and publications that can help you organize and learn about business planning. There are also various bureaus often affiliated with business schools that can assist you in developing your plans. Alternatively, contact the Small Business Administration for a list of their publications at P.O. Box 1000, Ft. Worth, TX 76119 or call them at 1-800-U ASK SBA to find out the nearest office to you. There is also the SBA Office of Women's Business Ownership that you can reach at (202) 205-6673. Founded in 1978, the National Association of Women Business Owners—now with over 7000 members and 50 chapters across the country—can also be of service to women seeking information and mentoring when opening a new business. They can be reached at (312) 922-0465 or by writing to 600 South Federal, #400, Chicago, IL 60605.

Picking your company name

One important aspect of your business plan is your company name. Now is the time to select the moniker by which you want to be known. Your company name is a critical factor in many businesses. Much has been written about this topic, but let's summarize a few points:

You can choose a name to reflect your location, your service, your goal, or your personal attention. Spend some time considering your business name, and don't settle too quickly on one. Sound out a few options with friends, and hopefully with people who are similar to your potential clientele. Make sure the name is memorable and portrays your best image given your market. Avoid names that sound like other companies in your area.

A note on partnerships

One possibility for some people to consider is that, through your planning or your background, you might find a person who is interested in forming a partnership with you. Some people in business recognize that they cannot handle all the work, or that they could use a partner who has different skills, such as marketing experience or a nursing background. While this option isn't for everyone—since some paralegal or legal related jobs cannot support more than one person—partnerships can be very profitable since you can take advantage of two minds that each contribute ideas, time, and contacts to help the business grow. A few people we interviewed were sharing a business with others or started as a collective of individuals initially to help each other for overload work. Some paralegal partnerships, however, have not fared well. If you plan a partnership, give it a lot of thought, and draw up a detailed partnership agreement to cover all the eventualities.

Step 3: Organize & plan your financial resources

Calculate your start-up costs

Start-up capital is a critical issue in anyone's decision to leave a job and go solo. Many freelance paralegals agree that you must be financially prepared for an uncertain future, although the definition of how uncertain it can be varied. We recommend the following steps.

Begin by determining what start-up costs you will have. Regardless of whether you are working for an agency or for yourself in your home, you will probably need to invest in a few items such as equipment, books, phone, answering machine, or more.

Your minimum set-up might be as little as a few hundred dollars or as high as several thousand, depending on what you need, and how elaborate the stationery and supplies you choose. Of course, if you already have the equipment you need, your start-up costs will be minimal—apart from the cost of supporting yourself until you get enough business coming in.

Use the list in Fig. 7-2 to estimate your start-up costs. Add more money if you know or think you will need any of the other equipment on the list. Also add in an account for cash you will need to cover initial operating expenses until you receive your first income.

7-2

Start-up costs. Estimate a high and low for how much you will need to spend on each item.

	Low	High
Business cards, letterhead, envelopes, etc.	_____	_____
Business licenses & other fees	_____	_____
Consulting & training fees (legal, tax, computor tutor, etc.)	_____	_____
Initial marketing costs of brochures, etc.	_____	_____
Office equipment	_____	_____
Telephone	_____	_____
Answering machine or voice mail	_____	_____
Computer	_____	_____
Monitor	_____	_____
Printer	_____	_____
Fax machine	_____	_____
Modem	_____	_____
Copier	_____	_____
Scanner	_____	_____
Software	_____	_____
Office furnishings	_____	_____
Desk, chair, filing cabinets, lighting, etc.	_____	_____

	Low	High
Remodeling of home office (if needed)	_____	_____
Telephone installation costs	_____	_____
Initial operating expenses (if any)	_____	_____
Other start-up expenses specific to your business	_____	_____
Total start-up costs	$_____	$_____

Next, determine how much money you need to have coming in each month by calculating the following three items, then take a look at Fig. 7-3, which contains a worksheet to calculate these costs.

Calculate your gross income needs per month

- Living expenses—How much do you need to live on? This is the "salary" you will need to support yourself and your family. Be sure to include taxes and fringe benefits such as health insurance formerly covered by your employer.
- Direct costs—How much it will cost you to be in business, including the cost for travel, phone charges, and materials and supplies used in serving your clients.
- Overhead—How much does it cost you to run your business each month in general expenses not attributable to any particular client? These include the costs of being in business: general marketing, advertising, utilities, office furniture, and equipment.

Calculating gross salary	Low	High
Auto expenses	_____	_____
Clothing	_____	_____
Food	_____	_____
Health insurance	_____	_____
Home maintenance	_____	_____
Entertainment	_____	_____
Education	_____	_____
Medical and dental care	_____	_____
Personal care	_____	_____
Rent or mortgage	_____	_____
Taxes (federal, state, self-employment)	_____	_____
Utilities	_____	_____
Other living expenses	_____	_____
_____	_____	_____
Subtotal salary	$_____	$_____
Calculating direct costs		
Cost of materials	_____	_____
Travel to and from client sites	_____	_____
Long-distance phone calls	_____	_____
Supplies	_____	_____

7-3
Calculating gross income per month. Estimate a high and low for how much you would need to spend each month on each item.

Calculating direct costs	Low	High
Other	_____	_____
_____	_____	_____
Subtotal direct costs	$_____	$_____

Calculating overhead

	Low	High
Insurance	_____	_____
Interest or loan payments	_____	_____
Marketing costs (advertising, publicity)	_____	_____
Maintenance	_____	_____
Office supplies	_____	_____
Postage	_____	_____
Professional fees (legal, accounting)	_____	_____
Telephone & fax	_____	_____
Utilities (above household usage)	_____	_____
Other	_____	_____
_____	_____	_____
Total overhead	$_____	$_____
Total monthly needs	$━━━━	$━━━━

7-3
Continued

Compare income needs & work plans

Now that you know your three income needs, you are in a position to sit down and calculate a total monthly target income, including (a) how much you would have to collect to cover your total costs, and (b) how many hours you would have to work per month at a given hourly rate (using the going rate for your type of work in your area) to achieve those goals. It is important to consider that you must spend some number of hours each month doing nonbillable activities such as marketing, administration, and running errands. Be conservative, therefore, in calculating how many hours you can actually bill out each month. For example, many people automatically calculate that if they can charge $25 per hour, they can earn $1000 a week billing out at 40 hours per week. But that's a gross income of $50,000 a year—with two weeks vacation. Be practical and cut by 15 to 20 percent the number of billable hours you think you might have per week.

Alternatively, if you find that you would have to work more hours per week or month than are practical, reverse your calculation and assume you will work only a certain number of hours. Divide those hours into the total gross income you need per month to find out what you would need to charge. Now ask yourself, is it possible that you can charge this amount? Have you been underestimating how much you might be able to get? If you are more qualified, or can do what you offer faster, better, or more conveniently, then you might be able to charge more.

Calculating your needs is critical. Some people simply figure out how much they might need for living expenses and then add 30 percent to cover benefits and expenses. For example, if you're currently making $35,000 a year and want to maintain that level, you would calculate that working 52 weeks a year at 40 hours a week, that salary amounts to a little under $17 an hour. Therefore, if you were in your own business and you needed to cover your own benefits and expenses, adding another 30 percent would mean that you should charge $22 an hour as a freelance paralegal. We recommend, however, that you calculate as closely as possible what your expenses are, the salary you will need, and go into as much detail as you can about your direct costs and overhead.

Like many freelance paralegals, you might need to save or even borrow money to finance your start-up costs. Many paralegals also recommend that freelancers calculate the cash flow they will need and be sure they have enough potential clients to meet that need before giving up the security of a full-time job. Some recommend that you have at least a year's financial support ahead of time, and that includes the money necessary to cover business expenses, as well as meeting the family budget needs.

However, expecting a paralegal to have saved even six months' salary is asking too much, according to Cheryl Templeton. Rather than an amount of money, Cheryl suggests you prepare during the years you are getting your job experience, by paying off your debts and investing in the necessary equipment and supplies, especially a computer, software, and library materials—whatever you will need to do your work. Get your home office furnished and equipped while you are still employed. Develop a potential client base too, because the most important asset in starting an independent business is a potential and reliable client base, people you know will call you for work.

For example, Cheryl worked part-time developing her independent business while she was still employed, so that by the time she finally went entirely independent, she had her basic office ready, clients already loyal to her, and a business already going. In addition, she paid down her credit cards so she had no debt; that also gave her available credit should she need it for supplies or other expenses.

Do not be discouraged by the investment in training and experience necessary to develop a freelance paralegal business. The need for paralegals in every feasible arena continues to grow, and the need for freelance paralegals appears to be growing even faster, as the business and legal communities rely on more flexibility in their employment practices.

If you have a plan for an independent business when you are working in your early paralegal jobs, you are several leaps ahead of your coworkers, who are probably working along without a goal. You will have a goal and will be able to work toward it as you are building your experience base, your reputation for excellence and performance, as well as the necessary client base and your home office, so that when the time is right, you can achieve your dream. It might sound like a cliché, but it is absolutely true: the better your foundation work is, the more successful your own business will be.

Insurance issues

While examining your financial resources, don't forget to pay some attention to your health insurance. Although some kind of universal health insurance as proposed by either President Clinton or an alternative plan from Congress is likely to be passed in the next year (as we write), you must make sure your home-based business has adequate insurance at an affordable cost. Insurance has kept many people from going out on their own full-time. As many as one-third of the self-employed do not have health insurance.

The best health insurance option for many self-employed will probably still be to become part of a group policy, such as those offered by local or state business, trade, or professional associations you can affiliate with. Before buying a policy, however, check it out thoroughly. In addition, if you are the sole source of your income, you might want to obtain disability insurance to protect from loss of income when you are unable to work due to illness or injury. It's important if you are depending on your business as the sole source of your income and would have no other forms of income should illness or injury prevents you from carrying out your work for an extended period of time. Discuss all these insurance needs with your agent.

Step 4: Attend to business

This step involves resolving the many business details that home-based businesses face, from zoning issues to setting up an office.

Zoning

Every local community has ordinances governing what, if any, kind of commercial activity can be done in residential neighborhoods. In many cases, home-based professional work is acceptable. However, many local zoning ordinances have not been updated since the industrial era when communities wanted to protect residential neighborhoods from noise, pollution, danger, and congestion. Therefore, you need to find out exactly what you can and cannot do from your home and make your plans accordingly. To check your zoning situation, contact the zoning department at your city hall or county courthouse.

Business license

Most communities require a business license to operate any income-earning enterprise of any size. Going to the trouble to take out a business license says that you take your business seriously. So make it official; get your business license.

Office space

First, let's consider the tax consequences of having a home office. The space you use for your home office need not be a separate room. It can be a portion of a room such as your bedroom, but the portion of that room that you designate for your business must be used only for business. So if you don't have a separate room, you need to clearly mark out the portion of the room you use for work space with a divider, screen drape or furniture arrangement.

You are then able to deduct a pro-rated portion of your rent or mortgage interest, plus a proportional amount of your utilities bills and even upkeep on your home as business expenses. You must keep accurate records, of course, showing receipts and payments.

Concerning the physical aspects of your home office, we recommend that you read *Working from Home* by Paul and Sarah Edwards for additional information on how to set up an office for maximum efficiency and productivity. When you select which room you might be working in, it is important to think about things like noise level, interference from family and neighbors, ease of use, whether or not you need to add a door or a wall to enclose your office, or even if you have enough space to make it work.

Equipment

We highly recommend that, if at all possible, a home-based paralegal or legal-related business start out with as much basic office equipment as you can afford. It improves your productivity and adds to your professionalism. This means that having a computer, laser printer (or letter quality dot matrix), voice mail or high quality answering machine, fax machine, and even a modem. In today's environment, a reasonably equipped home office containing all the items named costs as little as $2000.

We also suggest these useful hardware items, if you can afford them.

Laptop computer   You can take it with you when you work on assignments outside your office, or use it as a backup when your regular computer is "down." As you might know, deadlines for legal work are rarely flexible, and attorneys count on you to have the required product to them promptly, no exceptions. If your sole computer crashes you could be looking disaster in the face. Be sure you are covered for that eventuality.

Fast letter-quality printer   Laser printers are what most law firms are using; your work product will look as if it came from a very professional law firm. The speed of the printer is important; printing a 35-page brief at 3 o'clock in the morning is a pain if you don't have a fast printer.

Modem   This is used both for transmitting documents electronically to clients and to log onto online services such as CompuServe, GEnie, and Dialog. Fortunately, the price of modems is now quite reasonable, but you should definitely buy the fastest modem you can afford, at least 9600 baud.

CD-ROM drive   As more and more products become available on CD-ROM, home-based businesses will benefit. The storage capacity of CD-ROM gives you access to entire libraries of information, and will without any doubt become the fastest-growing trend in the information business. Having a CD-ROM drive will enable you to compete with much larger businesses.

Copier   Depending on your area of practice, a high-speed, high-quality copier can also be critical. Cheryl Templeton says she would not be without her high quality copier. She is usually so busy she has more work than she can complete in an eight-hour day, and time to run to a copy shop is not possible. Remember that you might end up at the copy store behind another business with a bigger rush job of their own, and so your work has to take a back seat until the other job is done. Of course, if you work in a forms-intensive area such as estate administration, you will need to make multiple copies on a regular basis, and so you must own a good copier. Paralegals working in trial preparation and document management also rely on high-speed copiers when they have to produce copies of documents to provide them to an attorney on short notice.

Phones   Various individuals find other kinds of phone equipment imperative to their efficient functioning: a cellular phone for staying in contact with clients or family from your car; and at home, a telephone system with a voice mail option from your local phone company or a separate voice mail board in your computer, so callers never get a busy signal (attorneys cannot afford to be put on hold).

Although a wide spectrum of computer equipment is available, we recommend that you purchase the best equipment you can afford because your business depends on reliability and quality. You will also be better prepared for the future if you get the highest level of technology available for your budget. For example, we recommend buying the fastest PC computer available now, Intel's Pentium microprocessor (a 586 chip), or at least a 486 PC. Although much paralegal work does not require the fastest chip, you can benefit from the extra power in many other needed business uses, such as creating your marketing materials with sophisticated desktop publishing software, using spreadsheet programs to help you do your own financial work, or using a database program to help track your client contacts. Many of the best of these programs are Windows-based products that run best on 486 technology.

Software

As for software, most people in a legal-related business must have WordPerfect to use for word processing. Fortunately, the new version of WordPerfect (6.0) also contains a number of nice features, including desktop publishing and the ability to import spreadsheet files, both of which you could use to create marketing materials. For other business needs, we recommend the following:

Check-writing software   Many easy-to-learn check-writing software programs such as Quicken (Intuit), Managing Your Money (MECA), or Microsoft Money can handle your essential financial tasks. They make bookkeeping about as easy as writing checks and recording transactions in a checkbook register! The benefit of these programs is that they handle money in the same way that most home businesses generally keep their books.

Calendar and appointment programs These programs are particularly useful for home-based businesses to automate your calendar, appointment schedule, and address book. They have a wide variety of features ranging in complexity from simple to highly sophisticated. Some of the programs are TSRs; that is, they reside in your computer's memory while you are working at other tasks. If you need to search a phone number, no matter what other software you're using, you can simply push a combination of keys and bring the program to the foreground so you can check your list of numbers, or schedule an appointment, or look up an address.

With other calendar programs such as Lotus Organizer (Lotus), Personal Calendar (Microsoft), and Calendar Creator Plus (PowerUp), your screen looks like an open appointment book with tabs along the edge, and you simply use your mouse to point to a tab you want and then go to the pages you need for addresses, phone numbers, to-do lists, appointments, scheduler, and so on. Other programs allow you to view your calendar in different increments, such as two days at a time, or a week, month, or whole year at a time.

Many of these appointment and calendar programs also have an automatic alarm function to remind you of appointments by beeping at an assigned time. When you enter an appointment you simply indicate that you want the alarm to alert you as the scheduled time approaches. (Of course, your computer needs to be turned on.)

Personal information managers (PIMs) PIMs offer more powerful features than calendar programs. They are actually specialized database programs that let you make "records" of information far beyond simple names, numbers, appointments, and dates, although the programs also have those capabilities as well. For example, with a PIM, you can take lengthy notes, track client profiles, store references to magazine articles, make lists of all kinds, and link them all together in groups. Then, whenever you need to find something, you can search through all the information you've stored using keywords or phrases, and any record that contains those words will appear on your screen.

InfoSelect (MicroLogic), PackRat (Polaris), and Ascend (NewQuest) are among the personal information managers that have been well received. Some of these programs are described as free-form databases, in that you are not restricted to predefined fields for your entries, as is the case with many database programs.

For example, paralegal Bonnie Twigg does not have a lot of software on her computer; but she found herself at a loss when she worked on a class action suit for four years with a large number of documents. Because she did not have a database system or know how to use one, she was actually quite worried about the fact that she was the only person who knew what was in the files and where they were. Had she known how to use a database program, the job would have been more efficient and the information accessible to more people on the case.

Library

Finally, a well-equipped library is an absolute necessity. You should at least create a library reflecting your practice area, certainly including the code sections for the area you work in. For example, you might need medical books if you do personal injury work, as well as practical handbooks on state evidence, federal evidence, federal and state civil procedure (beyond just the code).

Because paralegals utilize a lot of resource material in their work, you need a basic library in your own office, comprising:

- Legal forms samples.
- *Black's Legal Dictionary* or another equally good one.
- The *Blue Book of Citations*.
- Copies of *Legal Assistant Today* magazine.
- Paralegal association periodicals, such as the NFPA *Paralegal Reporter* and/or NALA's *Facts and Findings*.
- Bar journals covering your practice area.
- Materials from seminars in your practice area.
- Textbooks from your paralegal training.
- Handbooks for all your computer software.
- Resource material tailored to your practice area.

Susan Kligerman, who works in litigation and also does case management and consulting, has a seven-shelf bookcase crammed with a broad variety of reference and resource materials including materials on general paralegal issues, legal ethics, management (for use in her consulting work with law firms), legal forms, copies of ABA Journals, paralegal periodicals, directories of addresses and services, the zip code directory, government studies, form books and court rules in her practice area (litigation), and a shelf of materials from other practice areas for reference. She also has books on software, including not only the software she uses but information on software she has reviewed; dictionaries and a legal thesaurus; books on accounting and administration; continuing legal education (CLE) training video tapes; and some skills-for-success type books.

In addition to your personal library, you need to have access to a good legal library in your community, when your work requires research extending beyond your personal library. Brenda Conner suggests you might be able to negotiate library privileges by doing some free work for an attorney who has a good library—for example, you can donate 5 free hours of work a month in exchange for use of the law library. With that arrangement you might be able to do research late at night that you couldn't do at a university library or supreme court library. A college law school library is another alternative, but there it might be harder to spread out and focus—a private library is a better deal if you can arrange it.

One tendency to be wary of in setting up your home office, however, is what Herman Holtz, prolific author of consulting and business guidance books, calls *Taj Mahalitis*, the compulsion to spend excessive amounts of money equipping your business. One rule of thumb is to buy only when you've earned the money to make the purchase. Another option is to buy only equipment that improves your productivity and pays for itself in your next job. For example, if you need to send out direct mail letters and you can save yourself $500 in typesetting, design, and mailing expenses (by purchasing a laser printer), you might decide that the extra sum you spend buying it rather than a dot matrix printer is worth the investment. Similarly, splurging on a newer model high-speed modem that achieves 14,400 bps rather than a 9600 bps modem might pay off in faster transmissions and therefore greater productivity. Time is money, especially when you run your own business and do everything from receptionist to CEO.

Caveats in equipping your office

Be certain to keep exact records of all your purchases and office supplies. While you might never be audited, you are best prepared by having receipts for everything you have deducted against earnings. Remember that you can write off many standard business expenses, including office supplies, stationery and business cards, business software, shipping/postage charges, professional publications and books, business insurance, and advertising expenses, so keeping accurate records is a must. You can also write off up to $17,500 in equipment purchases as of 1993 (such as computers, printers, and office furniture), as long as your write-off does not exceed income. (That is, you cannot use the write-off to generate a loss.)

About taxes & home office deductions

In addition, be sure to establish your home office in such a way that you can legally take a business deduction for using part of your living quarters as your office. Whatever space you use, it must be used exclusively for business, and be separated from living space. So, even if you use just a part of a bedroom, you can deduct it as an expense by prorating the percentage of space used for business against your mortgage or rent. If you make any improvements to that space for purposes of your home office, you can also deduct those direct expenses. Be sure to check with your accountant for many specific issues about deducting for your home office.

Finally, be aware that there has been a lot of focus lately by the IRS and by state tax authorities on who is and who is not an independent contractor. If you are determined not to be an independent contractor, the people who hire you might be considered your employer and could be charged with employment-related taxes. To protect your clients, it is important to establish yourself as thoroughly as possible as an independent contractor.

Independent contractor vs. employee status

The IRS considers a number of factors in determining whether you are independent or not. You should discuss these with a tax attorney or your accountant, and take steps to make your status clear.

Some freelance paralegals feel print advertising helps verify their independent status. Others take out a fictitious business name as a way to show they are serious about their business. Even having business cards might help. Contracts are another one of the factors; whenever possible, it is wise to sign a contract for your project, identifying the nature of the work, the time period, and the fee. (You might draw up your own contract based on your knowledge of contracts, or use a software template contract, or hire your own lawyer to draw up a standard contract that you can modify for each client.)

State tax regulations might affect your practice as much as the IRS. In some states you might need a state tax license in order to hire subcontractors to help you on a job. Susan Kligerman discovered that since she works in Pennsylvania as well as New Jersey, she must address the fact that tax consequences can be different in each state. Keep this in mind if you are in a similar situation.

Step 5: Resolving work-from-home issues

You need to think about and arrange for solutions to the many problems you will face as a home-based entrepreneur. The following issues are critical, and failing to understand how to overcome some of them have led to the downfall of many businesses.

Motivation

One of the first issues that comes to mind when a home-based entrepreneur is asked to identify problems is motivation. Without the trappings of "work,"—an office, colleagues, even the transition time of a commute—many people find that they simply cannot stay motivated to work independently. They might sit down in the morning at their desk, but find that their concentration is interrupted by a myriad of other issues: family, errands, dinner plans, children, and so on. They might worry about the next job, about cash flow, about a previous client, or they might simply daydream staring out the window.

Nothing defeats the purpose of being self-employed more than a lack of motivation. Starting your own enterprise especially demands that you maximize your work flow and personal habits. You need to stay motivated and upbeat, learn how to tackle challenges, overcome defeats, and work at your very best if you want to succeed and be happy in your own business. Poor management, one of the leading reasons for business failure, does not necessarily mean only that the owner did not understand accounting, cash flow, or marketing mix. Poor management also means that the owner has a bad attitude, alienates people, or becomes so discouraged that an opportunity to save the business passes right in front of his or her eyes.

We highly recommend the excellent advice found in *Making It On Your Own*, by Paul and Sarah Edwards, which focuses on the psychology of being your own boss and maintaining your motivation. There are also numerous other books in the field of personal performance improvement, from Steven Covey's

Seven Habits of Highly Effective People to Anthony Robbins' *Unlimited Power* and Mihaly Csikszentmihalyi's *Flow: The Psychology of Optimal Experiences*. In addition to reading business literature, you might also read in the literature of creativity, positive thinking, and peak learning to build your knowledge of how to improve your attitudinal habits toward work.

Work priorities

Deadlines are a serious matter in the practice of law. Real deadlines are not negotiable; on the other hand, some deadlines can be for convenience. An experienced person can tell which are which, but even when the deadline is for convenience, take it seriously. Attorneys will not use a business that does not respect their deadlines.

In addition, you must also be careful not to get yourself into a situation of conflicting priorities. As Cheryl Templeton said, freelancers do not have an outside recourse to help them sort out conflicting priorities. This is true whether they are paralegals, summarizers, court reporters, or others supporting attorneys. Consequently, it is important not to accept work that cannot be completed in the accepted time. When a paralegal in a law firm finds herself pressed with too many assignments to complete in the expected time, there are partners or supervisors who can be consulted to resolve the time conflict. At the least, the two attorneys who each want something from you at the same time can be left to "duke it out" and set the priorities for the paralegal.

Furthermore, remember that your situation can often be complicated by the fact that many attorneys, when they give an assignment, seriously underestimate the time it will take to complete it. As a precaution, it's a good idea to contact the attorney if it appears that the time—and therefore the resulting cost—involved in the project is grossly out of line with his expectation. You might be approaching the project differently from the way he intended. Or, you might do as some people end up doing when they have worked very long on a project, and in the end, they might feel as if they have put in more time than they were supposed to. When it comes time to bill, they therefore charge less than they should. These are all judgment calls, and this is where you must think of your own needs as well, so that you don't sell yourself short.

Court reporters and scopists also have very short deadlines for their work, because deposition transcripts are often requested to be delivered within 24 or 48 hours of the deposition. Reporters work many evenings and weekends getting the work out on time. They find they need a network of other reporters and scopists to help with overflow. They take great pride in perfect work and, in fact, find themselves liable for erroneous transcripts.

Paralegals, like Fran Turner, would rather turn down work when they are overcommitted than turn in a sloppy job. Fran says "One complaint clients have about attorneys is that they don't get enough attention from the attorney; the same is true of us, we need to be paying attention to the clients we are working with, and not taking on too much so that we aren't able to provide competent services to them."

Keeping personal time

Another aspect of being your own boss is that you must protect your personal time. It is easy to fall into the trap of working nonstop or cutting into your evenings and weekends without thinking about the effects of this on your family and your own need for relaxation. Many legal assistants (both salaried and contract) tend to work themselves to the bone for lawyers, and it can become a co-dependent relationship. It is not unusual for freelance paralegals and other entrepreneurs to suffer under the perception that "no work is too much," or that no matter how much is done, it isn't enough. You have to be able to draw the line.

You might be familiar with the kind of person who asks when a project is due, then works right up until the deadline, regardless of whether or not the work needed that amount of time. If the client had given the person an extra two days, he would have filled that time as well. Beware of creeping workitis and perfectionism. These traits cut into your income possibilities as well as into your personal satisfaction.

Getting a support network

Ninety-six percent of people who go out on their own to work from home are glad they did and say they would do it again. But there is one thing missing from most home offices and that's *other people*—colleagues, mentors, co-workers, business associates, and peers. To keep from feeling isolated and to make sure you keep abreast of current developments, you need to take some initiative to be sure you have regular contact with colleagues, peers, and mentors.

Paralegal Fran Turner comments, for example, that if you are a very social person and like being around a lot of people, freelance paralegal work might not be for you, unless you work in an office setting on your assignments. She is comfortable being alone, but she does set up lunches or go out for company to meet with friends and get a change of pace from time to time. In a sense, you need to replicate the following types of social interaction that usually happen automatically when you're employed by an organization:

- Brainstorming ideas with colleagues.
- Commiserating with a fellow worker who knows what you're up against.
- Celebrating a victory with someone who can appreciate what you've accomplished.
- Accessing the grapevine to keep you abreast of the latest developments and inside scoop in your field or industry.
- Having a mentor show you the ropes, introduce you to the right people, cheer you on, and guide you to success.

If you depend exclusively on your family or friends for these needs, you will quickly burn them out and alienate them from supporting you. It is far better to satisfy your work needs for camaraderie and support by using professional contacts from associations or by simply having regular lunch meetings with a colleague. For example, you might schedule a regular Wednesday breakfast every two weeks at a local restaurant with a colleague just to stay in touch with that person and maintain perspective on your own work. Such a mid-week break can be a good way to catch up on news from someone else, compare notes, empathize with another person's situation, and recapture your own energy.

The last issue in this section is learning how to set and negotiate your fees. Many independents and home-based people are not comfortable in this area. They might feel that they can work for a lot less money than others since their expenses are lower, or they might feel they need to charge less than others in order to get the business. However, your fee is the lifeline of your business and for each hour you undercut your potential income by a few dollars (or more), you take food out of your own mouth and you might even give clients the sense that your work is of less value than a higher priced competitor.

Setting & negotiating a fee

For example, freelancer Terrie Burton screens calls from new potential clients: she gets all the details she can; she asks the type of case, the time frames involved, where the office is, what the staffing is on the case, and whether she will have secretarial support in case she has to pay for it herself. Sometimes Terrie sets a higher rate for certain new cases if she feels that the attorney has underestimated her work. Also, if an attorney suggests that the client will pay her fee, she reminds the attorney her arrangement is with the attorney, not with the attorney's client. (She also makes sure the attorney's malpractice insurance covers her work.)

For paralegals, we recommend that you obtain a copy of a salary survey for your area, conducted by a local association, or use a national survey from NFPA or *Legal Assistant Today* magazine. Most contain a section that outlines a range of typical paralegal billing rates, the hourly rate at which attorneys typically bill out paralegal services. Be aware of whether or not attorneys in your area are likely to charge your fees out directly as an expense to their clients, or if they add a premium to your fees when they prepare the client's bill. Some attorneys consider paralegal services to be a profit center and bill your services at a higher rate than what you charge them.

For example, in some areas in 1993 lawyers billed paralegal services out to clients at a rate between $50 and $75 per hour. Freelance paralegals could probably not ask for that rate, and would more likely be billing out for their services at $25 to $35 per hour. So find out whether attorneys who want to use your services will pass through your fees as a direct cost or will bill your work out at a typical paralegal billing rate of $50 to $75 per hour, and make a profit on your work. (In some areas, this might be considered unethical; in others, it appears to be common practice. If this is common in your area, you can take it into account in setting your fees.)

The goal is to learn through every means you have what the traffic will bear. Using your networking efforts and your association affiliations, you might be able to learn what the competition is charging. All these factors considered together help you decide how to bill your fees. Of course, remember you will not be paid for holidays, sick days, or vacation.

Brenda Conner found that for some projects she had to do a proposal, and she would have to think long term and analyze before quoting a price—in one case a client wanted a price for a project comprised of 780 boxes of documents needing review, and she couldn't tell, without looking at some of the boxes, what type of documents were there—memos, correspondence, invoices, pages covered with writing or pages with little writing, etc.; Brenda added a stipulation to the proposal that she might have to amend the proposal once she saw the documents. Then she kept the client apprised of how the project was going, so there were no jolting surprises for her or the employer.

When negotiating, remember to start out with the highest fee you can reasonably quote. Attorneys will inevitably negotiate with you to try to get your services for less. By starting high, you give yourself some leverage and room to come down.

Related to this topic, always stay on top of your own billings. Send out invoices as soon as you complete a project, and don't let them become overdue more than 30 days. As soon as it happens the first time with a client, place a phone call to let the person know that you have completed the work and are counting on the payment for your own business.

Ultimately, consider any hesitations you have about making and deserving your own money, and refute them. Although some people say that they are really in business because they like the work, it is downright foolhardy to earn less than you deserve for your services—especially in the legal field where many lawyers earn over $100,000 or $150,000 per year. Why should you settle for $25,000 when you could be making $35,000 or more if you priced your service more honestly with the value of your labor? Don't underestimate your potential.

One statement to use if a client disagrees with you over money is to say: "I'm sorry, but the company policy is . . . ." In phrasing your position like this, you depersonalize the rebuttal, and make your "company" seem larger than the two of you locked in that battle now. You need to speak from a position of strength although you needn't hesitate to compromise when necessary.

Each of the chapters in this book has already focused to some extent on the marketing techniques pertinent to your business, and marketing is a business requirement one cannot underestimate or forget. Every home-based or independent business must squarely face this issue, because without customers, you aren't in business. There is competition out there today that will constantly do marketing, and might someday attract your best clients if you don't market also. The point is, you need to do at least some form of marketing *all the time*, even when you have enough business at the moment.

Innovative but cost-effective marketing techniques take another volume to explain in detail, and we do not have space in this book to cover this topic in depth. But there are many basic principles that apply to anyone who wants to sell freelance services to attorneys or law firms. This section outlines some basic principles, and also mentions other hints obtained from our interviews.

For anyone providing services to attorneys, your former employers and coworkers are a prime source of business. Never burn these bridges in your legal career; stay in touch with people who know your work style and ethic, and who are familiar with your skills and expertise.

With that in mind, it helps to make sure your clients are pleased with your work, and keep them happy. Freelance law librarian Doriana Fontanella has obtained all her new accounts from attorneys who worked in firms where she had been the librarian, or attorneys referred to her by someone she had worked for. Court reporter Jan Burnham relies on former employers and referrals for her freelance reporting assignments. Paralegal/consultant Susan Kligerman keeps in touch with her clients by contacting them after an assignment to do a follow-up and asking if what she did was useful or helpful; or, in the case of her consulting, if what she did or what she suggested worked. However, she warns, do this carefully; don't make a pain of yourself. Freelancers who do a good job at a reasonable price tend to acquire a client base that provides them with regular work, and nearly everyone we interviewed agreed that without word of mouth and repeat clients they would be out of work.

The next best source of work is personal referrals from people you know to their attorney acquaintances, particularly when the person doing the referring has an excellent reputation. Moral: do excellent work at all times, no matter how small or insignificant the job might seem to be at the time, because you never know when a well done job will get you more opportunities. That extra step you think of taking, to please the client or show the client you remembered his preferences or his situation, should always be taken. Your reputation for excellence is your job security.

Step 6: Determine your marketing strategy

Use your former employers & coworkers

Use referrals

Gatekeepers

Gatekeepers are people who can open doors for you to new business or to other people who can get you business. While the concept is simple, people often neglect to recognize that strategy. We suggest you identify early on in your business who your gatekeepers might be. One activity is to create a *gatekeepers network*, as follows. On a sheet of paper, write down the names of each person or client to whom you are planning to sell your services. Stemming from each name (as in a family tree pattern), write down names of people who these people do business with. Keep track of this network and add to it over time as you hear conversations and learn who knows whom. This kind of planning can pay off at some point in the future when you are pleasantly surprised to learn that you are only two phone calls away from someone who can bring you business.

For example, demonstrative evidence specialist Shelley English uses her legal friends and acquaintances to help her get a chance to do presentations at large law firms. These presentations eventually pay off, as associates begin to use her work in their cases. Her friends have gatekeeper power, and she makes use of it.

Networking

Besides your employment contacts, networking includes reaching out to other people who know you. Contacts in the legal community are your most valuable marketing tool if you have services to provide to lawyers or paralegals, whether you are a freelance paralegal, court reporter, deposition summarizer, consultant, or creator of demonstrative evidence. Because attorneys are, for very good reason, religiously cautious about the services they provide to their clients, they are reluctant to hire support services with whom they are not already familiar. In legal work, there is very little time or money available to spend on false starts or on poor work product. Everyone interviewed for this book listed networking as their prime marketing tool, second only to their contacts with former employers. The following is a list of good networking opportunities.

- Local and national professional associations.
- The local bar association. Many have associate memberships for nonlawyers.
- Participate in training programs by teaching or serving on an advisory board.
- Women's or men's professional or business groups.
- Chamber of commerce groups (especially helpful in small communities).

Join these organizations and read their publications to increase your own awareness of who in the legal community might have need for your services. Even if they do not have nonlawyer memberships, many bar associations permit nonlawyers to attend meetings and serve on committees.

In addition to a membership, use your professional, bar, and civic organizations to get involved in ways that demonstrate your professional and civic attitude and commitment. Doing a fundraiser or helping on a mailer provides you with an opportunity to contribute to your profession and the community while you form connections and increase your visibility. Some of these involvements might be:

- Bar and paralegal associations often have special committees for specific practice areas, so consider doing some committee work.
- Attend luncheons and seminars and meet people. More than likely you'll be asked what you do, an invitation to sell the value of your services.
- Attend or speak at seminars (CLE) and meetings.
- Volunteer to write articles for bar publications or professional journals.
- Volunteer to deliver legal services to the indigent.

Phyllis Cardoza is an excellent example of what association involvement can bring. Through her work with the Los Angeles Paralegal Association, and the Beverly Hills Bar Association, she got more and more involved in legislative issues in the area of probate law, and eventually served on committees that redrafted the California Probate Code. She was also responsible for getting a provision in that code that made paralegal fees a recoverable expense in probate. During that work she did a lot of writing and speaking, and is now a very visible and respected part of the probate law community in Los Angeles and California.

Computer consultant Cory Levenberg taught free seminars for lawyers as a way to develop his business contacts. By giving seminars on computers in law firms at local bar association meetings, he was invited to bid on consulting contracts that little by little built his business.

Meeting and socializing with people in activities help increase your visibility in the legal community. Talk to the people you meet and when they show an interest in what you do as a freelancer, give them your card. The next time you see them, they will probably remember, and after seeing you a few times, they might become comfortable using your service.

The paralegals, deposition summarizers, consultants, and court reporters we interviewed stressed that it's extremely important to join a professional association—they offer wonderful networking opportunities. Not only do you find out what's going on, and get support and advice, but you can meet other paralegals who are often asked for a contact by their bosses when a freelancer is needed. If that paralegal knows you from an organizational contact, you could be the hired freelancer.

Litigation freelancer Fran Turner regularly sees a number of probate paralegals at the paralegal association; they refer litigation work to paralegals they know who do work in the area. Brenda Connor met a number of attorneys at bar functions, and saw them again at CLE programs, where they became aware that she was also keeping herself current in the profession; Eileen Brown met a future client in a legal administration class; Phyllis

Cardoza goes to a lot of CLE sessions to educate herself and also because lawyers meet her again and again and the more they see her the more comfortable they feel with her; or they might see her up there giving a pitch on one of her projects. One attorney watched Phyllis this way for two years before he was finally comfortable entrusting work to her. She says it is a mistake for paralegals to sit with each other at these meetings, you never meet anybody that way.

Phyllis Cardoza finds paralegals are often too shy or timid to go out where attorneys are, talk to them confidently and give speeches. She admits she wasn't always confident either, but she has built up her confidence over time.

The personal touch in marketing

Everyone likes to do business with people they know and trust. To us, this means that the bottom-line objective of your marketing is to get to the potential client and find out what they need rather than focusing on your need for business. You need to get to know the client, and it also pays to like them and have them like you.

Boulder-area paralegal Cathy Schultheis (whom we profiled in chapter 2) gets most of her paralegal business from word of mouth and repeat clients because people like her work and recommend her. She explains "I spent a bunch of money on brochures, and I also put an ad in the Boulder Bar newsletter—and I got virtually nothing from these." She does mention that some attorneys kept her brochure, so she did gain a little name recognition, but she does not believe she gets much paralegal business from her advertising efforts.

By and large, Cathy says, word of mouth does the most: one client recommending her to another potential client, or one attorney recommending her to another. But she also has another promotional technique that she says is second best only to having a well-respected attorney recommend her—taking the attorney you want to get to know out to lunch. You have sixty minutes of undivided attention and since you're paying the bill—they listen to you. She suggests you find out first what kind of work they do, so you know if they have a need you can fulfill, and then sell yourself by telling them specifically how you could help. "Attorneys are generally not good at delegating, they tend to keep it all but then can't do it all, so tell them how exactly how you can save them time and money. For example, say the attorney has a case coming up and has stacks of documents; suggest something you know how to do, to help. If the person has no system, it's an easy sell. All you need to do is outline exactly how you can help: reviewing the files, looking at the documents, discussing the issues of the case, selecting what is critical and putting together a trial notebook, indexed and tabbed, etc. They can see from what you say that the result will be a more smoothly run case. The secret here is to focus on the needs of the attorney, not on yourself, your achievements, your credentials, or your need for business."

This personal method works well particularly in small communities, or with attorneys in a sole practice or small office. In a larger community and with attorneys in large firms, the personal contact might be harder to obtain. Cathy does recommend though that you join things like the local Chamber of Commerce and go to their meetings, to after hours meetings, and breakfast networking meetings.

Advertising

In general, we found that freelance paralegals found advertising of minimal value in their marketing efforts—it is extremely expensive and not cost-effective. Many people we interviewed tried it and found it unsuccessful. For example, Yellow Pages advertising attracts mostly the general public, not the attorneys who are the real targets of advertising for paralegals. Some advertising in bar journals was found helpful in promoting name recognition, but very few paralegals got work from the ads exclusively.

However, court reporters regularly place ads in legal publications, bar journals and directories. So do people who do computer consulting, demonstrative evidence, and videography. Court reporter Jan Burnham gets some jobs from her listing with the National Court Reporters Association.

Newsletters & postcards

Newsletters and postcards serve a dual purpose: they remind former clients of your name, and they update people about new information in the field or services you might offer. Some paralegals and consultants send occasional newsletters to clients, small law offices, former employers and others who might recognize the freelancer's name, highlighting some new capability the business is offering, a specialty service, recent or upcoming speaking engagements, or articles, etc. You can also remind clients of a change in a local court rule that will require certain steps to be taken in certain cases.

Newsletters, in particular, have become a popular tool with many businesses. Easily created using desktop publishing software, you can write your own articles (or pool with others in your field) to produce a sophisticated print piece for very little money. The newsletter can show people the quality of your writing, your knowledge of the law, or simply tell people about news events in your community that they might have an interest in.

Susan Kligerman plans to do a newsletter for her firm, discussing interactions of attorneys and paralegals, noting court recognitions of paralegal efficiencies. Susan is involved in numerous paralegal and bar associations and committees in New Jersey, primarily due to her sense of commitment to the profession—those involvements began years before she thought of becoming a freelancer. But the existing connections provide her with a natural, regular contact with a number of influential people. Susan says your exposure as a paralegal comes from attorneys' or paralegals' knowledge of you as an individual.

Stationery

A common mistake of new entrepreneurs is to underestimate the value of their company name, logo, and stationery. It truly pays off in the eyes of your clients to have well-designed and professionally printed stationery and business cards that portray your company well. Don't settle for the $29.95 special at the local office supply store. Standard business typefaces and logos are not distinctive enough for someone entering the legal service as an independent or home profession. Getting a logo designed can be expensive, however. We recommend that you design it yourself using a graphic design software program or that you hire a designer to create a very specialized logo for your company in exchange for services you can provide the designer.

Take stock regularly

Spend some time each month charting your progress. Although you might have started your business because you enjoy the work, you still need to be like a president or CEO who stands vigil at the control tower to be sure there are no accidents.

Step 7: Pay attention to details

Paying attention to details involves making sure that every aspect of your business reflects that you are a professional in every sense of the word. You are competent, punctual, honest, and forthright in your business dealings. In today's competitive environment, it is the little details that make a business stand out. This ranges from handing in clean documents and being prompt in your communications and calls to providing unsolicited advice and ideas, all the while being gracious to others. The following sections outline details we recommend you consider.

Keep a professional appearance

Nearly every freelance paralegal we interviewed stressed the importance of appearing professional whenever they had meetings with attorneys and their clients for any purpose. Brenda Conner felt that was an important factor in earning an attorney's respect and trust. Bonnie Twigg finds one of the advantages of being professionally dressed when she goes to any office is she has been asked to go to court or even to lunch with an expert witnesses or a client on the spur of the moment. You won't get these experiences if you are not professionally dressed.

Separate your life from your work

Clients usually don't want to hear about the travails of your life. In general, refrain from involving clients in your personal life, even if you think you are friends with them. It usually complicates your business, and people will unconsciously or consciously avoid you (even if they don't tell you so) if they think that your personal life will interfere with your ability to get the job done.

Schedule yourself

In the sections in chapter 2 on litigation paralegal practice, we discussed the importance of maintaining control of the docket (trial calendars) in order not to miss deadlines. A freelancer must also maintain a personal calendar or docket, in order to bear in mind the schedules of the various cases or projects on which she is working. Susan Kligerman uses Abacus Law (formerly called

Fast Tracker Plus) software for case management (from Abacus Data Systems, Inc., 6725 Mesa Ridge Rd. #204, San Diego, CA 92121 (800) 444-4979) for maintaining control of her docket and calendar. It has a conflict system, time and billing, and docket management that is especially valuable because it enables her to work with more than one set of court rules at a time.

Stay current

There are several attributes of a true professional, and paralegals have always considered themselves to be true professionals. They have taken responsibility for the direction paralegalism has taken in its 20–25 years of life; they have their own professional organizations and codes of conduct (the NFPA has a Model Code of Ethics and Professional Responsibility). They organize continuing education for themselves, and aspire to a high standard of excellence in their work. Several aspects of professionalism were stressed by the freelance paralegals in our interviews. They suggest strongly that anyone aspiring to be a freelance legal assistant be aware of the need to constantly stay informed on changes in their practice areas through continuing legal education (CLE); that they stay current on the issues affecting the paralegal profession; and that they work to demonstrate professionalism in the quality of the work and in their contacts with attorneys and clients.

In fact, Continuing Legal Education is a requirement for attorneys in many states. They are obligated to accumulate a certain number of credits in training, courses or seminars, to keep themselves current in ethical issues and in their practice areas. Although no such legal requirements exist for legal assistants, keeping themselves current in legal practice areas is a moral and professional obligation that paralegals take very seriously.

NALA offers a certificate called the CLA to demonstrate this professionalism. They require CLAs to maintain their status by taking courses regularly in ethics as well as in practice area updates. (See appendix for more information about the CLA designation.)

In its position paper on the issue of regulation of paralegals, NFPA endorses a two-tier regulatory scheme consisting of licensing and specialty licensing programs as a preferred form of regulation and states that such a program must include a CLE requirement. All the national paralegal professional associations provide seminars for such education, and most state and local associations also produce educational programs for legal assistants. In addition, most programs presented for attorneys welcome paralegal attendance (and some provide for reduced fees for paralegals).

Fran Turner, like most of the experienced legal assistants we interviewed, stressed the importance of staying current in the paralegal's area of practice. She feels that continuing education is critical to the effectiveness of a freelance paralegal. "The problem for a freelancer is that you have to pay for it out of your own pocket. In California it's required for attorneys, so costs have gone up a lot, and are almost prohibitive for paralegals."

Bonnie Twigg agrees that it is costly when you are on your own to get the necessary continuing education. She has convinced some firms or attorneys to split the fees with her, or to pay the cost for her. In return, she gives them the materials (copying a set for herself) and gives the firm a memo on the information gained. If she knows a case is coming up to which the topic particularly applies, she makes an arrangement with the firm to share the expense with her. She estimates that she ends up paying about two-thirds of the cost of her continuing education. She tries to get to ten or twelve sessions a year, including meetings. She goes to civil procedure updates, personal injury updates, programs put on by judges, and California Continuing Education for the Bar (CEB). The local bar association does a lot, as do the paralegal association, the women's bar group, and Sonoma county trial lawyers. Particularly now with mandatory CLE there is a lot available.

The "hot issues" facing the paralegal profession are volatile, changing constantly and causing debate and controversy. As discussed in appendix B, legal assistants are subject to a variety of potential changes in their ability to practice. It's a good idea to be sure you are tapped into an information source, so you know as soon as possible if any changes are "in the works."

Integrity

The most important aspect of integrity for all people who work with lawyers is absolute honesty and trustworthiness. You need to demonstrate the kind of character that assures the attorney he or she can rely on you to be completely open, to disclose immediately any mistake you make, or any problems you uncover that might compromise the attorney's position or the client's. The attorney must feel your absolute loyalty to him and to the client, and your sense of discretion with respect to the client's situation and the information that comes to you in your work. Without that sense of your integrity, the attorney will be reluctant to trust you with anything.

In short, you want people to know that they can trust you to do the best you can, even if you make a mistake occasionally. The key word is "integrity." Not every business person demonstrates integrity, but it is this quality that makes people respect you, refer you to others, and even admire you for what you do. There are many aspects to having integrity: it means avoiding personally oriented conflict with others, refraining from professionally inappropriate actions and language, and maintaining an even keel regardless of what occurs in your business.

One important element of this is knowing when to avoid situations you won't like and that drive you to lose your control. Often entrepreneurs feel they must accept business even though the customer brings in more problems than profits. To put it bluntly, we all know that the legal field has its share of egomaniacal personalities who can also be bad businesspeople. There are front office staff people who, faced with tremendous pressure to do more than one job, might take their anger out on you. Every situation is different.

Paralegal Terrie Burton recommends an "eyes up—pay attention" approach all the time. She has had some experiences with attorneys she would not work for again, and has learned to appraise the character of the office from her first contact. As part of sizing up a new client, the image of the office as you first enter it tells you a lot about the type of practice the firm is in.

If you are experiencing personality problems with a client, or what appear to you to be an unusual amount of snafus, you would be wise to do something about the situation. Sometimes speaking up is not worth it, since it might bring you a poor recommendation for the next client. This is why it might simply be better business to avoid difficult people, and work with people you enjoy. We are not suggesting you abandon clients at the drop of a dime if they are troublesome, but that you look for patterns of behavior that over and over again indicate to you that the client is disreputable, egotistical, sexist, or otherwise not worth your time.

On the other hand, situations like this actually give you an opportunity to test out your personal communication skills. Can you make the situation better by trying to find a way to clear the air? For example, if you have a client who keeps blaming you for mistakes, can you make the person conscious of the difficulty you have taking this blame by saying something like, "I'm awfully sorry, but we keep having this communication problem and I'd like to bring it out in the open and try to clear things up. Can we find some time to talk outside of the office when you are not so pressed for time?" Then when you get that time, explain to the person that you work on his or her projects in the same way that you do for other clients without any problems, and that you would be eager to find another way to resolve the dilemma rather than letting the situation deteriorate or continue.

In short, make your business to run *your* business according to your pleasure and taste. If you are to succeed, you might as well do it *your* way!

A view of the future

In the process of making legal services economical as well as maintaining excellence, the legal profession is in the midst of enormous change. The constant flux—contraction and explosion at the same time—makes law an extremely dynamic field of opportunity for a broad variety of intelligent professionals and entrepreneurs, people who love working with other bright, energetic, and curious professionals. Lawyers need a universe of support to manage the inevitable changes in methods of dispute resolution and the information explosion as it affects the legal profession. People working in legal support in the coming years will enjoy an exciting variety of opportunity.

Associations & organizations

National Federation of Paralegal Associations, Inc. (NFPA)
P.O. Box 33108
Kansas City, MO 64114-0108
Phone: 816-941-4000
Fax: 816-941-2725

National Association of Legal Assistants, Inc. (NALA)
1601 South Main, Suite 300
Tulsa, OK 74119-4464
Phone: 918-587-6828
Fax: 918-582-6772

Professional Legal Assistants, Inc.
120 Penmarc Drive, Suite 118
Raleigh, NC 27603

California Association of Freelance Paralegals
Post Office Box 3267
Berkeley, CA 94703-0267

(To find a state or local paralegal association near you, contact NFPA or
NALA, or a local bar association in your area.)

**Paralegal & legal
assistant
associations**

Court reporters associations

National Court Reporters Association (NCRA)
8224 Old Courthouse Road
Vienna, VA 22182-3878
Phone: 703-556-6272
Fax: 703-556-6291
TDD: 703-556-6289

There are also court reporter associations in most states. Contact NCRA for an association in your area.

Other organizations

American Association for Paralegal Education (AAfPE)
P.O. Box 40244
Overland Park, KS 66204
Phone: 913-381-4458
Fax: 913-381-9308

American Association of Law Librarians (AALL)
53 West Jackson Blvd.
Suite 940
Chicago, IL 60604
Phone: 312-939-4764

American Association of Legal Nurse Consultants (AALNC)
500 N. Michigan Avenue, #1400
Chicago, IL 60611
Phone: 312-670-0550
Fax: 312-661-0769

B Paralegal issues

The paralegals interviewed for this book worked for attorneys, not directly for consumers, in providing legal services. A growing number of individuals are performing legal-related services of certain limited types directly for the public (legal technicians, free-standing paralegals or independent paralegals).

Paralegals directly serving the public

The question of whether, and at what point, such practices might violate unauthorized practice of law statutes has not been finally determined but is being addressed in numerous states by way of state bar task forces or committees and in some cases through proposed legislation. As we go to press, those states include Arizona, Florida, Illinois, Maine, Minnesota, New Mexico, Oregon, Pennsylvania, Tennessee, Texas, Vermont, and Wisconsin. In California, several bills have been proposed over the past few years to regulate legal technicians but none has passed, and the issue continues to be studied.

Generally, paralegals are prohibited by law (termed "unauthorized practice of law" statutes or "UPL") from performing legal services directly for consumers. The structure of these laws varies from state to state and has typically been strictly interpreted. This is beginning to change, largely because of the need for economical legal services for the poor for simple legal procedures like no-fault divorce (if no children or assets are in dispute), adoptions, landlord/tenant matters, real estate closings, simple wills, and some immigration procedures.

Within a few years, some states may provide for limited licensure of nonlawyers to perform certain specific legal tasks for consumers without working under the direct supervision of an attorney. To date, however, no states have passed such laws. Some states are providing for nonlawyer court facilitators to work at courts, assisting consumers in selecting and filing appropriate forms and proceeding through some simple court processes. Virginia and Washington are two states that permit nonlawyers, under certain circumstances, to engage in certain duties for the transfer of real property.

The ABA has created a Commission on Nonlawyer Practice, comprised of members of the legal profession, representatives of paralegal associations, and the public. In 1993, the Commission has been holding hearings around the United States on the questions of regulation of paralegals and the delivery of legal services by nonlawyers directly to the public. Following the hearings, the Commission will submit a report containing findings and recommendations to the ABA House of Delegates.

Both the NFPA and NALA have considerable information available on the issue of limited licensure. In addition, if you are interested in becoming an independent paralegal and working directly for consumers, there is an excellent article in the March/April 1992 issue of *Legal Assistant Today* magazine by Catherine Elias-Jermany entitled "Independent Paralegals: Working for the Public." The book *Paralegal; An Insider's Guide to One of the Fastest Growing Occupations of the 1990's* by Barbara Bernardo (Peterson's Guides, updated in 1993) has a chapter, "Cutting-Edge Issues Affecting Your Paralegal Career" which is a clear and concise discussion of the issue. In addition, the book *Independent Paralegal's Handbook* by Jack Warner (Nolo Press Self-Help Law, last revision 1993) strongly promotes the practice of independent paralegals.

Regulating & licensing paralegals

The issue of regulating traditional paralegals (i.e., those working under the supervision of attorneys) is being addressed in many areas. In November 1990, the New Jersey Supreme Court's Committee on the Unauthorized Practice of Law issued Opinion 24, which found that independent (freelance) paralegals were engaged in the unauthorized practice of law and prohibited them from working even under the direct supervision of an attorney in New Jersey.

In May 1992, the New Jersey Supreme Court considered an appeal submitted jointly by 11 freelance paralegals in New Jersey, along with amicus curiae briefs, one submitted by the National Federation of Paralegal Associations and the American Association of Paralegal Educators and another submitted by the National Association of Legal Assistants. The New Jersey Supreme Court then modified Opinion 24 so that freelance paralegals working directly under the supervision of an attorney, whether employed or retained on a contract basis, are now acceptable. However, in New Jersey, as in many states, paralegals continue to be obligated to refrain from illegal acts and from UPL, to work only under the supervision of attorneys, and to conduct their professional behavior according to the Rules of Professional Conduct, which also governs attorneys.

Currently, committees have been established (of attorneys and/or paralegals, some as part of state bar association activity) and legislation proposed to regulate traditional paralegals in the states of Alabama, Arkansas, Georgia, Hawaii, Iowa, Kentucky, Montana, Nevada, New Jersey, Ohio, Texas, and Wisconsin. Several other states' bar associations have issued guidelines for the utilization of paralegals by attorneys.

It is possible that some state legislatures will pass legislation in the near future, state supreme courts will issue orders and/or state bar associations will issue opinions requiring paralegals to be licensed or to register in order to work as such. Such steps can drastically affect your ability to work as a paralegal, whether employed or freelance. Because each state may proceed differently, the best way to stay on top of these developments is to join the closest local paralegal association or, if there is no local association anywhere in your vicinity, to join one of the national associations as an individual member. (Call NFPA, NALA, or a nearby bar association for the name of the nearest paralegal association.)

The National Association of Legal Assistants (NALA) has a voluntary certification program for paralegals who meet the standards they have established through a rigorous testing procedure. Upon passing, the person is entitled the CLA (certified legal assistant) designation, suggesting a higher level of skill and knowledge. To date, thousands of paralegals have been awarded the CLA designation; however, many paralegals do not feel the certification is necessary for their career.

Ethics

In most states, paralegals are considered to be governed by the Rules of Professional Conduct or Codes of Professional Responsibility, which govern the ethics of attorneys. These codes spell out the boundaries of acceptable attorney (and paralegal) behavior with respect to conflicts of interest among clients, confidentiality of client information, and the nature of communications between attorney (or paralegal) and client, among other areas of ethical concern.

Good paralegal training programs include in the required curriculum a course on ethical considerations in the legal and paralegal professions. In addition, many employers reinforce the importance of keeping confidential all client information encountered during an employee's work. It is also incumbent on each individual paralegal to be familiar with the Rules of Professional Conduct in her particular jurisdiction and how it relates to paralegal practice.

Freelance paralegals carry a special responsibility in this area because they do not have a regular employer to provide ethical guidance. Because they work for a number of attorneys and clients, there is more likelihood of conflicts arising among clients than there would be for regularly employed legal assistants.

An additional ethical concern that arises particularly among freelance paralegals is the possibility of their being hired by an attorney in another practice area who is hoping to benefit from the paralegal's expertise in an area in which the attorney may be short of experience. This situation results in the paralegal being the expert on the case and the attorney not really being in a supervisory position. Such practice is not fair to clients or to the paralegal and does not comport with the standard of a paralegal working under the supervision of an attorney at all times. This concern was one of several that motivated the New Jersey Supreme Court's Unauthorized Practice of Law (UPL) Committee to issue its Opinion 24 that declared that freelance paralegals were guilty of UPL.

Confidentiality

As part of their ethics training, paralegals learn that everything they work on must be held in the strictest confidence. In fact, even the fact that certain clients are represented by a certain attorney is a confidential matter unless that client chooses to discuss the representation himself. Law firm employees are counseled not to discuss client business with anyone outside the office or even outside the team working on the matter and to never talk client issues in any public place or even among family members. This obligation lasts beyond the time of the representation and extends into the future, even after that employee leaves that particular employment.

For freelance paralegals, the obligation remains the same, and it extends to the information as to which lawyer that freelance paralegal may be working for at any time. That information is the lawyer's to choose to disclose or to keep confidential. The only exception arises in the event of a potential conflict between a current assignment and a past one. Should the freelance paralegal become aware, once into working on a case, that such a conflict might have occurred, this fact must be immediately disclosed to the attorney on the current case.

Freelancers have another critical concern regarding confidentiality that employed legal assistants do not encounter. Freelance paralegals often have in their homes the paperwork and files from a current case. While employed paralegals follow the guidelines of their employer and are often comfortable leaving papers on their desks in a locked office at night, freelancers may be working on materials in a home office that are less secure. Perhaps there is a guest bathroom off the office and guests walking through the office could inadvertently see client files and papers. Home-based paralegals must be scrupulous about keeping all work papers and client effects out of sight when they are not being worked on. Furthermore, meticulous organization is necessary to prevent the materials of different attorneys or clients from becoming intermingled in the paralegal's office.

Conflicts of interest

Paralegals who have been working as such for a period of time, and those who have attended a good paralegal training program, are aware of their obligations regarding potential conflicts of interest. However, among freelance paralegals, there is an even greater danger of the paralegal inadvertently finding herself working for someone who was on the opposing side in a previous matter or working opposed to someone who was a previous client or the client of an attorney she worked for in the past. Such a situation can represent a serious breach of ethics and, first, should be prevented at all costs; second, must be immediately addressed if it occurs. A law firm can be disqualified from a case based on the appearance of conflict of interest among employees working on the case.

Freelance paralegals should keep records of each case on which they work, listing the names of the parties and all attorneys. Before accepting a new assignment, this list must be checked against a list of parties and counsel in the new matter. Some paralegal services maintain sophisticated computer programs including the past clients and opposing parties of their freelance paralegal employees as well those of the service. Most potential conflicts reflect only a remote connection and turn out to be no problem. The paralegal must disclose any potential conflicts to the attorney to determine if any problem exists.

Some paralegals keep track of their clients using computers, listing the names of the parties of the cases they've worked with, perhaps even using a database program. At the beginning of a new matter, they then check all the initial client intake information, plaintiffs, defendants, and counsel. They also check again if new parties enter the case in one way or another.

Conflict issues are different in a small community where there are few attorneys. However, it is still important never to be working in a conflict situation and to maintain strict records. However, the same names come up more often. In a larger legal community, freelance paralegals might restrict themselves to working strictly for personal injury plaintiffs or personal injury defense. However, in a small community, the reality is that there are not a lot of attorneys so you are less likely to take exclusively one side or the other.

Conduct

Some state and local bar associations have guidelines for attorneys that govern the conduct of legal assistants when working under their supervision. While these vary to some extent from state to state, they generally cover the following areas of concern:

Contact with clients The paralegal may maintain general contact with a client so long as the client knows the paralegal is not an attorney, the contact is authorized by the attorney, and the attorney remains the client's primary contact.

Attorney supervision   The attorney remains ultimately responsible for the legal assistant's work product and conduct in his or her work and supervises the legal assistant's work performance.

Communications   Any correspondence from the paralegal must not include legal opinions or give legal advice, and it must designate that person as a paralegal or legal assistant and must not be misleading as to that person's nonlawyer status.

In addition, the status of the paralegal must be disclosed at the outset of any contact related to the paralegal's work, with a client, with other attorneys, courts, agencies, or members of the general public.

Prohibited conduct   The paralegal's work should not require the exercise of unsupervised legal judgment. It is never appropriate for legal assistants to solicit legal business for the attorney, to establish the client-attorney relationship, to set the legal fees, to give legal advice, or represent a client in court. And, of course, a legal assistant cannot do anything the attorney would be prohibited from doing.

UPL   A legal assistant also must not engage in any act which would constitute the unauthorized practice of law.

Contracts

Many freelance paralegals use an occasional written contract with attorneys who hire them on a case by case basis except with former employers or attorneys they knew well and have worked with before. If you decide to design a written contract, you will probably want to have an attorney help you draw it up. Based on the comments of the paralegals we interviewed, the contract a freelance paralegal makes with an attorney should include what the paralegal expects from the firm or attorney and what they can expect from her, for example:

1. What services are being contracted for (perhaps listed in an attachment);
2. How the paralegal will bill, and what the charges will be; whether a retainer or advance for expenses is required to be paid to the paralegal;
3. How expenses will be handled, such as mileage, copying expenses, courier services, long distance telephone, online computer and fax charges and subcontracted work;
4. Whether there is a premium added to the paralegal's rate for after hours work or expedited services;
5. Statement that the attorney, not the attorney's client, is responsible for payment, and payment is not to be delayed until the client pays the attorney;

6. Reminder that the attorney is ultimately responsible for the work product, the paralegal does not practice law;
7. What constitutes termination or renewal of the contract, and what happens if the case settles or work terminates, e.g., attorney will still be charged by the paralegal for the time already spent on the project;
8. Paralegal's assurance of treating materials confidentially; and
9. Whatever terms your attorney and CPA recommend in order to clarify your status as a non-employee for tax purposes, and to assure your coverage under the attorney's or firm's legal malpractice insurance.

Whether or not you use a written contract, you will want these matters understood between you and your client before you begin work. You should also make sure that the attorney's malpractice insurance will cover you as well or have your own malpractice insurance as described in the next section.

Malpractice insurance

Until very recently, there was no legal malpractice insurance available specifically to cover practicing paralegals. Employed paralegals were covered by the policies carried by their employers, along with attorneys and other law firm employees. In addition, freelance paralegals were also typically considered to be covered by the policies carried by the firms that hire them to work, with respect to that work for that client's attorneys. Some freelance paralegals have managed, with difficulty, to obtain errors and omissions policies (E&O) with private insurance carriers to cover the business. However, it is very difficult to get this type of insurance if you operate out of your home.

Recently, some coverage has become available in connection with a program offered by Meridian General Agency, Inc., developed jointly with and endorsed by the NFPA. (Information can be obtained by calling NFPA Risk Purchasing Group at 800-989-NFPA.) Two policies are available, one for employed paralegals, in case the firm does not carry coverage or its coverage does not cover paralegals; and one policy for freelance paralegals who work under the direction of an attorney client.

Paralegals should be aware that neither the firm's policy nor the newly available policy for paralegals will cover a case resulting from the paralegal giving legal advice—that is the unauthorized practice of law and is illegal. There is no insurance coverage for illegal acts.

The new NFPA-related insurance is not yet available in every state. Some states require the carrier to be admitted to practice in that state, and rates and forms must be approved in order to solicit in that state. Susan Kligerman says that New Jersey is one of the few states that cannot get it. She is in contact with, and educating, providers of broad E & O insurance.

Most freelance paralegals do not see a need for insurance separate from that held by the attorneys who use their services. In fact, some feel the existence of another "deep pocket," in addition to the lawyer's insurance, will only encourage lawsuits against paralegals. They believe freelancers should be covered by the attorneys they work for since they are working under the attorney's license and the attorney is ultimately responsible for the work.

You can take your own preventative measures: don't take on more than you can handle and watch all your deadlines closely. Set up a good calendaring system. For more detailed information on the issue of insurance for paralegals, see the article "Do You Need Professional Liability Insurance?" in the 1993 July/August issue of *Legal Assistant Today*.

C Training programs

There are currently more than 600 paralegal training programs in the country. To find a program near you, we recommend you contact your local paralegal association to obtain specific recommendations about schools in your area, or contact NALA or NFPA (see appendix A) for any information they can offer about programs they recommend.

Paralegal training

There is no specific standard curriculum or number of courses that comprise paralegal training. Each school develops its own program. As indicated in chapter 1, however, some schools have received Final Approval or Provisional Approval from the American Bar Association Standing Committee on Legal Assistants, indicating that the program has met standards established by the ABA. As we write, the National Federation of Paralegal Associations is also in the process of creating a model curriculum to recommend to training programs.

The following list of programs represent those approved by the National Court Reporters Association. These programs have met the general requirements and minimum standards established by the Board on Approved Student Education of the NCRA. Note that some schools offer day programs, others in the evening. We recommend contacting the school directly to obtain specific information about their program.

Court reporter education programs

Alabama

Gadsden State Community College
Gadsden
205-549-8626

Prince Institute of Professional
  Studies
Montgomery
205-271-1670

Arizona

American Institute of Court
  Reporting
Phoenix
602-252-4986

Parks College
Tucson
602-886-7979

Phoenix College
Phoenix
602-264-2492

California

Bryan College of Court Reporting
Los Angeles
310-484-8850

California School of Court Reporting
Santa Ana
714-541-6892

Merit College of Court Reporting
Van Nuys
818-988-6640

South Coast College of Court
  Reporting
Westminster
714-897-6464

Colorado

Denver Academy of Court Reporting
Denver
303-629-1291

Mile Hi College, Inc.
Lakewood
303-233-7973

Florida

Bay Area Legal Academy
Tampa
813-621-8074

Cooper Academy of Court Reporting
West Palm Beach
407-640-6999

Court Reporting Careers, Inc.
West Palm Beach
407-881-0220

Erwin Technical Center
Tampa
813-231-1800

Florida Career Institute
Fort Meyers
813-939-4766

Legal Career Institute
Ft. Lauderdale
305-581-2223

Legal Career Institute
Riviera Beach
407-848-2223

Orlando College
Orlando
407-628-5870

Sarasota County Tech. Institute
Sarasota
813-924-1365

Segal Institute of Court Reporting
Clearwater
813-535-0608

Sheridan Vocational Technical
  Center
Hollywood
305-985-3266

Stenotype Institute of Jacksonville
Jacksonville Beach
904-246-7466

Winter Park Adult Vocational Ctr.
Winter Park
407-647-6366

Georgia

Brown College of Court Reporting
Atlanta
404-876-1227

Illinois

Chicago College of Commerce
Chicago
312-236-3312

MacCormac Junior College
Elmhurst
708-941-1200

Midstate College
Peoria
309-673-6365

Midstate College
Carthage
217-357-6626

Southern Illinois Univ.
Carbondale
618-536-6682

Sparks College
Shelbyville
217-774-5112

Triton College
River Grove
708-456-0300

Indiana

College of Court Reporting
Hobart
219-942-1459

Iowa

American Institute of Business
Des Moines
515-244-4221

American Institute of Commerce
Davenport
319-355-3500

Kansas

The Brown Mackie College
Salina
913-825-5422

The Brown Mackie College
Overland Park
913-451-3856

Washburn University
Topeka
913-231-1010

Kentucky

Kentucky Career Institute
Florence
606-371-9393

Maine

Husson College
Bangor
207-947-1121

Maryland

Hagerstown Business College
Hagerstown
301-739-2670

Massachusetts

Mass. Bay Community College
Framingham
508-875-5300

Michigan

Central Michigan Univ.
Mt. Pleasant
517-774-3554/774-3778

Elsa Cooper Institute of Court
  Reporting
Southfield
313-552-0061

Great Lakes Junior College
Saginaw
517-755-3444

Lansing Community College
Lansing
517-483-1596

Minnesota

Southwestern Tech. College
Jackson
507-847-3320

Minnesota School of Business
Minneapolis
612-338-6721

Rasmussen Business College
Minnetonka
612-545-2000

Saint Cloud Business College
Saint Cloud
612-251-5600

University of Minnesota
Crookston
218-281-6510

Mississippi

University of Mississippi
University
601-232-7800

Nebraska

Lincoln School of Commerce
Lincoln
402-474-5315

Nebraska College of Business
Omaha
402-553-8500

Nevada

Phillips Junior College of Las Vegas
Las Vegas
702-434-0486

New Jersey

American Business Academy
Hackensack
201-488-9400

New Mexico

International Business College
Albuquerque
505-298-2750

Santa Fe School of Court Reporting
Santa Fe
505-983-5699

New York

Alfred State College
Alfred
607-587-3427

Central City Business
Syracuse
315-472-6233

Court Reporting Institute
Hicksville
516-937-3700

Long Island Business Institute
Commack
516-499-7100

Stenotype Academy
New York
212-962-0002

Ohio

Academy of Court Reporting
Cleveland
216-861-3222

Academy of Court Reporting
Akron
216-867-4030

Academy of Court Reporting
Columbus
614-221-7770

Clark State Comm. College
Springfield
513-325-0691

Clermont College
Batavia
513-732-5200

Cuyahoga Comm. College
Parma
216-987-5000

Stark Technical College
Canton
216-494-6170

Oklahoma

City College
Norman
405-329-5627

Oregon

College of Legal Arts
Portland
503-223-5100

Pennsylvania

Central Pennsylvania Business
  School
Summerdale
717-732-0702

Court Reporting Institute of
  Orleans Technical Institute
Philadelphia
215-854-1853

Duff's Business Institute
Pittsburgh
412-261-4530

Manor Junior College
Jenkintown
215-885-2360

Peirce Junior College
Philadelphia
215-545-6400

Rhode Island

Johnson & Wales Univ.
Providence
401-456-4626

South Carolina

Midlands Technical College
Columbia
803-822-3594

South Dakota

Stenotype Institute of South Dakota
Sioux Falls
605-336-1442

Tennessee

Court Reporting Institute of
Tennessee, Inc.
Nashville
615-885-9770

Middle Tenn. State University
Murfressboro
615-898-2902

Texas

Alvin Community College
Alvin
713-331-6111

Amarillo College
Amarillo
806-371-5000

Arlington Court Reporting College
Arlington
817-640-8852

Capitol City Careers
Austin
512-892-4270

Court Reporting Institute of Dallas
Dallas
214-350-9722

Iverson Institute of Court Reporting
Arlington
817-274-6465

Professional Court Reporting School
Richardson (Dallas)
214-231-9502

San Antonio Court Reporting
Institute
San Antonio
512-366-0144

Court Reporting School
Richardson (Dallas)
214-231-9502

Stenograph Institute of Texas
Abilene
915-677-2003

San Antonio Court Reporting
Institute
San Antonio
512-366-0846

Utah

Provo College
Provo
801-375-1861

Vermont

Champlain College
Burlington
802-658-0800

Virginia

Reporting Academy of Virginia
Virginia Beach
804-499-5447

Washington

Bates Technical College
Tacoma
206-596-1885

Court Reporting Institute
Seattle
206-363-8300

Green River Community College
Auburn
206-833-9111

West Virginia

Huntington Junior College of
  Business
Huntington
304-697-7550
800-344-4522

Wisconsin

Concordia University
Mequon
414-243-5700

Gateway Technical
Kenosha
414-656-6900

Lakeshore Technical
Cleveland
414-458-4183

Madison Area Technical College
Madison
608-246-6100

Wisconsin Indian Head Technical
  College
New Richmond
715-246-6561

Canada

Northern Alberta Institute of
  Technology
Edmonton
403-471-7857

Index

Index **233**

About the authors

Rick Benzel is a professional writer and editor focusing on business, technology, and health. He has been involved in publishing for more than 17 years, and has worked in various editorial and marketing positions for Houghton Mifflin, Prentice Hall, and Jeremy P. Tarcher, Inc., before he started his own business. He currently works and writes from his home-based PC in Los Angeles where he lives with his wife, Terry, and his two wonderful daughters, Rebecca and Sarah.

Katherine Sheehy Hussey holds a B.S. and B.A. in English and Library Science from the University of Minnesota and taught high school English before finding herself in the paralegal world. She has been active in the Denver, Colorado, paralegal community for the past 18 years as a corporate and securities paralegal and a paralegal manager in law firms and corporations. She has been active in paralegal associations and has authored numerous articles on issues in the paralegal profession. Katherine currently performs paralegal services on a contract basis from her home office and at law firms and corporations in the Denver area. She has a son and three stepdaughters, all grown, and lives in Westminster, Colorado, with her husband, Bob.

About the series editors

"People are thirsty for specific how-to information that can enable them to earn a living at home," say Paul and Sarah Edwards, authors of *Working from Home* and *Best Home-Based Businesses for the Nineties.*

The Windcrest/McGraw-Hill Entrepreneurial PC series is designed to fill the until-now unmet need for step-by-step guidance for people wanting to make the work–home transition. The Edwards' track the trends that yield opportunities for successful home-based businesses and then find authors to provide the nitty-gritty business-specific information that can spare the home-based entrepreneur months of frustration and costly mistakes.

Paul and Sarah have been working from their home since 1974. It didn't take them long to realize they were participating in what would become a major social and economic trend—the home-based business. That spurred them to want to help others make the transition from office to home and to professionalize the image of home-based business.

Paul and Sarah are contributing editors to *Home Office Computing* magazine and write the monthly column, "Ask Paul and Sarah." They founded and manage the *Working From Home Forum* on CompuServe Information Service, an electronic network with more than 30,000 people around the world who work from home. Paul and Sarah also cohost the hour-long national weekly radio program "Home Office" on the Business Radio Network.